ON LIVING WITH
TELEVISION

CONSOLE-ING PASSIONS
TELEVISION AND CULTURAL POWER
Edited by Lynn Spigel

ON LIVING WITH TELEVISION

AMY HOLDSWORTH

Duke University Press   *Durham and London*   2021

© 2021 Duke University Press
All rights reserved
Printed and bound by CPI Group (UK) Ltd, Croydon, CR0 4YY
Designed by Courtney Leigh Richardson
Typeset in Warnock Pro by Copperline Book Services

Library of Congress Cataloging-in-Publication Data
Names: Holdsworth, Amy, [date] author.
Title: On living with television / Amy Holdsworth.
Other titles: Console-ing passions.
Description: Durham : Duke University Press, 2021. | Series: Console-ing passions | Includes bibliographical references and index.
Identifiers: LCCN 2021010943 (print)
LCCN 2021010944 (ebook)
ISBN 9781478013839 (hardcover)
ISBN 9781478014751 (paperback)
ISBN 9781478022060 (ebook)
Subjects: LCSH: Television—Social aspects. | Television—Psychological aspects. | Feminist television criticism. | Queer theory. | Disability studies. | BISAC: PERFORMING ARTS / Television / History & Criticism
Classification: LCC PN1992.6.H585 2021 (print) |
LCC PN1992.6 (ebook) | DDC 302.23/45—dc23
LC record available at https://lccn.loc.gov/2021010943
LC ebook record available at https://lccn.loc.gov/2021010944

Cover art: Watching TV before bed. Amy and Jessica Holdsworth, ca. 1984.

For my family

CONTENTS

Acknowledgments ix

INTRODUCTION 1

1 TO (NOT) GROW UP WITH TELEVISION 31

2 BEDTIME STORIES 49

3 TV DINNERS 77

4 HOMECOMINGS AND GOINGS 107

EPILOGUE. (Un)pause 139

Notes 147

Bibliography 163

Index 175

ACKNOWLEDGMENTS

The acknowledgments are often the first thing I will read in any academic book. They map out the networks and frameworks of support that all authors are indebted to: whom the author works with; where they've traveled; the conversations they've had; the people who have championed them, challenged them, or been a shoulder to cry on; and the ones who have kept them calm, fed, and watered or offered (un)wanted distraction. My own life has been front and center of this project, but it simply wouldn't have come together in the form it is now without the belief and support of Lynn Spigel and Elizabeth Ault, who kept the faith from initial concept to the delivery of the final manuscript. I am also indebted to the reviewers who have pushed, challenged, and encouraged me to make this work the best it could be (even though I sometimes wished for an easier path). Karen Lury has been sounding board and pep squad throughout, and I couldn't wish for a more generous colleague, collaborator, and friend. Special thanks to Rachel Moseley, who has read numerous drafts at various stages, for her insights and enthusiasm, and to Alison Peirse: our shared experiences (always best to be the same) underpinned the ideas for chapter 4, and her writing tutorials helped me finish it.

The writing of this book has been generously supported by the College of Arts and the School of Culture and Creative Arts at the University of Glasgow through periods of research leave, teaching relief, and travel funding. Many thanks also to my colleagues in Film and Television Studies for the collegiality, check-ins, impromptu writing surgeries, study days, dinners, and drinks. The ideas in this book and the confidence to take them forward are also the result of conversations with friends and colleagues, whether brief or sustained, that helped me put the pieces of the puzzle together, in no particular order: Matthew Allen, Hannah Tweed, Zöe Shacklock, Amanda Ptolemy, Andrew Kötting, Paul Sutton, Anna McCarthy, Faye Woods, Kerr Castle, Lisa Kelly, Rowan Aust, Glyn Davis, and the members of the Northern Television Studies Research Group. Bryony Randall and Geraldine Parsons have also continued to provide much-needed "peer mentoring" and support. I am also particularly grateful to the organizers of the following conferences and symposia for giving me a space to try out my work in progress and for the audiences (often small but perfectly formed) for their thoughts and feedback: the Screen conference (University of Glasgow, 2013, 2015, 2017), "Television for Women" (University of Warwick, 2014), "Media and Place" (Leeds Beckett University, 2016), the Society for Cinema and Media Studies conference (University of Chicago, 2017), "Disability and Disciplines" (Liverpool Hope University, 2017), and "Ageing, Illness and Care in Cultural and Literary Narratives" (University of Huddersfield, 2019). I am also grateful for the invitations to give research presentations at the University of South Wales, University of St. Andrews, University of Hull, University of Warwick, and De Monfort University. However, my most significant testing ground has been in two of the television studies courses I have taught and continue to teach at Glasgow: Television Analysis and Advanced Topics in Television. The undergraduate and postgraduate students in these classes have been a constant source of inspiration—sharing their own thoughts and experiences of living with television while also being willing and good-humored participants in my TV-viewing experiments.

My family and friends are present throughout this book—whether on the page or in between the words—and none more so than our dear friend John Parker (1977–2019), whom we miss every day. In getting my life stories down on paper, I am beyond grateful to my mum, who has continually supported and contributed to this venture with her honesty, her resilience, and her candid reflections on our family life. In the words of most reality TV participants, "we've been on a journey together," and I thank her and the rest of my family for making the best (most annoying, amusing, nurturing, frustrating, loving, and loved) companions: Jessica, Sam and Annie, Dad, Briony and Ta. And not forgetting Doris and Geoffrey, Muriel and George, Joseph, and Alice (always).

Finally, to Michael, for the love, patience, and peace I once thought I might never find.

INTRODUCTION

Television has always been there for me. I have never lived without it and honestly find that prospect anxiety inducing. I admit to being immediately suspicious of those who don't have one in their home. When I moved to Glasgow in 2009, I drove up from Yorkshire the night before the moving van was due to arrive. Knowing the tenement flat I had rented would be bare, I packed my car with life's essentials: a kettle, tea bags, beer, crisps, and a small TV set. I ventured around the corner to a grocery store to buy a pint of milk but then quickly scurried back to the relative safety of my new home. I camped out in the front room that first night, alone and frankly terrified of the life decision I had made to leave my home and family for a new job, city, and country. So I got drunk, ate Monster Munch, and wrestled with a cable box in order to get a weak digital signal, and eventually settled in to watch *EastEnders* (figure Intro.1). Though I was in a new place, the experience was familiar. In 1998 the same TV set came with me to the University of Warwick when I started my undergraduate degree and moved into the residence halls. Rootes E50 was my designated cell, a small rectangular room with a single bed, a desk and chair, a couple of shelves, and a sink. It was the cheapest option on campus, which meant it did not have a bathroom. My dad and older sister, Jess, drove me down the motorway, and with each sign for the university we passed, the knot in my stomach would tighten. Taking advantage of our family Motability bus, I had packed it full, aiming to simply transfer my teenage bedroom to this new accommodation and to bring all that was familiar with me as an antidote to the blind fear and trepidation I felt. When we arrived, Jess, by that point an experienced student, helped me construct my home away from home. We put up posters and made the bed; we set up the stereo, TV, and VCR and located

FIGURE INTRO.1
First night in Turnberry
Road, Glasgow,
August 2009.

the communal kitchen; and when it was all unpacked, it was time for them to leave. Alone and immediately stricken with homesickness, I switched on the TV and opened a beer.

In 2004 I returned to Warwick to start my PhD. The experience was uncannily similar, and though the room was bigger there was still no private bathroom. The university housing office had given me a room in a former nursing home that now housed around twenty postgraduate students. I'd left the terraced house in the West Yorkshire village we grew up in, where I'd settled in with Jess and our cat for the last three years, to begin the next stage of an academic career that I had dreamed of since I was a child watching Inspector Morse stride around the hallowed halls of Oxford (the halls at Warwick were certainly less hallowed but fortunately less murderous). My dad and stepmother were in charge of crisis management, on this occasion rushing out to Argos to get me a TV cable when I realized I'd left it behind, resulting in a cross between a tantrum and a panic attack. I followed the same routine—we unpacked and said our goodbyes, and I turned on the TV and opened a beer before plucking up the courage to leave the room and meet my fellow residents.

There I was, and years later, here I am again. It is the summer of 2017 and I've arrived in Liverpool for a disability studies conference. I am older, I'm financially secure, I don't drink as much beer, and I don't do communal bathrooms. I find myself checking into a hall of residence on the Liverpool Hope University campus. The rectangular room is bare and austere, with a single bed, a desk and chair, a couple of shelves, and a private shower (I'm not sure if I'm going up in the world or coming down). I am rushed by a series of feelings as the anxiety and homesickness of those previous experiences loop themselves around who I am now. I set about making the room more palatable. I drape a scarf over the fluorescent light, plug in my laptop, and connect to the university Wi-Fi. I click on the livestream of BBC One through the iPlayer. *EastEnders* is playing. I haven't watched it in years, but the familiar sights and sounds of Albert Square spill into the drab room and immediately make me feel more at home.

THIS IS NOT AN unfamiliar story. Television in this account emerges as both a companion to the everyday and a way of managing crisis and transition. It speaks to the kinds of "ontological security" that forms of broadcasting have been imagined to provide and of a viewer who is well rehearsed in this particular cultural practice.[1] It may not tell us much about the text of television, but it alludes to a set of text-based experiences that are durational (the long-running soap opera, for instance) and iterative (a pattern of retreat and return that is captured in my own academic comings and goings). It also speaks to a series of continuities and discontinuities in both my life in general and my life with television. I recently turned forty, and my life (so far) might easily be split in two: my formative years as analog and adult years as digital. It's not that simple, though, as my own sense of self, like television's technologies, continues to loop, layer, and multiply, and I still insist on using VHS tapes in my lectures. This is a story that reminds us of the materiality of television and its ability to transform space and of the way it is used in these recurring scenes to turn an unfamiliar space into a home. As an object and a medium, it has been seen to connect the near and far, home and away, over space but also over time. In this instance it also acts as a meaningful object or locus around which my own multiple selves are summoned—as undergrad, postgrad, early career, and midcareer academic—reminding me of the opportunities and sacrifices that have accompanied each stage. It is also a story that, like the soap opera itself, is ongoing and incomplete.

In a 2006 essay John Caughie asks the following question: "When we as academics and intellectuals write about television, who do we think we are?"[2] While the question alludes to the anxious place of television studies within the academy, it is prompted by an observation of the ways in which the reflections of different scholars on their own histories, experiences, and engagements with television underpin their critical responses.[3] This is perhaps not unique to the film and television studies scholar: for instance, as educational theorist Wolff-Michael Roth argues, "Because we are the products of the world that we attempt to describe, our auto/biographies and our scholarly works are deeply integrated."[4] But what might an autobiography of television look like? This work might take the form of an individual's viewing history or an account of specific televisual moments that have punctuated a life story. Literary scholars and critics have certainly produced plentiful accounts of individual reading histories and particular acts of rereading. Alison Waller categorizes these into "'bibliomemoirs' and 'autobibliographies': the former taking books read over a lifespan as a starting point for exploring a life history narrative and the latter employing autobiographical anecdote to illuminate certain texts or aspects of literature."[5] My own use of autobiography in this book utilizes both modes, tracing a lifelong relationship with television forms and cultures and using the personal as a *way in* to specific television texts and experiences. I have written elsewhere about the idea of a television autobiography to refer to the memories, references, and associations that are built up across a life lived alongside television. This should be seen not simply as the accumulation of an archive of televisual sounds and images but as a knotting together of our on- and offscreen lives. The autobiographical emerges, I argue, as a way in which to unravel some of these knots and to explore those experiences of intimacy, familiarity, repetition, and duration that have come to characterize television. An autobiographical focus, then, can tell us not only something specific *about* television but also something more general about *living with* television—about (not) growing up and growing old at a particular time and in a particular society.

Caughie's question and discussion that follows attends to the generational differences in having or having not "grown up" with television: scholars who remember the arrival of television into their homes as an exciting novelty and those, like me, for whom it has always been there. I wonder about how we navigate, in both our scholarship and our teaching, a similar generational divide between those of us who "grew up" analog and the digital natives who supposedly now fill our classrooms. I refer to Caughie's question here because, intentionally or not, it is also one that appeals to a feminist approach I follow in this book, placing the stress on "situated knowledge," the value of experience and a recognition of the scholar as embodied and embedded in a particular culture.[6] Clearly, asking *who* we are also requires us to reflect on the *when*, *where*, and *with whom* of television viewing as well. This means not just looking to the present but also attending to where we have been and, indeed, *who* we have been and how this informs our writing about television. As feminist literary theorist Liz Stanley writes in her advocation of the term "auto/biography," we are all constituted by and connected to "a multiplicity of other people throughout [our] lives. No person is an island complete of itself."[7] But we should also understand the autobiographical past as "peopled by a succession of selves as the writer grows, develops and changes."[8]

What I want to do is not just to consider the significance of the generation of television from which we emerge but also to recognize how our experiences as viewers continue and change over the life course: as children, teenagers, students, scholars, parents, carers, siblings, friends, (time) poor or rich, at home or away, in crisis and in the routines of the everyday, in sickness and in health, till death do us part. At Glasgow I often teach a core course called Television Analysis, and we begin the semester with examples of preschool television. As they are often bored and frustrated by the endless repetitions within *In the Night Garden* (CBeebies, 2007–9), I remind the students that "not all television is *for them*" and ask them to talk to older or younger family members or friends about the different ways they use and watch TV. I encourage them to reflect on how they watched when they were children themselves or how they might imagine using TV in the future as they move through the life course. There is plenty of scholarship that addresses the notion of "television in transition," and while television has never been a technologically stable object, the pace of change brought about by digitization has amplified this line of inquiry. This research tends to focus on the effects of change on television technologies and industries, accounting for evolutions in patterns of consumption and the impact these have on production, form, and aesthetics. It is a line of argument that can often be teleological in impulse—TV is (apparently) getting better.[9] While others have clearly teased out the implications for this line of inquiry in relation to questions of value and the legitimation of an object of study that has *always been there* for a small band of scholars, what I call attention to is an acknowledgment of the viewer or audience as also in constant transition. In her ethnography of television use by parents of young children, Ksenia Frolova, for example, argues that audiences are "often presented as a homogenous group," with their "viewing practices studied in broad generic terms."[10] This relates directly to the value of particular demographics, audiences, and experiences to the industry and the academy. Those sections of society not seen to be "productive" or "autonomous" in socioeconomic terms, such as the very old and the very young, are often marginalized and neglected. In the UK, for example, our central public service broadcaster, the BBC, caught between austerity-era politics and neoliberal market forces and subjected to extensive budget cuts, recently made the controversial decision to abolish free TV licenses for people over the age of seventy-five. While concerns regarding neglect and social justice are implicit within this project, I am aware that I am writing from the vantage point of the "ideal" viewer—independent, healthy (relatively, anxiously), white, financially secure, gainfully employed, middle aged, and middle class—but what this book endeavors to trace are former and future selves encountered through the medium and the points of connection between subjectivities that might emerge in tracing the life lived with television. In an era of niche content and algorithmically targeted modes of address, is there a different way to use our own lives to think beyond our own immediate experiences?

While I privilege the term "autobiography" (converting to "auto/biography" in chapter 1 as it explores the relational aspects of televisual spectatorship through the story of my younger sister, Alice, and her use of Disney Home Video) the book adopts, at different stages, an autobiographical *and* an autoethnographic approach. The latter is not an uncommon strategy for studies of popular culture, though writing tends to focus on issues of representation and the possibilities for identity construction, identification, and (mis)recognition: for example, how we use popular narratives and characters to make sense of or inform our own lives and relationships and the personal and political ramifications of how and where we do or don't see ourselves onscreen.[11] These are questions that emerge in my final chapter. However, for the purposes of this project I suggest that the combination of autoethnography as, in Roth's words, an "exploration of culture" and autobiography as a "pattern of life history"[12] makes it possible to follow cultural practices that are often everyday, invisible, and ephemeral while also establishing, through memory and reflection, a sense of these experiences over time.[13]

Obviously, time is complicated—and philosophers and theorists have been wrestling with it for centuries. Writing this book to a deadline, I am also acutely aware of how time can dictate, determine, and regulate our lives and bodies. Elizabeth Freeman's notion of "chrononormativity" describes the emergence of "properly temporalized bodies" that cohere with linear, teleological, state-sponsored timelines of the heteronormative life course. The institution of marriage, the accumulation of health and wealth, and the practice of childrearing enact a "sequence of socioeconomically 'productive' moments" that determine "what it means to have a life at all."[14] Theorists from a number of academic traditions have sought to unsettle and disrupt this sequential logic and its ramifications for thinking about the personhood of those who exist outside a dominant temporal order and its cultural script, including, though not limited to, children, the elderly, queer people, the "childless," and the chronically ill and/or disabled. Freeman also reminds us that "having a life entails the ability to narrate it not only in these state-sanctioned terms but also in a novelistic framework: as event-centered, goal-oriented, intentional, and culminating in epiphanies or major transformations."[15] My experience of a life lived is more "televisual" in its narrative framework: looping, repetitive, banal, catastrophic, messy, and incomplete. This is not a project that focuses on the use of television at different "ages and stages" (these are developmental terms that I challenge both in this book and elsewhere); rather, in something like the critical equivalent of a reverse tracking shot or a dolly zoom, it focuses in while pulling back to reveal a series of patterns that emerge both in time—in the loops and routines of the everyday—and over time—in the durational aspects of television. The patterns I recognize are textual—characteristics of television's formal and narrative features—and experiential—the result of a life lived alongside television as both a visual medium and a material object.

Ultimately, what I want to suggest is how television itself, and our attention to its micro and macro temporalities and textualities, has the potential to offer a vehicle through which to challenge, in Jackie Stacey and Janet Wolff's words, "the modern imperatives towards linearity and sequence [that] promise an orderly sense of directional flow."[16] As domestic object, text, and experience, television has a much greater capacity for temporal complexity than the unidirectional "flow" metaphor suggests. "Complexity" has itself become a central and somewhat contentious term within television studies over the last decade. Employed by Jason Mittell to describe a high-end narrative mode characterized by puzzle shows such as *Lost* (ABC, 2004–10), the term has been subject to critique due to the hierarchies of cultural value it constructs by placing one subset of television (and, by extension, one subset of viewers) over another.[17] The poet Claire Schwartz, however, writes that "to hold complexity is to have many possible sites of connection."[18] Within this sense of the term I imagine television as a fragmented surface on which different times and spaces, bodies and worlds come together and depart, and a meeting point at which I find myself again and again.

Television in and over Time
Theories of time have been, like me, preoccupied with models, forms, and patterns as ways of characterizing our experience of the world. It was in Rita Felski's *Doing Time*, though, that the patterns I recognized in television emerged most clearly. Felski's approach is to challenge an existing and gendered binary between models of time as either linear or cyclical. Broadly speaking, a linear model of time (or the "arrow of time") is the time of history, evolution, and progress and symbolically associated with masculine, industrial, and Western cultures. Cyclical time, on the other hand, is characterized by repetition, the everyday, the feminine, and the natural world. For theorists such as Henri Lefebvre, cyclical time is also anathematic to the idea of progress and a "sign of women's enslavement in the ordinary."[19] Felski is writing against a masculine intellectual tradition that devalues both the everyday and those subjects and objects associated with it: "Everyday life," she writes, is a term "deployed by intellectuals to describe a nonintellectual relationship to the world. For Lukács and Heidegger, for example, the everyday is synonymous with an inauthentic, gray, aesthetically impoverished existence."[20] As the rich traditions of feminist television scholarship have taught us, the terrain of the everyday, and time as routine and repetition, is also that of television, and it has struggled with and against the same associations.

Felski's work offers us a way out of this binary thinking that continues to reproduce gendered hierarchies of social and cultural value by dismantling the division between cyclical and linear time and instead recognizing both as central to social life.[21] This means challenging the perception that "cyclical time is a uniquely female province"[22]—a notion that underpinned early feminist scholarship: for instance, the work of Tania Modleski and others on the housewife and the soap opera. Gendered experiences of the televisual everyday are not the central frame of this book, and while I acknowledge how they underline my own experiences and my critical approach, it is Felski's conceptualization of everyday time that I wish to foreground. For Felski, "The temporality of everyday life is internally complex; it combines repetition and linearity, recurrence with forward movement. The everyday cannot be opposed to the realm of history, but is rather the very means by which history is actualized and made real."[23] What emerges here is a series of loops: in the repetitions of our everyday (sleeping, eating, washing, caring) and over time (generational cycles, modes of inheritance, losses and recuperations). The textual aspects of television itself are also completely loopy: the running gag, the recurring joke, the before and after and before and after, the previously on and coming up, the remakes and reboots and resets, the templates and formats, the recaps and highlights, the maverick detective and the female victim, the monsters of the week and the big bads.[24] One of the central aims of my project is to see how these loops overlap and intersect, where they might unfold in unison, and where the threads can get tangled.

Felski's model of everyday time as "recurrence with forward movement" is also suggestive of an iterative pattern that has come to characterize the textuality and the experience of television. Iteration is, to employ the *Oxford English Dictionary* definition, "the repetition of an action or process (implying frequency or long continuance); repeated performance."[25] In this sense, iteration defines television in its operation as a storytelling medium, but the mathematical application of iteration is equally important. From a mathematical perspective, iteration as a repetitive process is done with the aim of approaching a desired goal, target, or result, but the process remains open-ended, where the results of one iteration are used as the starting point for the next iteration.[26] From this perspective, television is understood as a kind of folded media with a nonlinearity that is, once again, akin to a process of spiraling, looping, or doubling—continually moving backward and forward. The process here is, like the most recent celebrations of television's serial characteristics, cumulative, distinguished by an iterative process of repetition that is "lived" over time. Television iteration is therefore not simply a textual but also a temporal and spatial experience.

Television's "evolutionary logic"—the desired goal—may or may not be achieved: whether this is a sleeping child, a successful meal, or a satisfying ending.[27] Freeman's critique of "chrononormativity" is insightful as she argues that the "double time" of industrialization harnessed the sequence and its "dialectical companion," the cycle. Here the repetitions and routines of domestic life were seen to offer a space for the restoration and renewal of workers. The "idea of time as cyclical," she writes, "stabilizes its forward movement, promising renewal rather than rupture."[28] Renewal, though, is not always on the cards: the child won't sleep, the pot boils over, your favorite show is canceled or "jumps the shark," and what happens after the joke wears out? The disruptions and distractions of both television and the domestic are many, and in challenging the logic of linearity, there is a need to emphasize the contributions of queer theory and theorists such as Elizabeth Freeman. Freeman's work focuses on examples from literature and video art, but the investigation of television has been taken up by others with writers such as Gary Needham, Lynne Joyrich, Amy Villarejo, and Zoë Shacklock offering insights into the contradictions of television and its messy temporalities, informed by queer theory and experience. Villarejo's project *Ethereal Queer* examines the role of television in the construction of queer identities and subjectivities and how television time(s) experienced as "segmentation, repetition, seriality, frozen, paused, captured, looped, restored, lost, and found" might be used to "organize, disrupt, or otherwise confront queer temporalities."[29] The capacities of these temporal modes have arguably been intensified through on-demand services, time-shifting devices, streaming video, and the multiplication and layering of screens. This multiplicity has led some television studies scholars to endeavor to "bring some order to [a] volatile and messy media landscape,"[30] and while this analysis may be invaluable to those of us who are still catching our breath, I'm keen to stress an alternative direction or opportunity that is less a desire for order than an embrace or temporary untangling of what is volatile and messy.

Joyrich, for example, in her short essay on the possibilities of a "queer television studies," draws on queer and feminist challenges to the logic of linearity and reproductive futurism to critique television, with its "narrative and economic reliance on futurity," and tackles a series of temporalities and textualities that are much more complex and contradictory.[31] She argues: "Televisual temporality and narrativity hardly adhere to a linear model of simply positive progression. Rather, television operates via restarts and reversals, iterations and involutions, branchings and braidings. Its imaginary is thus one of futurity without direct forward thinking, involving propagation without necessarily measurable progress and generation without necessarily clear continuity.

Thus, with both problems and potential, TV offers a model of proliferation—of multiplications, hybridizations, disseminations—beyond and besides teleological, Oedipal conceptions of a linear track from past to future."[32]

The pattern that begins to emerge in Joyrich's description—of "futurity without direct forward thinking"—can also be found in Felski's model and in her description of iterative movement. Joyrich offers an example of these iterative loops at play in her description of sitcom form: one that "depends on a regular return to the defining situation, thus constituting an iterative practice that, with whatever hijinks, hilarities, and even relative changes to the character group ensue in weekly episodes, impedes the possibility of straightforward, linear futurity."[33] The recent NBC sitcom *The Good Place* (2016–20), for example, knowingly plays with the notion of the "reset button" that has been seen as key to sitcom form by folding this feature into its ethical and moral experiments. The situation revolves and plays around with a supernatural being (Michael) and his all-knowing AI assistant (Janet) as they test a group of flawed human characters (Eleanor, Chidi, Tahani, and Jason) to see if they can learn and change enough to eventually make it to the "Good Place." An actual reboot button is incorporated into the scenario and, if pressed, will wipe the characters' memories and reset the experiment. As our "soul squad" learn to become "better people," the comedy, narrative, and character development is based around ideas of repetition and progress, and as Felski reminds us, "repetition is one of the ways we organize the world. . . . Quite simply, we become who we are through acts of repetition."[34]

While queer (television) theory is not the central framework of my project, I use it here both for what it tells us about (television) time and as a recognition of the alliance that can be drawn between queer lives with writing on disability, "crip time," and a feminist ethics of care that emerge as central to various chapters in this project. These are critical frameworks that also challenge notions of linearity and the accompanying orthodoxies of growth and development that privilege a vision of the child as the "future adult." This is a cultural script that emphasizes notions of competence, individualism, and autonomy alongside compulsory heterosexuality and able-bodiedness.[35] In writing this book I have drawn on my own experiences of caregiving and -receiving—as the sister to a young girl with Rett syndrome (chapter 1), the aunt of a young boy and girl quickly growing up (chapter 2), a single woman dining alone (chapter 3), and a middle-aged homemaker (chapter 4)—as a way to think through where television conforms to and departs from this normative script and to deepen our frames of reference in order to recognize the breadth of television's audiences and their lived experiences.

In the context of these rich traditions of thought and how they open up the possibility for the inclusion of a wider range of subjectivities and experiences in our investigations of television, I've found myself increasingly frustrated with the narrowness of a dominant critical lexicon used to discuss contemporary, predominantly US television: the cinematic, the complex, and the separation of television into "linear" and "nonlinear" forms. These are terms that circulate in popular, academic, and industry discourse, and within each are a set of implicit, and sometimes clearly explicit, value judgments that position different types and experiences of television against one another. "Cinematic," for instance, a term succinctly taken apart by Brett Mills,[36] elevates one form of television (predominantly high-end drama) over the rest of television by linking it with a more prestigious cultural form (see also the descriptor "novelistic"). "Complex" television, as previously encountered, is a term employed by Mittell to describe a particular mode of contemporary series-serial storytelling, characterized by puzzle narratives, transmedia world-building, and heightened fan engagement and control. The term is problematically positioned against that which he describes as "conventional" or the more "traditional" forms of episodic and serial storytelling that do not inspire, according to Mittell, the same level of passion and commitment among audiences.[37] The flow of broadcast television, now categorized as "linear," is that of an impoverished ordinary or everyday medium still controlled by schedulers and at the mercy of domestic distractions. Nonlinear forms, those that exist outside of broadcast television's traditional flow, are instead celebrated as offering viewer control, choice, and concentrated or immersive viewing. Nonlinear forms, for instance, are more likely to be associated with "prized content," which Amanda Lotz places in opposition to "linear viewing" to describe content "so compelling that it suffers from interruption" and that might be characterized by viewers' or content producers' attempts to eliminate or reduce disruption.[38] Alongside dictating the cultural status of specific televisual forms, the risk here is also in reproducing hierarchies of engagement—for example, positioning the "distracted housewife" in opposition to the "absorbed fan"—that impacts on the kinds of subjectivities imagined by television and television studies. In the context of the puzzles and prizes of contemporary television, it is perhaps paradoxical that the teleological applications of the "complex" and the "nonlinear" returns us instead to the linear time of history, progress, and evolution.

As these terms imply, it is the notion of interruption that returns as a defining characteristic of the medium and one that is seen to reflect the way the television text is embedded in the everyday lives of its viewers. In the privileging of prized forms and immersive and mobile modes of engagement, certain scholars within the field have raised concerns regarding the "loss of the ordinary"[39] that has emerged with the growing interest in the ways in which "television has been liberated from time and space."[40] This is television that, with the emergence of DVRs, DVDs, on-demand and streaming services, and mobile platforms and technologies, affords the "viewser" with a new sense of agency. In this framework, television consumption is no longer subject to a program schedule or to the quotidian rhythms of the home. There may be a false equivalence in this argument, however, given that the removal of television content from a scheduled broadcast flow does not necessarily mean it is removed from the experience or its occupation of daily life. While this everyday is certainly of a more "privatized and individualized"[41] kind, which clearly has implications for how we think about the nation-binding project of television (particularly in a public service context like the UK), the relationship between television text and domestic context is still ripe for continued investigation and analysis.[42] Within the domestic context, therefore, interruption and distraction still have a part to play in our understanding of the viewing experience: misbehaving children still need putting to bed, sofa spills still need mopping up, ghosts continue to intrude, and life doesn't always go as planned. In chapter 3, for instance, I consider what it might mean to eat with television and how attitudes of distraction and mindlessness accompany both sides of this dynamic. But I also recognize that distraction and interruption are not the only experiences that characterize the ways in which television is embedded and embodied in the everyday. This project is less concerned with defining what television *is* than with finding ways to describe what television *does* to us and what *we do* with television. In relation to my own autobiography, home and the family are my central points of reference as I return to the embrace of television and, in Patricia Mellencamp's words, its "messy vitality."[43]

Television's Ordinary Affects

I appreciate that the domestic scenarios I explore in this book are not the only sites in which television is consumed, but the home remains a principal site of consumption, and one that is still alive with possibilities and resonances for the ways we might remain attentive to television. Television's placement within and influence on domestic space, family arrangements, and everyday lives has long been subject to the investigations and analysis of scholars and researchers.[44] The home and family are ambiguous and ambivalent sites, and everyday life, as Felski writes, "should not be conceptualized as a homogenous and predictable terrain. It embraces a diverse range of activities, attitudes, and forms of behavior; it contains 'broken patterns, non-rational and duplicitous actions, irresolvable conflicts and unpredictable events.' Nevertheless, we typically conduct our daily lives on the basis of numerous unstated and unexamined assumptions about the way things are, about the continuity, identity, and reliability of objects and individuals."[45] Expressed in these terms, everyday life is filled with both anxieties and securities, plans and revisions, and practices—such as television viewing—that work to ensure a sense of continuity, regularity, and familiarity but that are also alive to the possibilities of interruptions, accidents, and emergencies. This book seeks to explore the role of television within this diverse and often contradictory terrain and to highlight those "unstated and unexamined assumptions" that also underpin the taken-for-granted status of television. In her writing on what she refers to as "ordinary affects," Kathleen Stewart explores the ways in which we can become "tuned in" to the everyday and attentive to the practices, affects, and intensities of the ordinary.[46] One of the purposes of this project is to situate television among these ordinary affects in order to open up the resonances and potentialities that emerge in both specific moments of viewing but also in and across a life lived with or alongside television. Stewart writes of everyday life as "a continual motion of relations,"[47] and it is in this notion of both continuity and relationality that the taken-for-granted, "always there" status of television might be seen to have a particular affective power. This is not, however, to lock television into the time of the now (and television therefore as forgetful and forgettable) but to understand how continuity is always open to contingency and to look out for those loops between past, present, and future. I draw on Stewart's writing to situate television as part of a system of ordinary affects that rest on a particular understanding of the imaginative possibilities of everyday practices within the home.

"The home cocoon," Stewart writes, "lives in a vital state—open, emergent, vulnerable, and jumpy."[48] Certainly, early theorizations of television's liveness and copresence focused on the vulnerable and jumpy aspects of live broadcasting, from technical breakdowns to catastrophic irruptions and the threat to that home cocoon that television could pose. Anxiety, as theorized by Mellencamp, was "television's affect,"[49] but comfort, security, and familiarity could also be found in its emphasis on continuity and the promise of return to the same time and place tomorrow. In chapter 2, I explore this fluctuating dynamic of anxiety and security in more detail and in relation to the role of television in mediating the anxiety associated with children's bedtimes. The contingencies associated with television's liveness and its public address may have lost some of their affective power in a digital era in which audiences are more fragmented. The contingencies of everyday life, however, still create particular conditions in which the experience of viewing remains open and emergent. Stewart writes that the home "lives as a practiced possibility, emergent in projects like home remodeling, shopping, straightening up the house, rearranging furniture, making lists, keeping a diary, daydreaming, or buying lottery tickets."[50] These are practices that harbor the promise of the future. But the home is also filled with "traces of a past still resonant in things; on a dresser top are loose change, pens, receipts, books, scattered jewelry, knick-knacks, a kid's drawing, and a long-discarded urgent list of things to do."[51] Television in the home can also be seen to bear the weight of possibilities and promises of the future along with the traces and resonances of the past. Television's contingency, like that of the home, remains alive to the possibility that the viewer might travel in either direction: memory and remembrance as likely to be activated as fantasy, aspiration, and desire. The domestic practices that Stewart references (and I want to emphasize the implication of iteration within the word "practice") are ones that "stage the jump from ideal to matter and back again" and "that can fuse a dream world to the world of ordinary things."[52]

These imaginative and relational movements can be seen to enact a continual pattern of retreat and return, another set of loops that Karen Lury has also seen as central to the experience of television and that is also crucial to this book: "There is no escape from the everyday; or rather, in sleeping, dreaming, working, in sex and in watching television, each everyday is occupied by a series of escapes and returns. If it can be agreed that television criticism is addressing the encounter between viewer and text—recognizing this as offering opportunities to both escape from and return to the individual everyday—then this experience will be interesting, revealing and worth understanding, whether it is a two-year-old girl watching the *Teletubbies*, or a forty-year-old man watching *Deadwood*."[53] In this short essay Lury draws on Roland Barthes's notion of the punctum—a snag or trigger that pulls the viewer backward or forward to a different time and space—to argue that the work of television criticism should be alive or attentive to the contingencies of these unplanned affective responses. In both the repetitive aspects of the everyday and the accumulations of our autobiographies, this book seeks to capture the push and pull of television, how it exists alongside the patterns and rhythms of other everyday practices, such as caregiving, sleeping, eating, and traveling, but also how it can become braided within them, through the design, choice, and implementation of particular forms of texts. Alongside and related to the notion of iteration, this pattern of retreat and return recurs across the case studies I explore in this book. This movement backward and forward across times, spaces, borders, and boundaries emerges in a series of everyday materialities and affects that form the focus of this project; from the transitions between waking and sleeping, eating and digesting, to the losses and recuperations of remembrance, homesickness, and homemaking. These border crossings, segues, and transitions also remain a central feature of television's characteristic flow, whether we are gently pulled, coaxed, lured, or pushed between programs and content. Likewise, the television screen continues to be productively conceptualized as a threshold in and of itself, and one this book traverses alongside those of the bed, garden, body, home, and nation.[54]

Vanessa Feltz's Grandmother

Television not only facilitates but articulates in its textual forms and content those looping relationships between everyday time and life time and the different affective registers of contingency and continuity. *Cucumber*—an eight-part series written by Russell T. Davies and broadcast on Channel 4 in the UK in 2015—centers on the lives of a middle-aged gay couple, Henry and Lance, who live comfortably in the northern city of Manchester. It is a series that echoes Davies's hugely successful, controversial, and influential 1990s drama *Queer as Folk* (Channel 4, 2000–2005) by returning to the same town and community, though focusing on new characters at a different stage of their lives. In this sense both series mirror their queer author's experiences of growing up and growing old. The main catalyst for the later series is Henry's midlife crisis, prompted by his own sexual insecurities and the lure of a younger man, as he walks out of his relationship and the home he shares with Lance. So far, so familiar to regular viewers of soap opera, however, the series takes an unexpected turn in episode 6 to produce a remarkable and hugely affecting piece of television. The episode opens with Lance casually shopping in a brightly lit supermarket and accompanied by the show's familiar upbeat soundtrack. This rather banal scene is one that recurs across the series, with the supermarket invested with middle-aged desire and characters "cruising" down the aisles. In the closing shot of this particular scene, Lance turns a corner and walks away from camera, framed in the center of two supermarket aisles. It is here, in this most everyday of moments, that *Cucumber* unexpectedly announces Lance's imminent death with the following text appearing in the bottom half of the frame: "Lance Edward Sullivan 1966–2015." What follows in the next twenty minutes is the story of Lance's life up until the present day. We witness his birth, the death of his mother, and the grief of his father; we see the joyful child laughing in front of the TV and his revulsion at his father's "birds and bees" talk. The same boy runs through the woods wracked with shame as he tosses an illicit copy of *Playgirl* into the river. We follow as he leaves for university, where he meets his first girlfriend before acknowledging a different sexual identity and discovering a queer community. In a repeated scene that conveys the passing of years, we see Lance repeatedly return home at Christmas to deliver presents to his father and sister: first with his girlfriend, who is warmly welcomed in, and later with different same-sex partners in tow. In these later scenes Lance stands with each partner on the threshold as his disapproving father coldly answers the door (see figures Intro.2–7). These returns are intercut with a history of hope and broken hearts, casual encounters, and a loved one lost to the AIDS epidemic—a detail that emerges when Lance turns up for Christmas one year on his own. We are privy to this succession of relationships intertwined with a blossoming career and upward mobility. Across the years, fashions, haircuts, tastes, music, homes change, repeat, and accumulate. His father's acceptance is signaled as Lance finally crosses the threshold with his choice of partner. Then Henry eventually enters his life, the love of his life, supporting him through his father's death, and soon thereafter they make a new beginning by buying a house together. But then we witness the ways in which their relationship becomes cluttered by building irritations and unspoken resentments until that fateful argument in the first episode in which Lance and Henry eventually fall apart. The remaining thirty minutes of episode 6 chart Lance's final day. He is still hurt and angry but also nervously and excitedly preparing for a "date" with his new colleague, Daniel (a handsome but erratic "straight" man with whom he has developed a flirty relationship). At the end of the date, Lance goes back to Daniel's flat. Daniel's clearly unstable undertones are heightened by both the viewer's foreknowledge and the character's confusing sexual signals. We are simultaneously unsurprised and shocked when a moment of intimacy between the two men is quickly flipped: with hatred and self-loathing, Daniel turns on Lance and smashes him across the skull with a golfing iron. Just once. Quick and brutal and senseless, but not yet the end. The camera closes in to a close-up of Lance, sitting up straight as blood trickles down the side of his head and tears pool in his eyes. Silent. Still. His life flashing before his eyes as his death looms. The image of Lance is intercut with a montage that depicts his final thoughts and sensations. Blurred images and sounds of

FIGURES INTRO.2–7 Lance on the threshold. *Cucumber* (Channel 4, 2015), episode 6.

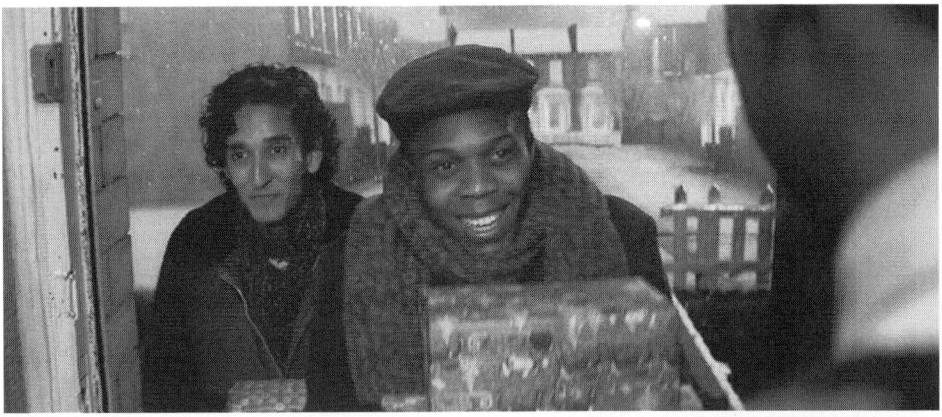

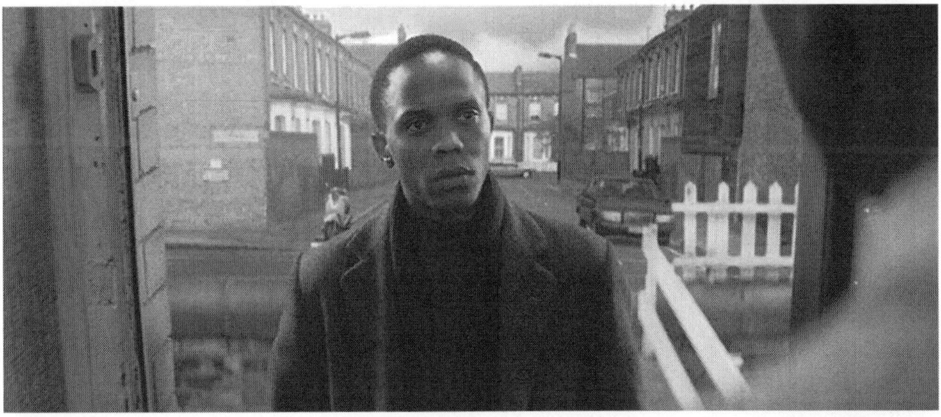

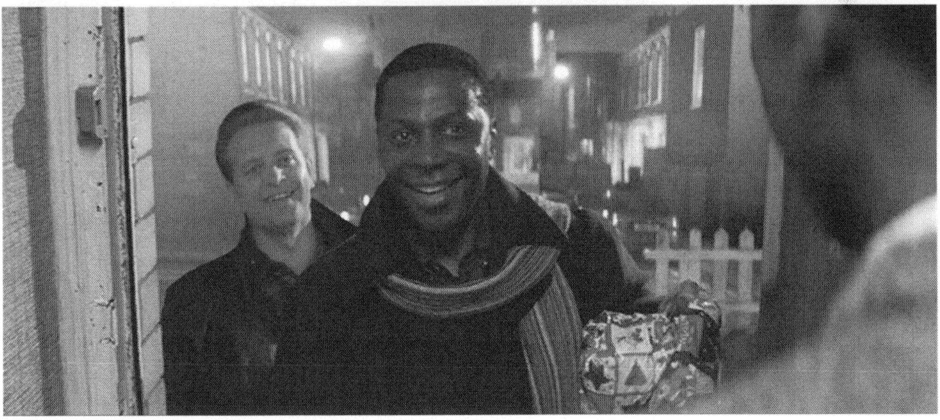

his immediate surroundings are mixed with a fragmentary collage of his most vital and banal memories drawn from across the life we've just witnessed. Among the fragments are images and sounds that fill in some of the gaps—a panicked boy horrified as pages of a pornographic magazine float up to the surface of the river; his lover dying in a hospital bed. There is sex, love, grief, loss, joy, judgment, music, laughter, dancing, light, and Henry. And then blackness and silence.

This example articulates several of the ideas that I have sought to establish in this chapter. The first is the intertwining of what Felski has referred to as everyday time with life time and the looping effect created by a pattern of repetition with forward movement. The chronological charting of Lance's life and death moves forward in time while capturing a series of cycles that characterize the life course: love, sex, death, betrayal, departures and returns, the fodder of any good soap opera or the "best bits" of the reality television show participant. Lance's perpetual, seasonal return to the threshold of his family home dramatizes both a history of queer exclusion and acceptance but also illustrates the border crossings—between bodies, homes, and relationships—that become a central theme of the drama and its exploration of modern queer identities and communities. The series also folds these dramatic moments into an attentiveness to the affective qualities of the everyday and both the banality and significance of popular culture's role within it. Lance's dying moments are infected by an earworm he has been unable to shake all day as televised images of Massiel singing "La, La, La" at the Eurovision Song Contest in 1968 infiltrate that last series of associations. The song is there to visualize a conversation Lance had earlier in the day when a remorseful and contrite Henry comes round to the house to try and make amends. Trying to appear upbeat and unfazed but seething with anger, Lance, while putting his shopping away in the kitchen, chatters about the song he's had stuck in his head:

> That stupid song, keeps going round and round and round. Some stupid piece of shit from thirty years ago. It's like—I read this article once, by Vanessa Feltz. About twenty years ago when she used to write for the *Mirror*. She said her grandmother always used to do the washing up in the same way: water too hot to the touch. I remember reading it because that's exactly how I wash up. The thing is, every time I wash up, I think of Vanessa Feltz's grandmother. Isn't that ridiculous? Every single day of my life. Just for a second. I think of Vanessa Feltz's grandmother. 'Cause she's in there, she's stuck; she's this tiny little thing that won't go

away. 'Cause that's all we are, Henry. Heads full of shit. All the stuff that just gathers over the years whether we want it or not. Stupid old song. Water too hot to the touch. I love you. So what?!

Despite Lance's disenchantment in this scene, the affect of this speech and the way in which that "head full of shit" is captured in the final moment of the episode is invested with urgency and poignancy, both momentary and momentous. The episode loads up the weight of this man's life, both ordinary and extraordinary, then discharges that weight in one senseless act of hate. The sense of loss is devastating. But Lance's anecdote also captures that push and pull of the everyday "that can fuse a dream world to the world of ordinary things." Associations become memories become habits, and now, every time I wash up, I think of both Lance and Vanessa Feltz's grandmother.[55]

Despite the violent nature of Lance's death, the pattern of return that I want to highlight is not constituted by the hauntings and hallucinations that might characterize forms of trauma. There is clear potential for trauma in Lance's story and its depiction of a violent crime enacted on a queer Black body,[56] but as I have argued elsewhere, trauma has come to dominate discussions of television and its relationship to memory.[57] In such models television is *taken to* task for reproducing and repeating traumatic images and narratives or is *put to* task as a therapeutic machine that can "work through" the recurrence of such extreme emotions. Instead, here I draw on Lance's story for the way it dramatizes the interweaving of temporal patterns: in the episode we are invited into Lance's everyday time—the repetitive act of washing up, the song or reference that goes round and round and round—and Lance's lifetime. What the episode conveys is a relationship between different temporal scales, micro and macro, that informs my own understanding and experience of television. This configuration is different to the relationship between "part" and "whole" that is often the preoccupation of writing on television's serial forms. I wish not to return us to this completist sensibility but, instead, to foreground the "ongoing-ness" of the everyday. As Ben Highmore argues: "The sense that the artwork completes sensual experience (resolves it into more satisfying and morally superior forms) is a central tenet within aesthetic discourse, and it immediately suggests that there is something generally incomplete and unsatisfactory about day-to-day experience . . . aesthetic satisfaction (in its dominant mode) is satisfaction in the end form of a process, rather than in the messy *informe* of the ongoing-ness of process. Most of what constitutes the day-to-day is irresolvable and desperately incomplete, yet, for all that, also most vital."[58] It is this last line that seems to me to perfectly capture the power of Lance's story, but it also opens up a way in which to value and understand television on its own terms and precisely for its incompleteness. The possible textual manifestations of this idea are diverse, and this project remains attentive to those fragments that become buried, stuck, or lost and that can prompt a range of affective responses—from frustration, grief, and desperation to resilience, hope, and care. Attentiveness has itself been central to understandings of care and how we recognize and respond to the needs of others (in both caring and being cared for). This has taken the form of an attentiveness to embodied forms of knowledge and the "small moments" that have been seen to evidence the existence of care (moments that become central to the scenes of care I revisit in chapters 1 and 2). But the attentiveness that this book advocates is also fundamental to the work of textual analysis. In its cultivation of a close reader, one who lingers and dallies,[59] the labor of textual analysis can uncover, unfold, or untangle those "small" pleasures, moments, and movements that constitute the ordinary affective realm of television in order to begin to build an incremental and iterative portrait of a life.

On Living with Television

This book is populated by my own encounters with television: sometimes momentary, sometimes durational, often repetitive either through form, feeling, or routine. They are encounters that I've chosen in an endeavor to capture those patterns of television that emerge within both everyday time and across our lifetimes, and my choice of examples is motivated by a desire to interrogate how television can become folded into our lives and how our lives, in turn, activate our uses of television. Alongside autobiographical anecdote, memory, and reflection, my approach draws on the analysis of a range of television texts that, during the writing of this book, became central to these various encounters. My use of textual analysis can be characterized as operating in two distinct but interrelated modes that are indebted to feminist critical traditions within television studies and beyond. The first explores the relationship between the text of television and the domestic context of viewing to account for both textual and experiential characteristics of the medium. The second turns to the relationship between the text and the self as a key site for the production of meaning.

Early theories of television broadcasting understood the ways in which the medium, as technology and cultural form, was entangled with the rituals, rhythms, and routines of our private and public lives: bound to the repetitive experiences of domestic labor and the cyclical patterns of the nation. Returning to where Carol Lopate and Tania Modleski began, I remain captivated by the ways in which the textual object is activated by the material and affective dimensions of everyday life. Tackling issues of cultural value, women's genres, feminine aesthetics, and "reading" positions, this scholarship established a common understanding of television's medium specificity as tied to its spatiotemporal arrangements: the housewife emerged as the model viewer, and domestic space and culture as the principal zone of consumption. Here the textual and the experiential qualities of television were seen to be both activated and constituted by the times and spaces of the home and its quotidian rhythms. Charlotte Brunsdon writes that it was Lopate "who first formulate[d] the correlation between the rhythm of daytime programming and housework."[60] For instance, Lopate observed how the busy aesthetics of the morning game show and the anesthetic qualities of the afternoon serial rhymed with daily patterns of women's work and rest in the home.[61] However, it was Modleski's development of this observation in *Loving with a Vengeance* that had a lasting impact.[62] Modleski considered the soap opera as both an archetypal televisual and feminine form and worked to illuminate the ways in which the context of viewing (the home) and the experience of the viewer (the housewife) were inscribed within the text. This particular alignment produced two couplings that became central to early understandings of television's medium specificity: the repetition and endlessness of the soap opera's "eternal return" to the "same time tomorrow"[63] and the characteristics of interruption and distraction that emerged through the endless deferral of narrative resolution, the fragmentation of television flow and the distractions of the domestic environment. In her emphasis on the feminine aspects of soap opera form and its ambivalences, Modleski argued for an understanding of its narrative pleasures and unpleasures as "thoroughly adapted to the rhythms of women's lives in the home."[64]

For Modleski, the entanglement of text and context is read through the subjectivity of the "housewife." However, one of the central critiques of her argument is the reference to a female subject that is seen to be a "historically unchanging and universal category."[65] While I wish to pay a debt to Modleski's legacy, I will decenter the position of the wife and mother in this particular study of television. My own approach has been to acknowledge a viewer that is, like television itself, both changing and unchanging and a subject position that depends on a notion of relationality. For example, in the stories I draw on I am neither a wife nor a mother, but a sister, daughter, aunt, child, adolescent, and adult. Sometimes these different selves are alone with television and sometimes they watch together. And while the experiences I write about—eating, sleeping, homemaking, driving, caring—will be recognized by many readers, I understand that the stories and encounters I draw on won't necessarily be. This, however, is a fundamental aspect of an autoethnographic approach it opens: a space for the reader to consider how they do or don't recognize themselves or their experiences in the description of familiar everyday practices. As Carolyn Ellis, Tony Adams, and Arthur Bochner write, "In autoethnography, the focus of generalizability moves from respondents to readers, and is always being tested by readers as they determine if a story speaks to them about their experience or about the lives of others they know."[66] There is certainly a parallel to be drawn here with aspects of reader-response theory that inform my other use of textual analysis within the book. Within this particular tradition, "the virtual space between text and reader" is understood to be a site for "meaningful interpretation or communication."[67] Here the attentiveness that textual analysis requires is central to my project—not just as an illustration or representation of a particular everyday practice but as a demonstration of how television articulates memory, emotion, and affect. More specifically, I draw on feminist writings and understandings of the text-reader relationship that have given us, as Lynne Pearce has argued, "a new model of how the text-reader relation can be used to make sense of the world(s) we inhabit: and, in particular, the way in which we can creatively combine the texts of others with the textual productions of the self to gain a new perspective on our complex 'locatedness' within contemporary culture."[68] Out of this tradition, Pearce herself devises an intertextual autobiographical approach that I have employed at certain points in this book and that accounts for "the emotional fabric of the reading process" as one dependent on "an interweaving of textual and extra-textual associations, as some cue in the text prompts us to the scripting of a parallel text based on some aspect of our personal or intertextual experience."[69] The modes of analysis I employ offer me a way into the intertwining of television's texts with everyday domestic practices and life histories and allow me to get at the intimate, durational, and ordinary affects of the television experience.

The soap opera or the serial itself might have seemed like the obvious texts to analyze in this way. Scholars such as Robert Allen and Christine Geraghty recognized early on the ways in which long-term engagement with soap opera narratives carried the accumulative weight of both characters' and viewers' memories and histories.[70] Instead I have chosen an approach that has been led by different examples of routine and everyday practices, performances, and affects that are experienced in relation to the home and the family in order to investigate how they are inscribed within and activated by television. I adopt a multigeneric approach as a way to think more holistically about the diversity of texts and experiences that television offers and to suggest that these diverse texts (when and because they are television) can act in this way: from the seemingly most simple (preschool television) to the apparently most complex (high-end drama). A secondary purpose of this has been to widen the frames of reference and analysis beyond television's legitimated forms and to pay attention to different kinds of viewers and experiences that are often marginalized by film and television studies. My opening two chapters, for example, revolve around the use of television (Disney Home Video and preschool TV) by the dis/abled child and those who care for them. But I also maintain that it is necessary to see how, rather than arresting and rescuing them from the polluted flow of the rest of television, those legitimated forms still sit within our everyday lives. For instance, my discussion of *Hannibal* (NBC, 2013–15) in chapter 3 frames the series in relation to practices of eating and digesting to insist on an understanding of television as existing within an embodied everyday rather than as a prized or rarefied commodity. To put it simply, this book describes the life lived with television while asking questions about what it means to "grow up" with and to live alongside television in the process. In doing so it reembraces the loopiness of television: its contradictions, oscillations, and ambivalences, its multiplications and layers, its againness and its endlessness. This is television again in Patricia Mellencamp's terms, as "both/and" rather than "either/or."[71]

Coming Up . . .
Chapters 1 and 2 explore the role of television as a scene or site of care. The material and affective qualities of care are central within our everyday lives, especially within the context of the home and family. However, caring practices have received little attention in relation to domestic media cultures. Across these chapters, then, I argue for an understanding of television as a technology of care by exploring the ways in which it finds itself embedded within complex routines of care within the home, specifically in relation to the child, child care, and children's television. Through a feminist ethics of care I uncover the forms of love and labor associated with both caring and being cared for and the role that specific forms of television can play in the constitution of these bonds and relationships. Chapter 1 employs an auto/biographical approach as it opens with the tale of my younger sister, Alice, and the significance of her repetitive viewing of Disney Home Videos throughout

our childhoods and adolescences. Here I consider how Alice's experience, as a child with profound and multiple disabilities and an obsession with Disney films and songs, widens our understanding of media use and complicates notions of "growing up" and prevalent (normative) conceptions of childhood. In this context, the patterns of time and feeling that this book explores disrupt linear notions of growth and development and, alongside an ethics of care and practices of life-writing, challenge the sovereignty of the autonomous subject that is often imagined in writing about film and television spectatorship. My use of an auto/biographical approach interweaves Alice's story into my own and operates, in this chapter, to emphasize the relational and interdependent aspects of both care and life-writing that, I argue, have particular political resonance for the stories we tell about disability.

Chapter 2 continues the exploration of discourses and experiences of care in relation to television through its focus on preschool scheduling and programming, exemplified by the CBeebies Bedtime Hour and the series *In the Night Garden*. Though the use of autobiography is less sustained in this chapter, it employs a series of vignettes charting my own experiences of caring for my young niece and nephew as it reflects on the design of television intended to be used by the carer and child as part of a bedtime routine. This is a routine that has been characterized as one that moves between conflict and comfort, anxiety and security as the child and carer negotiate the transitions between times and spaces within the home. Children's bedtime television emerges as a potent example through which to renew our attention to both the "dailiness" of television and the patterns of anxiety and security that have been central to theorizations of the medium through the work of scholars such as Patricia Mellencamp and Roger Silverstone. Preschool television's attempts to manage this experience in the home is an example of the way in which it can be seen to "care for" its audience. This is framed within a public service context and as part of the "duty of care" undertaken by broadcasters and tied to a history of paternalism that seeks to protect, control, and manage the child and instill "proper" notions of parenting within the home. This history also relies on a normative conception of childhood by positioning the child as the future adult and citizen to construct a fantasy of the family unit that assumes in its address both a dutiful child and a caring parent. However, as Charlotte Brunsdon has written in relation to the fantasy image of the housewife, "Fantasies of the real and the everyday can be as powerful as fantasies of the unrealistic/fantastic." Brunsdon remarks on the continuities between soap opera viewing and the little girls' imagination of the "tidy house" as a "fantasy of an everyday life of gendered order."[72] Here the CBeebies Bedtime Hour emerges as a fantasy of an everyday life of *generational* order as I explore the ways in which the Bedtime Hour is constructed as a "useful tool" for carers and parents and a space for intergenerational engagement. *In the Night Garden* is a product of this specific intergenerational use and address, catching the viewer somewhere between an adult's memory and a child's dream. In this chapter, I continue to interweave television's texts and contexts to uncover how the motions and patterns of the bedtime routine are mirrored by their textual manifestations. In this context, television, with its repeated patterns and journeys of retreat and return, is used to help negotiate the transitions between times and spaces faced by the child (between day and night; waking and sleeping; today and tomorrow; diegetic and domestic; being with others and being alone). Through these negotiations, the Bedtime Hour works to alleviate anxiety and ensure a sense of continuity for the child. Here we cross thresholds represented by the bed, home, and garden, and these are aligned with the threshold of the television screen, representing permeable borders between inside and outside, the self and the world, the private and the public.

Chapter 3, "TV Dinners," continues to investigate the relationships between inside and outside, individual and social, though this time focusing on the threshold of the body. Unlike in the previous two chapters, the viewing context is that of living alone with television. The image of the lone viewer is one that populates advertisements for newer forms of "platform mobility" that celebrate ideas of individualism and the freedom to move, unhindered, both around and outside the home. These images and promises of the fluid transitions between times and spaces are also suggestive of the imagined porosity of the television screen. Here an alignment can be drawn between the threshold of the screen and that of the body, one that is illuminated through the act of eating with television. As Annemarie Mol has written: "Neither tightly closed off, nor completely open, an eater has semi-permeable boundaries."[73] This chapter seeks to explore the alignments and synergies between eating and television through both theoretical understandings of the two practices and in relation to each as part of our routinized and everyday behaviors within the home. The metaphorical associations between television viewing and eating have long invoked a set of cultural anxieties that rehearse the discourses of distraction and attention that have dominated discussions of television. But these associations also call into being the material conditions of both viewing and eating and how they work together as an often-overlooked mode of engagement, and in which one can be seen to act as an accompaniment to the other. This chapter asks what the consequences of this layered engagement might be for our experiences of texts, tastes, and textures alongside what it can tell us about the forms of intersubjectivity that television enables. Drawing attention to a series of "eating scenes" both on and in front of the screen, I consider how these moments have informed, and been informed by, the ambivalences of eating within my own life. Here I consider how, for example, the protean affects of a series such as *Man v. Food* (Travel Channel, 2008–10) are created through those parallel texts of program and viewer. Through a discussion of the series *Hannibal*, I argue that scenes and performances of eating also offer another lens through which to make visible the iterative patterns of television forms (from the serial to the GIF) and experiences. And despite the contemporary sovereignty of the individualized and autonomous viewer, this relationship offers a prime site through which to explore the continuing connections that television can forge between the self and others.

Returning to where this book began, the final chapter continues to reflect on the comings and goings that have characterized my adult life so far. Whether by choice or necessity, a range of life events and experiences— work, study, romance, estrangement, exile—can take us away from the places and landscapes in which we grew up. My own experience of traveling between my family home in Yorkshire and my working home in Scotland forms the basis for this chapter as I consider how these repetitive journeys and the associated feelings of disorientation and indeterminacy have informed the views of "home" I see on TV. Here I draw on the BBC family drama *Last Tango in Halifax* (2012–), set in my home county of West Yorkshire in northern England, for the particular view of the north it offers. The series sits within a tradition of representation that is underpinned by northern writers' experiences of departure and return, and an experience that also heavily features in the shuttling to and fro of the choreography and characters in the drama itself. This pattern of movement through the landscape evokes my own experiences of travel but also points toward a more unsettled point of view, one that sits on both the inside and the outside, always yet never quite at home. These unsettled feelings are produced, in part, through the copresence of times and places that characterize television as, in Mimi White's terms, always "a relation between at least two places or identities, and often more."[74] But it is also symptomatic of the temporal, experiential, and textual loops of television that similarly shuttle us between past, present, and future. Through an analysis of the midlife terrain of the sitcom *Catastrophe* (Channel 4, 2015–19) I consider how past experiences and imagined futures have shaped the decisions I've made in the present. Caught in between past and future, here and there, I conclude by reflecting on the necessary incompleteness of both television and the life-writing project.

With this incompleteness in mind, and because the events of 2020 perfectly illustrate the contingency that characterizes our domestic and televisual lives, I felt the need to add an epilogue. The COVID-19 pandemic and the national and local lockdowns that followed have presented, for many though not all, a radical break in our everyday lives. But it has also made the experience of living with television highly visible: viewers have turned to the medium—in both its broadcast and online variants—in record numbers. In line with the themes of this book, the epilogue reflects on the affordances and avoidances of television viewing and how they shaped my own experiences of an unsettled and unsettling period in recent history.

Television, in each of these chapters, is understood as a relational object, but importantly, the television viewer is recognized as a relational being in their connection to other people—regardless of whether those other people are in the room or not—and to their previous selves. Despite these experiences of disorientation I am lucky to have a family that has given me such steady foundations. For that, for them, for our sadnesses and our joys, the conflicts and the comforts, I am beyond grateful. This book is for all of them, present and absent, whether they want it or not. The losses and gains, the securities and anxieties I explore in this book won't be everyone's, but they might resonate beyond my own life to capture a broader sense of the ambivalences, oscillations, and iterations that emerge through the everyday nexus of television, the home, and the family. The analysis, criticism, and appreciation of television, I argue, should remain alive to the contingencies and continuities of everyday life and to the passing of time, thus enabling us to access the full range of television's uses, meanings, and patterns of feeling.

1 TO (NOT) GROW UP WITH TELEVISION

I begin this chapter with a photograph (figure 1.1). I present it here as evidence for the story I want to tell. This is a well-established beginning, in the spirit of Annette Kuhn's use of family photographs and memoir in her study *Family Secrets*, and the search for clues, traces, and markers that comprise her account of "memory work."[1] It is also inspired by Lynn Spigel's collection and analysis of hundreds of "family snapshots of people posing with their TV sets" that provide, in her words, "an archive of everyday life."[2] What does this specific remnant from an everyday family archive have to say?

In the image is my younger sister, Alice. It is her birthday and she is being presented with a cake. There are six candles on top, but I can tell she is older— ten, I suspect. She sits in her red wheelchair; characteristically, she is leaning to the left (a result of her scoliosis) with one hand raised to her mouth and

FIGURE 1.1 Alice's birthday (ca. 1995).

the other clasping the opposite arm. She looks pretty. Curls of hair frame her face and she wears a soft yellow party dress. She is looking not at the cake but toward whoever is taking the picture. Behind her is a fourteen-inch CRT television encased in white plastic, and on it sit several figurines, all characters from Disney's *The Lion King* (1994)—Simba, Zazu, Rafiki, Pumba, and Timon. The space around the TV has been tidied up for the family party, but I know that the cupboard underneath the set is crammed with VHS tapes of Disney animated films and "Sing-Along Song" compilation videos. They usually spill out of the oak cabinet, preventing us from shutting the door. I can still hear the *ping* of the catch as the door is forced shut on the bulky tapes but refuses to stay closed and pops open. The memory reminds me of the drawers and cupboards that run wild with magic after Mary Poppins's "Spoonful of Sugar" routine. Hidden inside the cabinet—and the photo—is Alice's archive.

I have wanted to write about Alice's relationship with television for a long time, specifically her repetitive viewing of Disney films and videos, as I think this might be where my interest in memory and television began. As in many other families, they accompanied so much of our early lives, entwining enchantment with the everyday: after-school routines and tea parties on ceilings, wet afternoons and magic carpet rides. Living with a sister with complex physical and cognitive disabilities (and an obsession with Disney), home video was also fundamental to our practices of both caring and being cared for, emerging as a key site of pleasure, comfort, and play as well as pacification, frustration, and boredom. It is this conflation of labor and love (Eva Feder Kittay's seminal collection on the ethics of care is itself titled *Love's Labor*)[3] that marks many of the tensions and dynamics within the various sections of this book that explore the role of television as a scene or site of care. Care is a political as well as a personal issue, consistently marginalized and devalued because of its connection with feminized, domestic, and low-paid forms of labor but also through entrenched fears and dismissals of forms of dependency and vulnerability. This chapter seeks to explore a number of routes through which to challenge such orthodoxies and their consequences for the lives of children with disabilities and their families. For example, Alice's and our family's use of Disney offers a lens not only through which to make visible routines of care as, in Marian Barnes's words, "difficult, situated, and complex," but also through which to witness how these routines are woven into our patterns of media and television consumption.[4] To position this more strongly, both this and the following chapter seek to argue for television, in both its texts and practices, as a technology of care.

But Alice's story also invites us into another world, one shaped by disability. Disability studies theorists Tanya Titchkosky and Rod Michalko have argued for disability as "a rupture in the clarity and unquestioned flow of daily life, and thus almost a 'natural' starting place for thinking about the workings of culture."[5] Alice's life and relationship with Disney offer both familiar and alternative ways of thinking about the temporalities of childhood, growth, and development, and in doing so challenge the dominant kinds of subjectivities, that is, able-bodied and able-minded, that are more often than not imagined when we write about film and television spectatorship. Ultimately, as an auto/biographical narrative inhabited from within a world of disability, this chapter is about what it might mean to (not) grow up with television. Not as in living without television but in complicating what it means to "grow up." Here I want to draw together both the challenge to linear notions of development with the insights of studies of memory and remembering. In their work on experiential psychology and memory Steven D. Brown and Paula Reavey remind us that "we are not a 'thing' that moves through time, but rather an ongoing pattern or series of knots made of diverse materials that repeats and reiterates as our life unfolds."[6] This chapter entwining Alice's story with my own concludes by exploring the knotting together of our lives with television and the residues, resonances, and inheritances that (re)activate our memories and our encounters with both television and the world.

Self and Sister

As the introduction has already outlined, the autobiographical lens I employ is indebted to long traditions within feminist scholarship across the sciences and the arts and humanities regarding the value of the personal and an understanding of the scholar as embodied and situated. For example, Kittay's challenge to the notion of "objectivity" within her field of moral philosophy and the abstract dehumanization of people with intellectual disabilities is informed by her position as the mother of a woman with such disabilities: "There is no view from nowhere," she maintains.[7] An auto/biographical lens, in this sense, might be adopted to tell us more about what it means to (not) grow up with television in a particular time and place. Alice's story, for instance, largely takes place during the period of the Disney renaissance (1989–99): a decade that saw the production and release of artistically and commercially successful films such as *The Little Mermaid* (1989), *Beauty and the Beast* (1991), *Aladdin* (1992), and *The Lion King* (1994) and that Chris Pallant has described as "a phase of aesthetic and industrial growth."[8] In other words, not only did the feature films of the Disney renaissance quickly acquire "classic" status, but the studio, along with a few others, was also able to capitalize on emerging synergies between home video and theatrical exhibition.[9] These commercial strategies were enabled by the increasing affordability, throughout the 1980s, of the VCR, which finally made an appearance in the Holdsworth household in the late 1980s. The particular confluence of events that framed Alice's emerging spectatorship should also be situated within a history of attitudes toward children with disabilities and the policies and practices that determined both the availability of resources and support and the capacity for Alice to have a full family life. As Ariella Meltzer and John Kramer have argued, histories of institutionalization and deinstitutionalization have shaped and been shaped by the attention to sibling relationships. For example, in the 1940s and 1950s parents were encouraged to send their children with disabilities to institutions in order to "protect" the psychological well-being of siblings.[10] I am also mindful of the battles my mum waged for education, respite care, and adaptations to our home (a lift between floors and ceiling-mounted hoists), battles that were hard fought and won. Yet I imagine that these battles would be more likely lost in recent years, during which a decade of austerity politics and the further rollback of the welfare state in the UK have hit children and adults with disabilities and their families the hardest.[11] In another time and place this story of a disabled childhood and a relationship between sisters would be very different; however, this chapter aims not to map these much broader histories but to highlight where they intersect. A rudimentary communication aid put together by my parents when Alice was a toddler offers an initial snapshot of this constellation and the role of media within the everyday life of a young disabled girl. A small photobook that could be carried to playdates and appointments operated as both a way for Alice to indicate her choices and to inform an army of medics, therapists, social workers, and carers who she was by situating her within the context of a family and a community, and as a keen media user. The book included images of important people and objects in her life: my older sister and I, our grandparents' house, her group of friends at the Child Development Centre, Special Ted, a box of Corn Flakes, our freestanding hi-fi stereo, and a large boxy television set (pre-VCR) (see figure 1.2). The selection of photographs compiled within the short album extends Alice's archive of everyday life to situate our television cultures, in line with the aims of this book, among other domestic practices such as sleeping and eating, as it points toward a set of activities and identities that are entirely relational.

It is important here to stress that my understanding and use of auto/

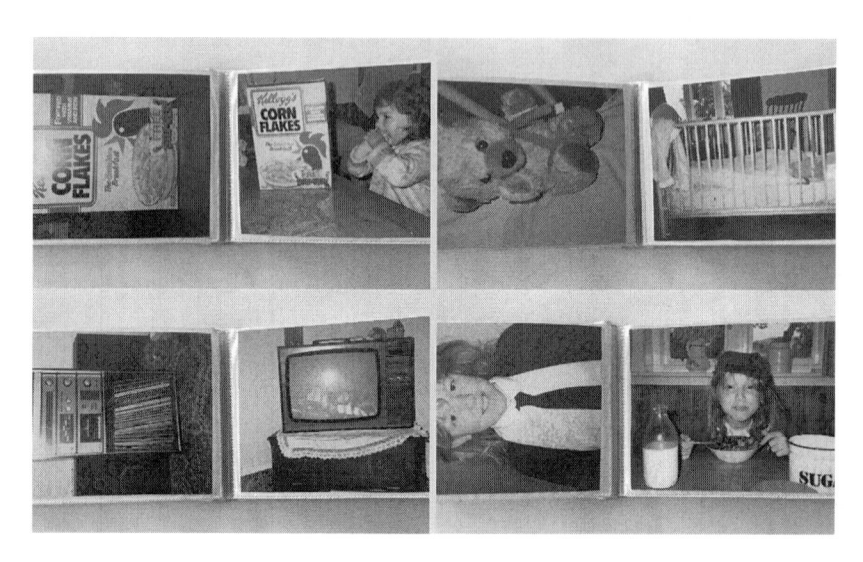

FIGURE 1.2 Images from Alice's photobook (ca. 1987).

biography within this chapter is informed by studies of life-writing and the family memoir that have challenged, alongside the work of Liz Stanley, the notion of the autobiographical "I" and the myth of the autonomous subject. Paul John Eakin, for example, refers to relational lives, "a term used to describe the story of a relational model of identity, developed collaboratively with others, often family members,"[12] while C. Thomas Couser, in his study *Vulnerable Subjects*, examines the notion of collaborative life-writing and the unstable oscillation between biography and autobiography.[13] My piecing together of Alice's story in this chapter comes from both the family archive and the conversations, memories, and recollections shared with my mum and older sister, Jess. The story is Alice's, mine, and ours. The stress on collaboration and relationality, in the practice of both memory work and life-writing, also has a particular political importance in relation to narratives of disability, where the emphasis on the singular voice has been seen to reinforce the perceived limitation of stories of individualism and the continued isolation of people with disabilities and their families within society and culture.[14]

Eakin writes that from a relational perspective the boundaries between self and other are hard to determine.[15] This is arguably amplified by the "nested relationships" of caregiving and -receiving.[16] A parallel can be easily drawn here with feminist scholarship on the ethics of care. This body of work similarly emphasizes relationality and interdependence as a challenge to the primacy of the neoliberal subject. However, material realities and an emphasis on agency have led to understandable hostilities toward "care" within disability activism. As Ann Fudge Schormans points out, "For many in the disabled people's movement the word 'care' has become synonymous with the pathologization and medicalization of impairment and disability, with exclusion, disempowerment and loss of rights: an oppressive practice to be actively resisted."[17] Yet underpinning this perspective is the continued belief in the sovereignty of the autonomous subject resulting in the association between care and paternalism. The consequence of such beliefs, as Schormans and others have argued, enables the persistent stigmatization of vulnerability and dependency, devaluing both those who give and those who are in need of care. What we need, Schormans suggests, are "alternative understandings of what care might be" and "the forms it might take."[18] Part of this project, then, is to reexamine what these forms might be and the role of television within the "matrices of care."[19] This also requires thinking about television as a relational object, not sitting outside these webs of caring relations but situated and enmeshed within them.

These studies of both autobiography and care ask us to consider how we conceive of subjectivity and identity, and they offer a lens through which to see ourselves through our relationships with others. To repeat Caughie's question: "Who do we think we are?" Who I am and the history of my engagement with television is bound up with Alice. Writing in her study of *Sisters on Screen*, Eva Rueschmann argues, "Sisters intimately mirror and challenge the self through time. Witnesses to one another's youthful passages into worldly experience and mature self-knowledge, sisters in adulthood often remain bound together through time and memory under the spell of their likenesses and their differences."[20] While the quote from Rueschmann implies a unified and upward trajectory shared by siblings, their lateral relationships invite comparison and make visible patterns of sameness and difference. Alice's presence both interrupts and intensifies these directions and patterns as disability disrupts the time and narrative of the "typically" developing child, requiring a more expansive frame of reference and the need to pay attention to a range of potential movements. As Kathryn Bond Stockton, writing on the queer child, neatly asserts: "There are ways of growing that are not growing up."[21] In response to this fact, Stockton considers the possibility of "growing sideways" as a challenge to the hegemony of vertical growth, and it is here that a clear alliance can be drawn between queer and disabled children and childhoods. But it is also within this lateral movement that sibling relations might be seen to harbor particular affordances.

Both disability studies and the scholarship on life-writing emphasize the relationships between parents and children. This is perhaps a logical consequence of psychoanalyst Juliet Mitchell's argument that "our understandings of psychic and social relationships [have] foregrounded vertical interaction—lines of ascent and descent between ancestors, parents and children."[22] Indeed, Mitchell's call for a "paradigm shift" from the vertical to the lateral has implications for how we understand the relationships between media technologies as less teleological and more *inter*dependent. In this context Michael Newman's reference to film, video, and television as "audio-visual siblings" seems particularly apposite,[23] and Mitchell's description of the love/hate of sibling relationships and replacements color the anxieties surrounding debates on medium specificity and cultural value: "The sibling is *par excellence* someone who threatens the subject's uniqueness. The ecstasy of loving one who is like oneself is experienced at the same time as the trauma of being annihilated by one who stands in one's place."[24] In this sibling relationship, television is perhaps the overlooked middle child, nestled between the "older" form of film and "new" media. This is a position I can empathize with.[25] When framed within the context of disability, the lateral shift Mitchell proposes is charged with a political significance that this chapter will endeavor to tease out: "A decline of the importance of descent," Mitchell writes, might be replaced by "a rise of the importance of alliance."[26]

Lives, Animated

Alice was born on June 5, 1985. My mum described her as a lovely, happy, and placid baby. At six months she began to notice that she wasn't physically developing in the same way my elder sister and I had or in comparison with her peers. A routine check with the health visitor also prompted initial concerns when she questioned what Alice could and couldn't do—measuring her against a script of "typical" or "normative" development. My mum was confused by the questioning; she recalls saying, "But she's lovely and happy. She loves music, she's sociable, and she smiles." At around twelve months it became clearer that Alice's development had slowed further, and she began to lose the skills, the few words, she was only just beginning to acquire. A bout of measles marked this period of regression, and after that, despite my parents' best attempts, she stopped saying words. After months and years of tests, at age five, unable to walk unassisted or to use language to communicate, Alice was diagnosed with Rett syndrome. In medical terms, Rett syndrome is "a progressive neurodevelopmental disorder caused by X-linked genetic mutations that occur almost exclusively in females" and one of the most common causes of profound or multiple disabilities in girls.[27] As Alice grew older, her mobility lessened, her hand movements became more limited, and her muscles more rigid. Both her weight and the severity of her scoliosis meant we couldn't walk with her anymore (we used to hold her up underneath her armpits and be guided by her footsteps). Physiologically she continued to grow up, but in clinical and developmental terms she would "deteriorate," "decelerate," "regress" over a series of prescribed stages.

Much like Stockton, scholars from a range of fields have challenged the idea of the "becoming" child, where value is centered on the child as the future adult.[28] Disability emerges as a prime site to challenge the assumptions and myths of this "typically developing child" and the linear passage from dependent childhood into independent adulthood, marked by milestones and monitored by culture and society. Simultaneously growing and declining, changing and unchanging, Alice's life invited us into a different understanding and experience of temporality. Out of sync or out of time with her able-bodied peers, Alice's atypical development might be framed by what disability scholars and activists have referred to as "crip time." Alison Kafer, for example, describes crip time as "time not just expanded but exploded; it requires reimagining our notions of what can and should happen in time, or recognizing how expectations of 'how long things take' are based on very particular minds and bodies."[29] Within the context of discourses of growth and development, this experience of time and disability should be understood not just in regard to "how long things take"—that the child, like the proverbial tortoise, will get there eventually—but as a way of exploding and reimagining the assumed goals and measurements of human development and competency. For us it was an invitation to develop attentiveness toward and value different modes of communication, expression, and understanding.

My own childhood and adolescence might have been seen to follow a well-worn path, but growing "up" with Alice also took our family on a "detour from the time of normative progress."[30] What I want to suggest is how Alice's relationship with Disney Home Video and her repetitive viewing of compilation videos and feature films might illuminate these alternative and multiple temporalities. On the one hand, she remained much the same, a young child locked into an obsessive pattern of consumption—like any eighteen-month-old who wants the same story, again, again. On the other hand, these films became an avenue through which to develop in other ways and to express her desires, needs, and blossoming personality. For us this looping temporality was further enabled by the possibilities and popularity of VHS technology and home video in the 1980s and 1990s. There is arguably something in the world of Disney itself that evokes a more complex temporality, one that also loops and repeats rather than offering a straight line. Disney fairy tales, for example, offer repeated fantasies of "growing up." Stories like *The Little Mermaid* or *Beauty and the Beast* end, in David Forgacs's words, "with the passage of the hero or heroine from the world of childhood to that of adulthood."[31] But these stories also loop through forms of cultural inheritance and reproduction. Disney's newest cycle of live-action remakes of its "classic" animated films is but one example of such cultural and commercial recycling.[32] Disney offers a dominant, though not exclusive, canon of texts and experiences that are continually renewed alongside generational cycles of childhood and parenthood, creating a series of "relays between past and present, adult, adolescent and child."[33] These iterative loops blur any rigid category of age and ability.

Forgacs's essay "Disney Animation and the Business of Childhood" focuses on the commodification of childhood, the cult of cuteness, and the infantilization of adulthood in and through popular culture. However, the image of the eternal child invoked by the "perennial, timeless fantasies" associated with Disney also has particularly problematic implications when viewed through the lens of disability.[34] In this context, how does one reconcile Disney's "magic of eternal youth" with the continued and enforced infantilization of people with disabilities who do not "grow up" in the conventional sense? As Katherine Runswick-Cole and Dan Goodley argue, the "conflation of 'learning disabled' and 'childlike' has had devastating consequences on the lives of learning disabled people who have been denied the right to vote, love, have children, work and to make choices about where they live and who they live with."[35] This complex intersection between Disney, disability, and "growing up" is also evident in the 2016 documentary feature *Life Animated* as it explores the affordances of Disney Home Video in the life of Owen Suskind, a young American man with autism. The film offers a coming-of-age portrait of Owen as he moves out of his family home and into independent housing alongside the story of his early years and childhood. Based on the memoir by his father, Ron Suskind, *Life Animated* recounts how Owen, like Alice, presented as a "normal" baby and a "chatty" toddler before taking an unplanned detour. Owen's "regression" (the first chapter is titled "Growing Backwards") and diagnosis is documented through the recollections of his family members, doctors, and therapists and charted in sequences from the Suskind's home videotapes. Following Owen's diagnosis, he is presented as a nonverbal, confused, and unhappy young boy who finds it difficult to engage and communicate with those around him. Yet he finds particular comfort in his repetitive viewing of Disney videos, his life spent "more and more, in front of the screen" in the family's basement TV room, his brother Walt often at his side.[36] Owen's early years are structured as a story of loss, imprisonment, and recovery, principally through the emphasis on his ability to communicate verbally and rehearsing, in part, a familiar trope of "overcoming adversity" popular in stories of disability. For example, when Owen's constant repetition of the gibberish "juicervose" was finally understood to be dialogue from *The Little Mermaid* ("just your voice"), the moment of epiphany is loaded both with narrative and symbolic meaning (*The Little Mermaid* is staged around Ariel's giving up and regaining her voice in order to win the heart of Prince Eric), and Owen's repossession of his voice marked the Suskind's tentative recovery of their son ("Thank god . . . he's in there," they recount in the film). It is important to note the problematic equivalence drawn here between the voice and verbal communication with agency and subjectivity that precludes other forms and ways of being seen and heard.

Putting these concerns to one side, for Owen, Disney emerged as a vital framework for and point of connection with his family and a means for expression and communication. The film documents how Owen's relationships were and continue to be mediated by Disney characters, stories, and dialogue.

As a child he would communicate through Disney dialogue and role-play, but he also learned to make emotional and moral sense of the world by fitting it to a Disney script. For example, the film illustrates the rhyming of events in Owen's life with scenarios from Disney feature films: as Owen packs to leave home for the first time, he watches Dumbo leave the circus, and during the first night in his own apartment we see him watching Bambi's abandonment after the death of his mother.[37] Because Disney's world is desexualized, though, some life lessons are less easy to comprehend: we see Owen struggle with concepts of French kissing, sex, and the breakup of a relationship. A welcome attempt is made to see Owen as a sexual being—his brother, for example, offers him guidance—yet the film comically emphasizes Owen's lack of comprehension rather than the further exploration of his sexual curiosity.

Anthropologist Cheryl Mattingly has written of the ways in which "Disney serves as a potent (if unacknowledged) cultural resource" in the lives of children with disabilities and their families, offering a point of resistance to stigmatization and the bleakness of biomedical prognoses.[38] For the families taking part in her ethnography, the consumption of Disney texts and products were seen as acts of "imaginative appropriation in which children and families creatively remake Disney characters and plots by *making them similar to* the lives they live and especially the lives they hope for."[39] These children (and their families) were seen to create points of identification from narrative resemblances with their own lives—specifically narratives of difference and exclusion found in *Toy Story* or *The Little Mermaid*—and hopeful futures from their happy endings. Both *Life Animated* and Mattingly's study emphasize the role of Disney as a map for living, drawing on literal and metaphoric narrative and thematic resemblances between the lives of characters and the lives of viewers. In such instances, the security and familiarity of the repeated text offers a way of processing information and mediating "real-world" experiences and emotions, while the hopeful, utopian promise of entertainment as an emancipatory form unveils possibilities for the role of imagination in our making of disabled futures.[40]

But what resonated for me most in *Life Animated* was both Owen's deep emotional bond with the world of Disney and how home video became central to everyday routines of care. Through it I recalled the ways in which the home viewing of Disney videos became deeply embedded in our family life through particular routines and rituals that are both common and everyday and specific to caring for a child with complex needs. Here I want to emphasize care as both a practice and a value and to recount the material, embodied, and emotional ways in which Disney played a part in caring for and about Alice.

Both Alice's and Owen's use of and relationships with Disney were facilitated by the domestication of VCR and VHS technologies in US and UK homes in the 1980s. Disney, for example, released its first "Sing-Along Song" compilation video in 1986, the year after Alice's birth.[41] It was also the first video my parents bought for Alice a couple of years later, when we got our first VCR machine, and following its successful integration into our lives, the release of each subsequent compilation was quickly purchased. At that point they were perhaps unaware of what they had let themselves in for. Alice had always enjoyed and responded to music. As a very young child, she used to kneel up against the record player and bang on the glass door to ask us to turn it on. Disney video quickly became part of our lives and a key source of pleasure and entertainment that could also, for me and my elder sister, Jess, become torturous in its endless repetition. It was, like the use of screen media in many children's lives, a way to pacify and keep her happy, perhaps evoking the often-anxious use of television as babysitter while other chores and labors are completed. It was a familiar part of her routine, accompanying breakfasts, the return from school, and bedtimes, with time and tasks measured by the length of video: thirty-minute compilation or ninety-minute feature film. VHS is clearly seen here as a predecessor to the self-scheduling of digital television practices.

Anxieties surrounding both children with disabilities and children's use of screen media might construct this narrative of consumption in particular ways: the child distracted by television from more healthy or culturally acceptable pursuits, or as a tragic figure imprisoned in the home with television a poor substitute for friends and community relations. Both are underpinned by a notion of passivity associated with television *and* with disability that I would like to challenge. Alice's spectatorship is not reducible to these terms. The family came to realize that the pleasure Alice gained from these videos was not just about "keeping her happy"; the videos were also becoming central to her development and growth (it is hard not to revert to these terms) as a child and a human being. It was her way of absorbing, enjoying, and learning about the world—not in terms of the more literal, moral, and didactic aspects of the Disney world but in her response to its emotional and affective landscape. Studies of film music have taught us how it offers a guide to stories, characterizations, feeling, and affects.[42] This type of sensitivity is what Alice brought to and learned from Disney. Sometimes she would sob so heavily we would have to turn it off; at other times she would laugh until tears rolled down her face. Through Disney she was recognized by the family and all her key workers as having a "banana-skin sense of humor"—something my dad, like our very own Basil Fawlty, played to endlessly.

Repetition also allowed her to understand sequencing, to anticipate, to recognize every "cue for a song." It didn't allow her to "find her voice" the way Owen Suskind did, but through these abilities our viewing with her offered us another avenue for communication and community that was embodied rather than verbal. Nestled in next to her, we would cheer the goodies and hiss at the baddies; we would excitedly anticipate our favorite scenes or songs, perform entire numbers, and endlessly recite catchphrases. In the hours between returning from school and teatime, with Jess away at university and my parents at work, it would often be just the two of us in the house. I remember throwing myself into a performance of the entirety of *Mary Poppins* with Alice as my delighted audience. Music therapists have written about how girls with Rett syndrome are highly responsive to music and of the ways music can be instrumentalized to "facilitate and to expose all those hidden skills" in a "population perceived as uneducable until not long ago."[43] But play, for the child with disabilities, is so often managed and monitored in the service of therapy and rehabilitation,[44] and I don't want to reinforce that sense here. In the context of Alice's spectatorship and the forms of pleasure, play, and performance that surrounded it, Disney was not only resource and resistance, in Mattingly's terms, but also an everyday expression of familial bonds and affections.

Alice could be willful, though. She would let us know when she wanted to watch her videos. She would scream and scream until she got her way. When she was younger and we could help her to walk, she would march straight to the television to indicate what she wanted, and it came as a big point of frustration for her when she couldn't do this anymore. But what is significant here is the way Alice's determined spectatorship made visible and evidenced to those professionals, who wouldn't believe that she could think and make choices, both her abilities and the strength of her personality. For example, her ability to select from a series of videos held up in front of her, her ability to make and communicate deliberate choices through purposive hand movements about what she wanted to watch and the agency this afforded her, convinced her school to rethink their interactions with her and allow her to use a basic yes/no communication button. Kittay has written of the layered work of socialization undertaken by parents of children with cognitive disabilities "to help the child make her way in the world and to help shape a world that will accept her."[45] As we cared for and about Alice, Disney facilitated her emotional needs, amplified her abilities for nonverbal communication, and enabled us to communicate with the outside world about her—a project this chapter continues.

For me as Alice's sister, Disney also came to mark the labors and emotional demands of care in our family life. For example, each bedtime video was accompanied by the use of a ventilator to ease Alice's chronic respiratory problems. This disposition of caring technologies can be seen in the opening photograph, where the ventilator machine, similarly encased in white plastic, is tucked down the side of the television cabinet. Disney tunes were entangled with the smell and mist of chemicalized vapor in the air. Alongside the repetition of medical routines were the battles to get her to swallow medicine, disguising tablets in fruit juice, or the never-ending attempts to take her hands out of her mouth (a quirk of Rett syndrome). There were also the regular hospital visits and stays, her VIP status and priority use of the limited TV/VCR units on Ward 17, but also how her lack of response to her videos (or to chocolate) signaled to me just how unwell she was. As previously discussed, there is an emphasis both in scholarship on life-writing and in disability studies on the relationships between parents and children, and much of what I share here comes from conversations with my mother. As a sibling, though, my memories are a mix of childhood and adult perspectives, and my recounting of Alice's life is informed by new insights as I learn more, as an adult, not only from my parents but also from reading disability studies scholarship. I feel guilt and complicity, for example, for playing on the periphery while she underwent monitoring, assessment, and medical interventions and for the teenage resentment of the restrictions placed on my own burgeoning freedom.

As Juliet Mitchell reminds us, frustrations and resentments are part and parcel of sibling relationships, and Alice's occupation of the television set could prompt such discord. I can still feel the groan of despair when we would have to watch *Pocahontas* for the umpteenth time. Both Jess and I remember that when allowing her to select a video to watch, we would sometimes try and guide her choice, nudging one tape in front of another or asking her to choose multiple times, so as not to be forced to watch a particular film—a strategy, we recall, that rarely worked. These memories supplement my experience as Alice's sister and carer but never usurp memories of the love and delight on her face when I greeted her on returning from school.

Debts and Inheritances

Jess and I grew out of and back into Disney, and it now reaccompanies our lives through my niece and nephew. These cycles of cultural inheritance reveal much about our different relationships toward and within care. As Marian Barnes observes, "People's caring histories mean that they are involved in different caring relationships throughout their lifetime, not only moving between identities as care givers and care receivers, but also experiencing what care means in very different ways."[46] Disney Home Video, for example, has become a way of charting my own "caring history." But in my niece's and nephew's use of Disney we are reminded of the shared culture that Alice had with all different types of children and young adults. She was not just a girl who sat in a wheelchair and couldn't do anything. By sixteen she had had her first taste of beer, and posters of the Irish boy band Westlife adorned her bedroom walls. Yet in many ways she stayed the same, a young child with a perennial love for Disney. Described in these terms, both changing and unchanging, Alice's story is perhaps not so different from those of the annual cluster of female undergraduates writing dissertations on Disney princesses.

This story, though, has a premature ending. In February 2002, after years of progressively more serious chest infections and an increasing resistance to antibiotics, Alice died at the age of sixteen. It was a Sunday morning in the familiar surroundings of Ward 17, and in our final moments together, just me and her, I sang her the lullaby from *Mary Poppins*. Disability is so often figured in terms of loss, grief, tragedy, and deficit that I was worried about the implications of this particular ending. These narratives haunt disability studies, but, as Katherine Runswick-Cole has suggested, it is this anxiety that has reproduced a silence around the lives of children with life-shortening conditions and more broadly around the discussion of death and disability.[47] Death does not mark the end of care. So, instead, I wish to reframe Alice's life and death not in terms of loss but in relation to ideas of inheritance and debt that might help, in the words of Faye Ginsberg and Rayna Rapp, to reorient us "to a place of possibility, as opposed to disappointment."[48]

If television has taught us anything, it is that stories rarely end.

There are certain embodied legacies of giving care and of helping to raise a child with physical disabilities. The years of carrying and lifting have left my parents and older sister with numerous neck and shoulder problems, musculoskeletal issues that might be said to "run in the family." Each of us also has a series of lifelong earworms. An internal Disney soundtrack has accompanied my writing of this chapter; each memory, each mention of a film title summons a song or scene, lyrics, and dialogue embedded in my brain through years of repetition. There are also the inheritances and heirlooms of children's culture.[49] The *Lion King* figurines that once stood on top of Alice's television now belong to my nephew Sam. In figure 1.3, here he is playing with them in the garden. My five-year-old niece, Annie, looks a lot like Alice. They share the same complexion, round face, and gapped front teeth. She often likes to

FIGURE 1.3 Sam, with Simba and Pumba (June 2017).

talk about her other aunt, and at her recent Pirate Day at primary school she named her costumed character Captain Alice. Not everything remains, and Alice's VHS archive became a victim of the cycles of obsolescence that accompany those of generational return and renewal, reminding us that forgetting and disposability are also built into cultural cycles of inheritance. You could probably get a good price for those VHS tapes on eBay today, and I wonder if they are still in circulation, with Alice's name written in pen and carefully taped inside their front covers.

Michael Davidson has argued that a value of disability is how it can be understood as the practice of "making normal life strange" and how it presents an avenue through which to rethink the taken-for-granted and normalized uses of television (within which I include film and home video) in everyday life.[50] Alice's relationship with these media offers a way to widen our understanding of media use and to complicate notions of "growing up" and prevalent (normative) conceptions of childhood. The stories of Owen and Alice also point toward a more expansive model of film and television spectatorship that might challenge, in Alison Kafer's words, the "ableist assumptions about how bodies look, move, sense, communicate and think" that pervade writing in film and television studies.[51]

There is also a political significance, not just in being more inclusive of differently abled audiences but in valuing the joys and pleasures of children with physical and cognitive disabilities precisely because they are so often marginalized, framed as objects of pity or tragedy, and, in worst-case scenarios, not seen as having the capacity for a full emotional life. As a sister and a scholar I am invested in articulating ways for us to harness the energies of film and television as audiovisual texts and experiences to offer a sense of life and vitality to those whom other aspects of our culture and our academy try to deny. This is the debt I owe.

Annie is two. She looks a lot like her other aunt—the one she has never met, the one she shares her middle name with. Same complexion, round face, and gapped front teeth. The familiarity can sometimes snag, an angle or a gesture reminding me of her namesake, but it quickly dissipates. Like many toddlers, she is also very much herself.

It is that strange, restful, restless period between Christmas and New Year's Day, winding down from one celebration and gearing up for the next. I'm with my older sister and her family in a single-story holiday cottage on the Northumberland coast, nestled between the moorland and the sand dunes. The latter run like a veil separating the cluster of former farm buildings from the North Sea just yards away. It is 9:30 p.m. and Annie won't go to bed. She bounces down the corridor between bedroom and front room, where her mum and I are trying to watch television. Her mum gets up and coaxes her back to her bedroom. She lies with her as she wriggles around, settled one minute, restless the next. This is the one, though; she is sure she has cracked it. Her mum tiptoes back to the front room, bemused, exasperated, and insisting, "She's not like this at home." A few minutes later the toddler reappears. Her eyes sparkle, a mischievous grin spreads across her face, and the game begins again.

MARIA TATAR HAS WRITTEN of the child's bedtime as a "conflict zone,"[1] a moment when adult and child are potentially at odds with each other—battle lines are drawn, leisure time is abandoned, and sleep becomes the final labor of the day. It is a moment of tensions and transitions. Stuart Albert and William Jones describe the psychological issues addressed by bedtime stories as "deep and potentially troubling: the problems of legitimate authority; of fear of separation, and of being left, abandoned, exiled, coerced, and compelled; of knowing that one will not die but merely sleep; of knowing that one will continue to be cared for and protected."[2] Various accounts of the emergence and use of the child's bedtime story as a familial ritual demonstrate a dialectic of authority and intimacy (where moments of conflict might be appeased by the storybook and its telling), of anxiety induced by the shift between times and spaces and the comfort provided by ritual and routine. The provision of television as a "useful" part of the child's bedtime ritual is the focus of this chapter. It opens with an exploration of notions of use and care within the context of preschool television, focusing specifically on the construction and function of the CBeebies Bedtime Hour. Here I argue that television's mediation of this temporal boundary for the child and carer offers a way of accessing the presence of television in domestic spaces and its imbrication into everyday routines or structures of care. The motions and patterns of these routines, I will demonstrate, are mirrored by their textual manifestations within the bedtime schedules of children's digital channels CBeebies and Nick Jr. and specifically in programs such as *In the Night Garden* and *Pajanimals* (Sprout, 2008–13), which are designed to enable the child's preparation for sleep. The second half of the chapter continues with close textual analysis of *In the Night Garden* and its negotiation of times and spaces for the child and the adult. For the young child (and the carer) television offers repeated patterns and journeys of retreat and return that negotiate the transitions between times and spaces (between light and dark, daytime and nighttime, waking and sleeping, today and tomorrow, fantasy and reality, diegetic and domestic).

Through these bedtime schedules and programs a(n) (e)motional rhythm is established, one that ferries the child between the social and the individual, the public and the private. This is an experience that has wider implications for thinking through the meanings and uses of television as it accompanies our lives. Here the experience emphasizes the temporal and spatial dimensions of everyday life in the transitions between being together (with television; with others and with television) to being alone (with or without television). Roger Silverstone's understanding of television as a "transitional object" (in D. W. Winnicott's terms) is characterized by the separation anxiety that "being alone" can induce.[3] In such instances, television takes on the role of babysitter or companion, a voice in the background, a connection to the world, whereby "the continuities of sound and image, of voices or music, can be easily appropriated as a comfort and a security, simply because they are there."[4] For Silverstone, television is both cause and cure of an ontological (in)security, both "disturber and comforter."[5] He sees the medium as responsible for the creation, mediation, and resolution of anxiety.[6] Silverstone's exploration of television's textual features is minimal, though, and he, like many others, turns to news programming to illustrate the point. What might be gained from remaining with children's culture and the figures of the child and carer that are central to Silverstone's psychoanalytic reading of television's object relations? In his "ontological circle at play" I am reminded of a familiar lullaby where the repetition of the lyrics enacts that same emotional dynamic of security and anxiety—a cradle that continually rises and falls.

> Rock-a-bye baby, in the treetop,
> When the wind blows, the cradle will rock,
> When the bough breaks, the cradle will fall,
> And down will come baby, cradle and all.

This book is preoccupied with the motions and rhythms of television within a largely domestic space: the repetitive and cumulative experiences of living with the medium. Like the above lullaby and through Silverstone's thesis, this chapter reimagines these movements within a specific context and for a particular purpose as this rocking motif emerges in television designed to aid the young child's journey to bed. These oscillations are paralleled by another movement, as Amy Villarejo has written: "Television requires that we shuttle between the macroindustrial and the microindividual; it is a machine that produces its value from that very movement."[7] Such bedtime programming and scheduling reminds us of the fusing of the institutional rhythms of television and the family, and offers a textual site through which to make visible the weaving of television's institutional logics into lived, imagined, and idealized domestic lives.[8]

Useful Television

The Bedtime Hour is a scheduling block broadcast daily between six and seven o'clock on the BBC's digital preschool channel, CBeebies.[9] The schedule is kept the same for a series of months, and parents are given ample warning of any forthcoming changes to the lineup (in order to accommodate the different tastes of their young audience) through the *CBeebies Grown-ups* blog and social media announcements. Programs with a slower pace are often scheduled within the Bedtime Hour, and while the lineup occasionally shifts, *In the Night Garden* and the CBeebies *Bedtime Story*—a picture book narrated by a celebrity—have been consistently scheduled at the close of the channel's day.[10]

SUNDAY THROUGH THURSDAY

6:00 pm Waybuloo
6:20 pm In the Night Garden
6:50 pm CBeebies Bedtime Story
7:00 pm Channel closedown

FRIDAY AND SATURDAY

6:00 pm 64 Zoo Lane
6:10 pm Driver Dan's Story Train
6:20 pm In the Night Garden
6:50 pm CBeebies Bedtime Story
7:00 pm Channel closedown

It is textually marked as distinct from the rest of the day's flow. For example, the end of the day is initially signaled by one of the daytime presenters putting on her coat and going home before the transfer to a different presenter in a more intimate part of the studio space for the Bedtime Hour. This transfer is also accompanied by interstitial songs that signal the transition into nighttime, such as "Goodbye Sun, Hello Moon." The young child's socialization into temporal rhythms extends beyond this daily occurrence to accommodate seasonal cycles. Songs, station identifications, and images emphasize the sights, sounds, and activities associated with specific seasons. For example, children are viewed wrapping up warm in the song "Cozy in the Winter" or jumping with lambs in fields in "The Spring Song," while the lyrics emphasize the darker nights or longer days. The Bedtime Hour, as an iterative process, offers us a scene repeated every day at the same time but with textual variations that correspond to the time of year and that can be used to accompany the child's passage both to bed and through early childhood.

Nick Jr. has scheduled its own version of the Bedtime Hour, but because it is a twenty-four-hour digital channel, the boundaries of this scheduling practice are much less well defined, and the cohesion and tone of the hour are problematized by the lack of a definite "end" to the day. Similar textual motifs are shared specifically in the use of station identifications and interstitials that correspond with the time of the day and the incorporation of songs that indicate the start or end of the bedtime routine. The "Jimmer Jammer Song," for example, depicts the child's bedtime routine of brushing teeth and getting into pajamas. The "Hey There Sleepy Head" song sees the Nick Jr. pop group Go!Go!Go! sing and dance while getting ready for bed on the CGI Sleepy Head island. As the song ends and the camera pulls back from the nighttime island, waves can be heard softly lapping the shore, a bell chimes in the distance, and the tranquil image is quietly held for twenty-five seconds. The moment of calm generated is quickly dispelled by a station ID, trailer, or ad that shuttles the viewer into the next program or points toward upcoming events. Because Nick Jr. is a commercial digital channel, the design of its bedtime hour is caught between another tension: the discourses of care that structure a routine for the child and parent and the need to keep viewers watching.

Earlier theoretical accounts of the experience of television, produced within the British context of public service broadcasting, considered the notion of "dailiness" as forming the medium's "unifying structure."[11] The project of both Paddy Scannell and Silverstone was to make visible the "taken-for-granted" and commonsense aspects of television that had become naturalized within the routines and entitlements of everyday life. This is broadcast television's mediation and management of daily rituals and routines and its structuring of time to produce a sense of daily, weekly, and yearly cycles. Through these accounts, television emerges as both clock and calendar, binding individual viewers into institutional and national rhythms that emphasize both the *here and now* and the *promise of a future*. It is this sense of continuity that, according to Albert and Jones, emerges as a significant counterpoint to the child's bedtime anxieties; to repeat, "of knowing that one will not die but merely sleep; of knowing that one will continue to be cared for and protected." Within television's "consistency of care," as Silverstone terms it, we can imagine how the characteristics of broadcast television might be used to shore up the child's sense of the world and their place within it.[12] Here the unifying structures of broadcast television find an explicit application within the niche address of a digital children's television channel, an address that reiterates previous incarnations of the management of children's domestic lives through cultural and artistic forms.

WHEN I WAS SIX or seven, after a nightly bath my mother would sometimes dry and brush my hair in front of the television. This didn't happen every evening—there were three of us and Alice took up most of my mother's time. But when it did, I would kneel on the floor in front of her, both of us facing the small screen, as she ran the brush through damp tangled hair, the hot whirr of the hairdryer around my head drowning out the noise of the TV. This didn't bother me; at this time of night *Wogan* was always on: a tedious chat show fronted by a gray, old, and uninteresting host.[13] Occasionally I would protest, but I watched anyway, eyes fixed on the screen, a hairbrush locking me in place, nestled in front of my mum.

ANOTHER CENTRAL FACET of Scannell's argument is a notion of "care" that is employed to highlight why we should both care about the place of broadcasting in everyday life and be concerned with how and why it is meaningful. He writes: "That things matter for us (no matter what), the ways in which they matter and the extent to which they do so, mark out the boundaries of our concerns."[14] Scannell deliberately distances his discussion of care from an understanding of the term as an ethical concern (i.e., caring *for*), but what might be revealed by placing this understanding at the center of our concerns? Television's "duty of care" (within both public service and commercial systems) is arguably heightened in its recognition of and (anxious) responsibility for the child audience.[15] This sense of responsibility is clearly underpinned by normative understandings of the child as a future adult and ideal citizen that I sought to disrupt and critique in the previous chapter. For example, within the public service context of the origins of children's broadcasting in Britain, Derek McCulloch, director of the first BBC radio program for children—*Children's Hour* (1922–64)—"conceived of the role of children's broadcasting and the formation of citizenship as constitutive of a form of pastoral care. He formulated the duties of the children's broadcaster thus: 'Our wish is to stimulate their imagination, direct their reading, encourage their various interests, widen their outlook, and inculcate the Christian principles of love of God and their neighbour. It is our desire to try to help mold the listening tastes of future citizens. There is no smugness in our attitude towards this vital task—only feeling of great responsibility.'"[16] David Oswell's study of the careful construction of the child television audience in Britain imagines that audience as both an object of governance and a "collective needing protection."[17] Within this regulation and control of the child *for their own good* is an understanding of care as a paternalistic and civic concern that has produced within public services a long-standing tension between needs and wants—the dynamic of parent and child mapped onto institution and audience/user. From a very different context, writing in relation to an ethnography of diabetes health care, Annemarie Mol considers how the paternalist mode has been replaced by a language and logic of choice.[18] Within the context of anxieties surrounding children's media, this shift presents itself as a transfer from the effective molding of future citizens to a fear that television creates only future consumers.

These concerns foreground a notion of care and responsibility that is linear and instrumental. Joan Tronto's groundbreaking study of the politics and ethics of care, however, presents a discussion of the "phases of caring" that allows us to think through this duty of care as part of a dynamic caring process of giving and receiving. Her systematic approach identifies four distinct phases. "Caring about" and "taking care of" refer to the recognition of an identified need and the assumption of a responsibility to meet that need.[19] "Caregiving" and "care-receiving" refer to the direct meeting of these care needs and the reception and response of the object of care.[20] The forms of mutuality and interdependence that Tronto's polemic emphasizes allow a consideration of television's "structures of care" functioning at the levels of production and reception, provision and use. For example, the Bedtime Hour provides a service for both young children and their carers through the crafting and scheduling of programs like *In the Night Garden*. CBeebies can be seen to "care for" its viewers, while this care is woven into the pleasures and labors of care that viewers do for themselves and each other within the space of television (as a site of care). In its stress on mutuality, Tronto's model also makes visible the tensions and imbalances of practices of care that might be embodied in the tug-of-war between carer and child at bedtime.

Although Mol's study shares much with Tronto's theorizations of the ethics and politics of care, what Mol emphasizes is the role of technology in practices and processes of care as shared work between human and nonhuman actors. The above vignette describes a particular assemblage of material things and a child *caught* by and between technologies (a hairbrush and television) that rehearse practices or motives of care. While *Wogan* might have been accidentally and reluctantly implemented as part of a bedtime routine, television presents itself as, like the hairbrush, "useful" and "usable": a tool or technology to be *grasped*.[21] It is the tangibility of television as a material object and a visual medium (and the cultural and textual practices that weave through both) that have been seen to have specific resonance for its preschool programs and audience. For example, former controller of CBeebies Kay Benbow commented in the *Guardian* in 2010: "I want CBeebies to be accessible and tangible, as if the audience can *touch* it, so that it is part of their lives, a positive thing."[22] Here the spatiotemporal arrangement of television is emphasized. The broadcaster's intention is not only for the channel to be carefully woven into the temporal rhythms of the child's days, months, and years but also for it to have a specific textural and tactual presence within the home, a quality of preschool television that has been highlighted by other scholars. Matt Briggs, for example, in his autoethnographic discussion of his son's interaction with the *Teletubbies*, describes how Isaac "kisses them as they appear on the screen and the glass is smudged by his handprints as he tries to touch them."[23] There are clearly resonances with the emergence of the touchscreen device but also forms of interaction that emphasize the porosity of the screen and the blurring of borders between diegetic and domestic worlds. For Briggs and his son the "boundaries between 'his world' and the 'diegetic space' are negotiable and porous," and the child's ability to distinguish between ontological realms of reality and fantasy (destabilized by modes of parasocial interaction within the program) is specifically linked to their developmental stage. Jonathan Bignell, also writing on *Teletubbies*, similarly describes "an interactive experience that spills out of the television set and occupies the viewer's space."[24] In the context of children's television this spillage might be seen to take the form of extensions of the text in the forms of mimetic play encouraged by the program's commercial surround and the selling and buying of toys and other merchandise associated with the program. The image here is of the child watching and playing with their favorite characters simultaneously (or their attention alternating between the two), sitting on the floor in front of the screen.

This study understands this porosity and the movement from and return to the domestic as a quality of television across a broader range of programs, practices, and stages but also recognizes these interactions as local and specific. As part of a nexus of everyday (caring) practices within the home, the tangibility of television offers two lines of inquiry. First, this operates in relation to the manifestations of touch and texture that have a specific purpose and heritage within preschool television.[25] Second, this sentiment is reiterated in a CBeebies blog on the Bedtime Hour authored by the institution: "A really *useful tool* to help you establish a night time routine for your little ones. You can set key points around the programmes for your children to get ready for bed, or use it as wind down time before they go to sleep."[26] Whether this routine is scheduled by the broadcaster or by the parent (using on-demand platforms), within it, television functions as a pivot within a mess of connections between domestic spaces, objects, and technologies, designed to be used as part of bedtime rituals, routines, and practices of care and self-care (encouraging children to get themselves ready for bed, to brush their teeth, put on their pajamas, etc.). Perhaps more explicitly, these practices and accompanying bedtime anxieties form a central part of the storylines featured and worked through in the Nick Jr./PBS Sprout series *Pajanimals* (see figure 2.1). Produced by the Jim Henson Company, the series features a family of animal characters—each reminiscent of a child's soft toy—who live together under the watchful eye of their unseen parents (whose voices are heard instructing the characters on their bedtime routine and singing a lullaby as they go to sleep). Each installment is located in their shared bedroom during the last moments of the day as day turns to dusk and dusk turns to night through the large bay window in the center of the bedroom across the duration of the eleven-minute episodes. Described by parental guidance site Common Sense Media as "gentle wind-down viewing," the program also deals with "common sources of bedtime strain"[27]—the child's restlessness or excitement, separation from parents, brushing teeth and washing faces, fear of the dark. Between toothbrushes and hairbrushes, television as a "useful" technology and its logic of care presents for its young (and old) audience a way of gathering knowledge that "is not a matter of providing better maps *of* reality, but of crafting more bearable ways of living *with*, or *in*, reality."[28]

Time for Bed

While a program such as *Pajanimals* can be seen to deal directly with the child's bedtime anxieties (fear of losing a favorite toy; fear of dreaming), historical scheduling practices reveal a continued concern with the temporal regulation of the child, prompting the question "Useful for whom?" The Bedtime Hour reiterates much earlier scheduling policies and decisions that tied programs (or their absence) to the real and imagined normative temporalities

FIGURE 2.1 Squacky wakes up early in "How Do You Know When It's Morningtime?" *Jim Henson's Pajanimals* (Sprout, 2008–13), season 1, episode 4.

and routines of children and families. For example, *Children's Hour* (named after Henry Wadsworth Longfellow's poem describing the paternal bliss of daily play with his three girls when they sneak up on him in his study at early evening) was scheduled in a 5–6 p.m. teatime slot that positioned the nation's children within a domestic and familial context but was also seen to be a demarcation for the child between school time and home time—the "pause" in the "day's occupations."[29]

> Between the dusk and the daylight,
> When the Night is beginning to lower,
> Comes a pause in the day's occupations,
> That is known as the Children's Hour.[30]

The Toddlers' Truce prohibited the broadcast of programs between 6 and 7 p.m. (now the Bedtime Hour) in order to help parents get their children to bed.[31] Separated from content for older children, the first preschool strand on the BBC, *Watch with Mother*, was scheduled at 3:45–4:00 p.m. and was designed to offer a space for mother and young child to occupy together before older siblings returned from school. Scheduled to follow on from the programming slot For Women, the banner was also intended to "deflect fears that television might become a nursemaid to children and encourage 'bad mothering,'" emphasizing the construction of a viewing position that would be occupied by child and mother *together*.[32] Here we see the invention of preschool television in Britain as, according to Jeanette Steemers, "part of a broader public service initiative which contributed to the public good by fitting 1950s notions of motherhood and family life."[33] Both then and now the BBC can be seen to construct and reflect contemporary values and discourses of parenting, family life, and education through its preschool programming, finding ways to "shape the child at home."[34]

Both *Watch with Mother* and the Bedtime Hour can be seen to remediate existing storytelling practices that celebrate intergenerational contact. In her study of children's literature, *Enchanted Hunters*, Maria Tatar offers a series of pictures and scenes that project an ideal image of what she terms a "literary contact zone," with the bodies of parent and child nestled together under a book. With regard to the practice of the bedtime story, Tatar suggests how "we cherish a model of bedtime reading as an opportunity for providing comfort as the child makes the transition to sleep, for sharing the magic, and for bonding between parent and child."[35] More recently, Alice Webb (former director of BBC Children's) has stressed this potential within the intergenerational address of children's television, commenting, "There's some fabulous programs that bring generations together. Look at the Bedtime Hour. Where parents and little ones snuggle up together as part of their daily routine."[36] Webb's remark was itself a response to the critique posed by her interviewers that television was used by lazy parents as a babysitter. The intimacy of the cradle or nook between caring bodies, of child watching with parent or carer, seems to be an ideal image that hasn't effectively translated to television viewing. Despite the viewing position insisted on within the history of preschool programming and the discursive spaces that surround it, children's television is still encircled by societal and parental anxieties regarding the passivity of the practice and worries over its use as an electronic babysitter.[37]

Once again, television fluctuates between positions of security and anxiety as discourses surrounding the child and effective parenting place the medium and the technology within frameworks of care or of harm. Yet whether television is regarded as benign or as damaging, both positions emphasize the governance and management of the young child by an adult or carer acting as a "gatekeeper" between them and the screen. The intended result of the Bedtime Hour as an iterative process is to have a well-trained child who goes to bed at exactly 7 p.m. In this fantasy, television fulfills its long-held promise as a social technology responsible for the management of designated times, spaces, and behaviors.[38] But this approach has implications for the agency and experience of the child, as Karen Lury has written: "By accepting and participating in adult-enforced temporality the child must forgo their own experience of duration, one that is often characterized as having a greater elasticity than the regimented, clock-bound time keeping of adult lives."[39] The provision of television content at bedtime reveals its connection to other forms of children's culture and the role played in the negotiation of freedom and control, intimacy and authority. For Tatar, bedtime reading (and, for our purposes, viewing) enacts a "double desire on the part of adults: a wish to instill discipline and 'good behavior' in children by getting them to bed at the right time, but also the hope of enchanting them—effortlessly and exquisitely—with the power of story."[40] Here both the book and the television enter into an intermedial relationship. They are used and designed as instruments of coercion—the promise of a story, the threat of its removal. This relationship between the bedtime storybook and television is also textually present in a number of ways. For example, a Nick Jr. station identification constructs the roof pitch of an animated house from an upturned book, and both Nick Jr. and CBeebies produce bedtime stories that feature celebrities reading storybooks to the young audience and that simulate the comfort zone between adult and child.[41]

In this opening half of the chapter I have attempted to situate these bedtime stories within discourses of use and of care. Here the notion of television as a domestic practice emerges most strongly. It also clearly operates as an instrument of socialization and management where the duty of the (public service) broadcaster plays its part in the creation of the dutiful child (and parent). Here the metaphor of the garden has particular significance, and I want to move on to consider one particular program, *In the Night Garden*, to examine how the series negotiates and manages the transition between times and spaces for the young child at bedtime. Here the movement across borders and patterns of return are written into the program. Within this study of the domestic and diegetic journeys taken with television, I continue by forging an alliance between the bed, the garden, and the television screen as particular domestic thresholds that mark a permeable border between the self and the world, the private and the public.

There and Back Again

Made by Ragdoll Productions for the BBC and broadcast on children's networks worldwide, *In the Night Garden* was produced by Andrew Davenport and Anne Wood (the team that also cocreated worldwide phenomenon *Teletubbies*) and was specifically aimed at children up to four years old to alleviate bedtime anxieties.[42] Filmed on a real woodland set, combined with stop-motion, 2D animation, and digital postproduction, it features a cast of live-action characters and puppets, including Iggle Piggle, Upsy Daisy, Makka Pakka, the Tombliboos, and the Pontipines. Like its predecessor *Teletubbies*, *In the Night Garden* utilizes a now-commonplace pedagogical practice within preschool television shows that are explicitly child-centered, employing extensive use of repetition, expressive movement, bright colors, and shifting scales and soundscapes. These programs draw on the mnemonics of repetition and a distinctive sensory and kinesthetic engagement with the world. As Karen Lury has written: "In this model of learning it is understood that children learn most effectively by gradually building an understanding of the world through a process of testing, repetition and imitation—learning is structured around a narrative that is generated via a series of questions and answers; answers are recalled through repetition and imitation is constantly encouraged."[43] What I want to explore is less the pedagogical style than how the series is designed to structure a particular everyday routine and experience for the child (and the adult). Anne Wood has commented that Ragdoll Productions "wanted to explore the difference between being asleep and being awake from a child's point of view."[44] What is evident from the aims of the program makers is an understanding of bedtime as a transitional moment in the child's routine. As Tatar observes, "At nighttime, children are in an in-between state, on the threshold of waking and sleeping, activity and rest, sociability and solitude, light and dark."[45] So while adhering to a particular CBeebies pedagogy of "learning through play" that coheres with the rest of the programs on the channel, *In the Night Garden* has a specific purpose of negotiating this transitional state at a particular time of the day. The opening sequence of the program marks the journey taken and the threshold crossed.

The stars are shining in the night sky. A few are larger and brighter than the others, and as they pulse in the midnight blue they appear to sound out a musical rhyme—a steady sequence of six clear notes played on a glockenspiel that mimics their twinkling. As the sequence repeats, a soft female voice (Celia Wickham-Anderson) begins to sing about the scene: "The night is black and the stars are bright and the sea is dark and deep." The image of the night sky cross-fades into a softly lit scene of a young child tucked up in bed, her hand resting, palm up, on her pillow. An adult's hand is seen tracing a circle with their index finger on the child's palm, and as the camera is gently pulled toward the circular motion, the child, sleepy and smiling, looks between the offscreen carer and the sensation drawn on her palm. The woman's voice, now humming, harmonizes with the simple musical sequence, and the voice of our narrator (Derek Jacobi) is introduced, picking up the description of the scene: "But someone I know is safe and snug and they're drifting off to sleep." The narrator's familiarity with the child is suggestive of an intimacy that is also evoked through the soft and round timbre of his spoken voice. The humming ends and the music pauses, but the narrator's rhyme continues as the camera pulls closer to the child's palm and the fingerplay—a circular gesture tracing out an entrance to an imaginary world: "Round and round a little boat no bigger than your hand, out on the ocean far away from land" (see figure 2.2). A cross-fade returns us to the night sky, this time enveloping a small boat on a calm, animated ocean. Motion is simulated by the sound of the waves gently lapping and a breeze that shivers the boat's red sail. Inside the boat is Iggle Piggle, a blue cloth humanlike figure that jingles and jangles like a baby's rattle, bells, squeakers, and shakers secreted within his toweling limbs. Iggle Piggle dutifully follows the narrator's instructions for the journey about to begin: "Take the little sail down, light the little light. This is the way to the garden in the night." Through the use of stop-motion animation, the boat bobs up and down on the waves as Iggle Piggle removes the sail, which

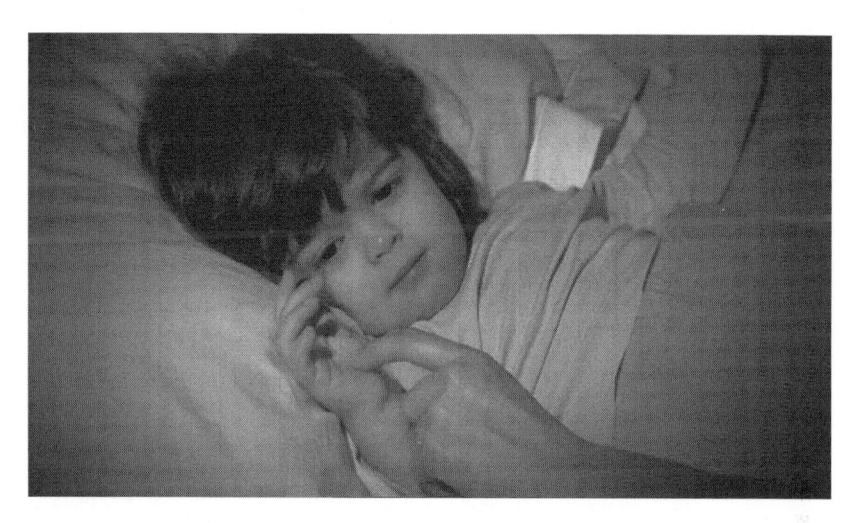

FIGURE 2.2 "Round and round a little boat...": opening finger-play in *In the Night Garden* (CBeebies, 2007–9).

becomes a blanket, and raises a light to the top of the small mast. As Iggle Piggle prepares for his journey and the final line of the opening rhyme is spoken, our musical theme returns. The high notes of the glockenspiel are alternated with bass notes played on a guitar that then also takes on the main theme (a theme that becomes Iggle Piggle's "song" across the series). Iggle Piggle then lies back and closes his eyes as the boat rocks out toward the horizon. This rocking motif is underscored by the music. While a flute takes over the principal melodic theme at this point, and strings fill out the arrangement, a piano accompaniment emphasizes the regularity of the rhythm, and a rocking motion is implied by the distribution of the chord (bass notes are played lower down the piano's register by the left hand and upper notes higher up by the right, so the alternation between the two simulates a back-and-forth motion).

As the boat arrives at the meeting of sky and sea, our attention is drawn to the gentle *ping* of a large star with a bluish hue in the center of the frame. With the strings taking a more prominent role, the theme swells and a rise through the musical scale is aligned with the star as it shoots up and into the heavens. Surrounding stars begin to burst into white cherry blossoms, and the flowers slowly subsume the sky and the frame (the flowers themselves are reminiscent of the single white blossom that gently unfolds in the title frame of *Watch with Mother*). Through the blossoms we spy our first glimpse of the Night Garden and return to the basic musical theme of glockenspiel and guitar. High up among the flowers, now secure on the tree branches, we see a yellow and blue bandstand in the middle distance; the same blue star now forms a light at the top of its canopy. The bandstand is nestled among tall thin tree trunks, yet on a manicured lawn (this is at once garden, park, and woodland), and someone is calling from it. As we move down through the branches, a series of "yoo-hoos" and squeaks greet Iggle Piggle's entrance to the garden as he skips down the path toward his friends, who are excitedly waiting in the distance (figure 2.3). We do not follow: instead the camera drops down behind a dense green hedge, obscuring the magical world from view. Coming to rest on the grass at the base of the hedge, the program's title is spelled across the screen and voiced by the narrator. While the final *ping* of the glockenspiel brings the sequence to a close (and tops the "i" of "Night" with the guiding blue star), the ellipsis at the end of the title anticipates its continuation and our hopeful, eventual entrance into the garden.

Creator and producer Andrew Davenport has spoken of the specific inspiration for the series as being drawn from a memory of the fingerplay rhyme that his grandmother used to perform on/for him:[46]

FIGURE. 2.3 Iggle Piggle crosses over into the Night Garden and greets his friends, *In the Night Garden* (CBeebies, 2007–9).

> Round and round the garden,
> Like a teddy bear.
> One step, two step,
> Tickle you under there.

The rhyme is accompanied by the movement of the fingers circling the child's palm, then walking up the limb to tickle the child under the arm or chin. A reference to this game and sensation finds its way directly into the opening of the program, performed by the onscreen carer or sometimes by the child themselves on their own body. The idea of the garden has a particular significance for understandings of childhood, as, for example, an imaginary site of childhood innocence, nature, and imagination.[47] But the body of the child also becomes the garden in this rhyme and action.[48] As Roni Natov writes, "The child may lead us to the garden, but also may become the garden, that which blooms, is cultivated, and nurtured."[49] (The PBS Sprout name and logo is a simple illustration of this sentiment.) We might think, for example, about the word "nursery" as a place of food, nourishment, training, and education and that marks an explicit link between the horticultural and the prosocial goals of early years development and education. The garden, like the figure of the malleable and amenable child, offers us an idealization of the ordering, management, and control of nature and culture.

In the opening sequence of *In the Night Garden*, the garden is revealed as a hidden sanctuary, a secret place, with Iggle Piggle and the viewer traveling over the sea and through the night sky until it is tantalizingly revealed behind a dense green hedge. The Night Garden as an enclosed space is one of safety and reassurance;[50] consider, for example, the significance of the crane shot that reveals the garden and its inhabitants yet drops down in front of the thicket, obscuring the magical world from view. Yet it is also a threshold to be crossed. The sedate opening sequence is followed by the appearance of either of the garden's two main means of transportation—the Ninky Nonk (a train) or the Pinky Ponk (an airbus)—that collect the viewer and then frenetically either burst through the thicket into the garden or rise up and over the border.

Here is a world that is contained and can be held in the palm of the hand yet is also as expansive and limitless as the night sky and the deep, dark sea. There is a playfulness with size and scale across the series. For example, the Ninky Nonk and the Pinky Ponk are at times both knee-high to the main (human-sized) characters and large enough for these characters to travel within them. This, among other features of the program, has prompted (comic) consternation online, where some adults describe the series as unsettling and surreal.[51] But it is a "child-centered" program, of course, and these features are consistent with an understanding of the child's experience of the world. The differing and inconsistent sizes and scales within the program, for example, are suggestive of the child's physical experience of the world, caught between the miniature and the macro—toys and figures that fit in the palm of the hand (though hopefully not small enough to be swallowed), houses for dolls, chairs, and beds that are "just right," and those that are too big, that are clambered onto with space aplenty to roll and jump around. The typically developing child is also continually growing, so their relation to the objects around them is also continually changing. As part of this experience of size and scale are the differences between the character on the screen and the toy in the hand. To this we might also consider their experience of shifting shot scales and the logic of continuity editing that seems obvious and natural to the adult but for the child is part of the consistent inconsistency of object sizes. For an adult the physical relationship with the material world (in terms of scale) is more constant (though certainly not fixed). But our reencounters with children's culture are also informed by the memory of once being small—of the previous bodies we occupied.

This is not to imply that the child (or indeed the adult) is unfazed by these experiences but to suggest that the crossing of thresholds, continuous change, is a daily occurrence for children and forms part of their accumulation of experience. Cultural geographer Owain Jones has written of the child's response to emotional stimulus as not being "flattened by the memory of experience. Children are still literally 'finding their way in the world' in a very obvious sense."[52] His argument, which cites Hilary Mantel, evokes the child's *greenness*: "Children are struggling to get a fix on the world. . . . Knowledge is revised from moment to moment, often from second to second. . . . Every moment the world shifts, and you shift within it [as] childhood brings continual change, tiny crises every day."[53] It is these tiny crises that form much of the narrative content of programs like *In the Night Garden* and *Pajanimals*: a Tombliboo is separated from his friends, a pair of trousers goes missing, a favorite toy is lost, somebody feels left out. But I also note the tiny crises that can often take place in the experience of viewing and the perpetual seesaw between anxiety and security.

ANNIE AND SAM USE television in many familiar ways but are also constantly growing in and out of fads and phases. I've watched them watching television over the past few years. I've watched with them, traveled with them to the Night Garden and back, and, though tucked safe under the nook of an arm, the journey doesn't always run smooth. The familiar notes and soft voice of the program's opening are heard, and Sam, now eighteen months old, bolts from his spot next to me in front of the screen to the back of the room, where his mother is sitting. He looks back in fear at the scene unfolding on the screen, then burrows his face in his mother's arm. "Off, off," he calls. I laugh with confusion as the softly lit image of a finger tracing a circle on a child's palm plays onscreen. The scene transitions to one of a little boat bobbing on the sea. All is well again. Sam takes a deep breath and returns to his spot on the floor next to me.

DESPITE THESE TINY CRISES, the garden, returned to every bedtime, is designed to offer safety and reassurance along with continual change and growth (reminiscent of the iterative pattern of everyday time as combining "recurrence with forward movement").[54] Natov writes of an additional movement associated with the pastoral as "a retreat from and a return to the world"—a movement that I have also aligned elsewhere with an experience of the everyday.[55] Certainly the garden itself might be considered as an intermediary space—between the home and the world outside. I want to explore further this repeated pattern of retreat and return that negotiates transitions between times and spaces for the child at the end of the day by looking at the closing moments of the program and how it repeats and reverses the opening. First, this pattern is common to children's picture books. For example, in Maria Nikolajeva and Liz Taylor's study of the meaning of beds in children's books they identify a common trope that involves the main character taking a real or imagined journey, starting and ending at their bed. "This structure," they write, "suggests the bed as a site of slightly boring, yet comforting, permanence—to be resisted when the protagonist is feeling adventurous, but returned to almost gratefully at the end of the story. The final location is the same, but the place is not the same because the child has changed, having gained ideas and experiences through the journeying."[56] Across the picture books discussed in their study and extended to other forms of children's media, the bed and the bedroom take on a complex symbolism: as a site of exclusion (the child denied food and company and sent to bed without supper), a site of anxiety (fear of dreams and things that go bump in the night), or a "liminal space for imaginative play" (stories of flying beds and magical transportation—in each episode of *Pajanimals*, for example, the characters take a magical trip on one of their beds to a special land, where a guide helps them to work through their anxieties).⁵⁷ Maurice Sendak's *Where the Wild Things Are* (1963) and *In the Night Kitchen* (1970), both of which are clearly referenced in *In the Night Garden* (Iggle Piggle's journey across the sea to a magical world mirrors Max's in *Where the Wild Things Are*), are perhaps archetypal in this regard: "The contrast between the opening and closing images emphasize the child's successful conquest of anxieties" and of childish behaviors.⁵⁸

In the closing moments of *In the Night Garden*, too, we return to where we started, but not before all the characters are tucked away in bed and read a bedtime story, a sequence that is repeated each episode (though the details change depending on the day's adventures) and that depicts the bedtime routine of the characters. High up in the treetops (superimposed onto the branches) are the Tittifers, a species of exotic birds that live in the Night Garden. Rocking back and forth and accompanied by the buzz of a kazoo, they sing their song at the end of the day's adventures. It is now "time to go to sleep." In the episode "Makka Pakka Washes Faces," the tiny Pontipines (ten little wooden figures clothed in matching red outfits and animated through stop-motion), who live in a semidetached house with a white picket fence at the foot of a tree, file in through the front door and away to bed. The tiny family (consisting of mother, father, and eight identical children) share one bedroom with beds symmetrically aligned. They chatter away, making high-pitched *mi-mi-mi* sounds until the narrator interrupts: "A story," he gently yet firmly promises, and the Pontipines go silent. We cut to the bandstand, accompanied by a simple circus march. It slowly cranks into action, the columns begin to spin, and the mechanical canopy rises as colored lamps emerge from underneath. "Once upon a time in the Night Garden . . ." From the rotating bandstand, now a story machine, a short tale is recounted that simplifies and emphasizes the causal chain of the day's events (Makka Pakka washed faces; they now have clean faces). This simple reiteration of the episode is accompanied by a series of basic two-dimensional picture-book-style images (see figures 2.4 and 2.5).

While offering a simple, linear narrative of cause and effect, within the frame of the program and the schedule, this specific iteration is more complex, making connections for the child between times and spaces. As a place of peace and security, *In the Night Garden* and its scheduling as part of the Bedtime Hour supplement this sense of reassurance and familiarity through messages of continuity that join together past, present, and future. For example, the uses of repetition, recall, and retelling within the narrative structure of the program have a particular pedagogical function tied to the child's accumulation of experience, but these also mirror the scaffolding of and distri-

FIGURES 2.4 AND 2.5 Makka Pakka *washes* faces / Makka Pakka *washed* faces. "Makka Pakka Washes Faces," *In the Night Garden* (CBeebies, 2007–9), season 1, episode 1.

bution of remembering between child and adult—"What did we do today? Didn't we have fun? Won't we have fun again tomorrow?"[59] The reflection on the day past and the promise of tomorrow that might alleviate the child's anxieties about going to bed (being alone in the dark, missing out on the fun) are also apparent in the channel's promises that it will return tomorrow and will be just as fun then (see figure 2.6). As I discussed earlier, Nick Jr.'s 24-7 broadcast offers a series of pauses in its spaces between programs, yet inevitably doesn't end. It therefore doesn't manage this transitional time for the child and family in the same way or with the same authority. What is amplified here is the significance of continuity as central to the child's sense of security, but it also has a specific textual and industrial role in relation to television. As Catherine Johnson has remarked on the continued relevance of interstitials and continuity within television as both industry and practice, there are "two potentially divergent aspects of the interstitial; that it is both communicating something about the experience of watching television, while also attempting to persuade or control the behavior of viewers."[60]

As the retelling of the day's events (as a bedtime story) concludes, the circus march returns and the bandstand folds away its accoutrements, its rotation slowing to a stop. The residents of the Night Garden are now ready for sleep. Softly yet firmly, the narrator directs each in turn to "go to sleep." While each character's musical theme is rearranged as a lullaby, they are seen tucked up in their beds, and they compliantly close their eyes at the narrator's command. The chattering Pontipines, now silent, close their eyes in descending order (each accompanied by a short muted xylophone note descending in scale). The three Tombliboos are tucked up inside their grassy cave, huddled together in striped sleeping bags. The large inflatable Haahoos visibly relax. Upsy Daisy lies under a duvet on her mobile bed out on the lawn, while Makka Pakka cuddles his pet stones in his underground cave. Each is the model child, submissive and willing to enter the world of sleep. The Night Garden is momentarily silent until a familiar squeak and bell are heard.

"*Wait a minute! Somebody's not in bed!*"

From the bottom of the frame Iggle Piggle skips down the garden path, cheekily turning to wave as he is spied by the narrator, then running away down the path toward the bandstand, his red blanket clutched in his hand. "Who's not in bed?!" the narrator exclaims. Cutting into the scene, Iggle Piggle pauses and turns around. "Iggle Piggle's not in bed!" He nods three times and then dramatically falls backward onto the path. But our kindly narrator does not scold ("Don't worry, Iggle Piggle"), and this unruly child does not es-

FIGURE 2.6 CBeebies closedown at 7 p.m.

cape his bedtime. Jumping up to his feet, he is told it is "time to go." Framed first in close-up and then in long shot within the context of the garden, Iggle Piggle waves dutifully at the audience, still clutching his blanket and gently rattling. Twilight now descends on the garden as the trees dapple the lawn with shadows. Once again, in the center of the frame is the bandstand, its blue lamp shining brightly. The music that brought us to the garden now returns, and the closing sequence reverses the opening pattern of movement and light. As twilight turns to night, we pull out from the garden, and the lights on the lawn, bridge, and bandstand transition into stars in the night sky; our guiding blue lamp/star shines brightest of all. Continuing to pull away, we eventually return to the rolling sea as a familiar lamp hung high on a mast enters the frame from the bottom of the screen. Iggle Piggle's boat bobs into view. Now he is sound asleep and drifting on the waves.

Significantly, the beginning and ending are not directly repeated, but the reversal of the pattern of movement enacts a rhythm of retreat and return that characterizes the journeys taken across this book. Here the textual motif of rocking (both visual and musical) is layered against the child viewer's movement between domestic and diegetic realms—the child is offered the space to adventure and learn yet is always safely returned and always has the promise of a tomorrow. Like a notion of the garden as both childhood and the child itself, Iggle Piggle occupies a dual position within the show: he is both the child's toy and the toy child. His softness and malleability, the toweling skin and large round head, communicating only through a series of bells and squeaks, mark him as an object of both play and control (to be managed by the program and the adult). Iggle Piggle and the other residents of the Night Garden are notably different from the animated toys in the feature film *Toy Story* (dir. John Lasseter, 1995) or programs like *Doc McStuffins* (Disney Jr., 2012–20) and *Woolly and Tig* (CBeebies, 2012–14). In these children's texts the toys, while tied to the child's imaginative play, occupy a separate existence; they belong to the child, yet also have a distinct agency of their own. While *In the Night Garden* attempts to capture a sense of the child's experience and subjectivity, working to alleviate specific anxieties prompted by bedtime, the child's own agency within this routine is always relational to the adult. The Night Garden is a world that is child centered but also informed by a collection of adult memories and desires. The text itself abounds with nostalgic gestures and intertextual references through the use of specific imagery and animation styles.[61] Cocreator Andrew Davenport referred to the idea for the series as coming from "a feeling you get when you look back on your own childhood and remember moments that summon up a sensation of comfort and security."[62] Here the Night Garden is entwined with notions of childhood as an escapist, nostalgic, and imaginative realm for anxious adults.[63] It is perhaps these allusions to childhoods past that lend the series something of its strangeness—caught somewhere between a child's dream and an adult's memory, it is the product of its complex and layered address to, and use by, an intergenerational audience.

This chapter has sought to examine the role of television within a commonplace routine and ritual and to reimagine early theoretical accounts of the medium—its "dailiness," its structures of care, and the oscillation between anxiety and security—by focusing on the relationship between the young child and the carer at bedtime. Here the spatiotemporal arrangement of television (both scheduled and on demand) is emphasized through notions of its tangibility and its role as a "useful tool" or technology of care (where we are also reminded of its role as a social technology in the effective management of the child). Television's mediation of times and spaces within the home presents particular textual possibilities that weave together domestic and diegetic worlds as the transitions and thresholds of the child's experience are imagined and negotiated through specific programming. *In the Night Garden* offers a complex and rich example that draws on metaphors of the garden and a series of intertextual references. The Night Garden is located on these thresholds but also binds together the perspectives and experiences of child and adult that call on the past, are lived in the present, and project into the future.

Alison Blunt and Ann Varley write of our geographies of homes as being both "material and symbolic . . . located on thresholds between memory and nostalgia for the past, everyday life in the present, and future dreams and fears."[64] Television, I argue, is central to these geographies of home, but it is also characterized, like the garden, as a border between the private and the public, the self (or the family) and the world, and it is this consistent crossing of thresholds, between inside and outside, home and away, that the next two chapters in this book continue to explore. To return to Silverstone's thesis, television's bedtime stories are the ones we tell ourselves and others to make life more bearable. But beyond narrative comprehension (and compensation), these examples of preschool television offer us a way of thinking about the affective use of media: in this instance, as a boat or cradle that gently rocks.

NEW YEAR'S HAS PASSED, and after a week by the sea in Northumberland I finally return home to Glasgow. Everything is still and quiet, and I feel a knot tug in the pit of my stomach. I miss them. I'm anxious about going back to work. I've only myself to look after again. I'll spend the next few days relearning how to live alone. The first thing I do is switch on the television.

In 2016 the British telecommunications company Sky launched a new digital delivery system called "fluid viewing." As one of many new examples of television technologies that embrace what Chuck Tryon describes as "platform mobility," it enables the viewer to watch content across multiple devices both inside and outside the home, allowing them to pick up each time from where they left off.[1] These new digital television practices, Tryon argues, have the potential to "disrupt traditional viewing habits and protocols" and promote, through marketing and advertisements, "a more fragmented, individualized notion of spectatorship"[2] while remaining couched in idealized images of domestic and family life.[3] Sky's television ad for its "fluid viewing" system adhered to a similar formula as it focused on an individual viewer, on this occasion a young woman in a comfortable and affluent middle-class suburban home complete with polished hardwood floors, a neutral color palette, and minimal clutter. The young woman is watching a battle scene from Marvel's *Avengers: Age of Ultron* (2015) on a large LCD screen in a spacious living room. As Thor begins to roar at his enemies—"Is that the best you can do?"—the action slows, and the sound drops and pulses as the image cuts to a side view of the screen in close-up. The surface shimmers and ripples, and the effect is like a slow-motion image of a stone dropped into a pool of water. As tension returns to the surface, a globule of color and sound breaks free, accompanied by the shift to the nondiegetic use of Sammy Davis Jr.'s recording of "I Gotta Be Me."[4] The lyrics to the song ("I'll go it alone"; "I gotta be free") perfectly capture the rhetorics of freedom, independence, and mobility that characterize the promises of new television technologies. Soon after that one droplet escapes, the screen suddenly bursts into hundreds of globules of color, image, and light (figure 3.1) that, in a series of short cuts, float and splash across the surfaces of the home: under the sofa—revealing a couple of forgotten toys—and across the kitchen worktops—scattering dusts of flour in their wake. Bouncing up the stairs, morphing and combining, they travel across the bedroom floor before finally pooling into a second LCD screen, where the Avengers' battle resumes at its original speed and the song concludes.

Once again, we see an example of television that is preoccupied with the transitions between times and spaces within the home. In chapter 2 I focused on how the Bedtime Hour relies on more traditional effects and uses of television scheduling to promote a sense of continuity for the child and to alleviate the stresses and tensions that might be triggered by such transitions. Such examples of platform mobility, however, emphasize a promise of domestic continuity that is unfettered by everyday disruptions and provides "convenient and seamless access" to content that fluidly crosses the thresholds and boundaries of the home.[5] The implications of such discourses are of television's liberation from the everyday times and spaces that once locked content to screens and schedules and of an immersive screen experience that leaves other distractions and duties—toys and baking—abandoned. New models of consumption and spectatorship enabled by these systems and technologies have provoked a great deal of discussion and debate, particularly in relation to the fluctuating fortunes of television's imagined cultural and artistic value. Yet what I've wanted to focus on across this book are the ways in which television continues to be productively theorized and analyzed in relation to its ongoing embeddedness in routinized and everyday behaviors and affects: as Graeme Turner has argued, there is "more to be done in terms of finding ways to describe and understand the cultures of use that have developed around the

FIGURE 3.1 The television screen erupts in an advert for Sky Q Fluid Viewing (2016).

multiple options available to consumers."[6] This chapter thus turns to questions regarding the personalized practices of television viewers by investigating the idea and practice of eating with television as an often-overlooked mode of engagement.

In recent years attention has been focused on newer forms of viewing behavior, such as the phenomenon of second-screen viewing. In her work on the app-based expansions of television series, Elizabeth Evans describes the "companion apps" that invite audiences to play or tweet along as offering a form of "layered engagement."[7] For Evans, these activities work to "promote old forms of television-related temporality" and support an economic model that keeps the viewer in sync with the broadcast series.[8] Her description of "two behaviors [that] are layered on top of each other" might enable us to position eating, instead, as a theoretical and experiential framework for thinking through the activities that occur alongside television consumption in the home.[9] And while Evans's later audience research on second-screen viewing has revealed "the *absence* of direct connections between the various devices being used,"[10] I wonder, What might the practice and performance of eating reveal about the direct and indirect connections that can be made between the two forms of consumption?

These potential connections and transmissions become clearer in relation to our theoretical models of both television and eating. Both, for example, have been seen to rehearse the continual making and remaking of the boundaries between inside and outside. Sky's "fluid viewing" ad and its porous screen presents us with the persistent image of television as a portal to other times and spaces. As a window on the world, television's association with mobility has been celebrated as a way of enabling viewers to travel far and wide from the comfort of the home, though the reversal of this movement has resulted in anxieties regarding the potential intrusion of these outside worlds into the private space of the living room.[11] Outside in or inside out, television has been partly responsible for, in Celia Lury's terms, the "dynamic re-making of the relation between inside and outside."[12] As the morphing and shifting screen of Sky's ad indicates, television is a topological object par excellence. Rather than imagining it as a fixed boundary, we might think of the television screen as a semipermeable surface that is looped, like a Möbius strip, into the everyday lives of viewers. Here I want to continue to conceptualize television as a relational object and an experience characterized by a push and pull between and across borders. The globules of color, image, and light that dance and seep from the screen in the fluid viewing campaign (see figure 3.1) also return us to metaphors of television's leakiness and its continuous multidirectional movement. Imagined as a constantly changing and semipermeable surface, then, it is also reminiscent of the eating body.

Accounts and theories of the various materialities and mobilities of food and eating have also emphasized how they bring the outside world into the home and the body. Theorists such as Maggie Kilgour and Elspeth Probyn have offered ways of articulating the practice of eating as located somewhere in between a series of potential oppositions: inside and outside, closeness and distance, individual and social, private and public.[13] It is these characteristics that so strongly recall those of television. Part open and part closed, the screen and body have a tentativeness that suggests both our connection to and removal from our everyday worlds, and as Probyn writes, eating "can be a mundane exposition of the visceral nature of our connectedness and distance from each other, from ourselves and from our social environment."[14] This understanding of the ambivalence of eating (and indeed our experience of this ambivalence) offers more than just an analogy with television: it reveals a significant experiential dimension of the medium and a rich yet overlooked mode of engagement. Often characterized by ritual and routine yet always open to contingency, eating presents another site or scene through which to investigate the ordinary affects and modes of (inter)subjectivity that television implements in the home.

This chapter, then, considers the significance of eating and television as iterative practices that accompany one another. In their study of television audiences in the 1990s, David Gauntlett and Annette Hill uncovered the commonplace use of television as an accompaniment to the evening meal. This correlation between the scheduling of mealtimes with television time emerged as a key indicator of how television acts as "a catalyst for forms of organization of time and space—or, to be more emphatic, often a primary determining factor in how households organize their internal geography and everyday timetables."[15] Longer cultural histories might tell us of the ways in which homes and lives were reoriented around the television in the mid-twentieth century. For example, the design of television-viewing accessories such as the TV tray table, portable toasters, mobile refrigerators, and the ready-made TV dinner enabled and promoted the experience of eating and drinking with television and testified to the coalescence of these forms of consumption.[16] Self-scheduling practices in an era of platform mobility might have switched the emphasis within this dynamic, with mealtimes determining patterns of television consumption rather than vice versa, but eating remains a significant dynamic within an everyday experience of television. When I have discussed television's continued relationship with everyday life with colleagues and students, conversation more often than not turns to their eating and viewing routines and rituals. As companion forms of consumption, they invite reflection on questions of intersubjectivity and the ways we construct our immediate social relations through acts of eating with television, even, or perhaps especially, when we live alone.

Within the frame of my own autobiography I want to situate this chapter in relation to my own experiences of eating with television and, more specifically, the experience of living alone, and eating alone, with television. For the best part of the last decade I lived on my own in a tenement flat in Glasgow (as Sammy Davis Jr.'s song goes, "I'll go it alone, that's how it must be"). The lone viewer, as featured in the kinds of advertisements discussed by Tryon, is still more often than not situated within an idealized context of kith and kin and the security that this is imagined to provide. For example, in Sky's ad the presence of other inhabitants is signaled through the domestic scenes that the droplets navigate—the toys under the sofa and the baking underway in the kitchen. As a single woman, living alone and miles from my family, television offered me a continued sense of security and companionship, and as the opening of this book described, it has consistently acted as an important transitional object as I set up each new home or temporary residence. In my flat in Glasgow the television in its multiple forms (LCD screen, laptop, iPad, mobile) was nearly always on, accompanying my movements around the modest space. The journeys I took with television were the paths worn between rooms: from sofa to kitchen and back again; from bathroom to bedroom at the end of the day. I would often fall asleep with the laptop lying next to me or the mobile screen resting inches from my face. I ate nearly all my meals with television, sitting on the sofa with a plate balanced on my knee and a cup of tea on the armrest.

Images of single women eating alone *on* television are often couched in humor, anxiety, and desperation. Liz Lemon's penchant for cheesy corn-based snacks in *30 Rock* (NBC, 2006–13), for example, comically signals her desperate state as overworked and unloved. Likewise, Miranda in *Sex and the City* (HBO, 1998–2004) spirals into anxiety when she finds herself alone and choking on a mouthful, feeling mocked by the Chinese takeaway service or eating cake out of the trash. I've not yet resorted to the latter, but I have been known to share a bag of Wotsits with Liz, finding in the experience a strange sense of solidarity and camaraderie. Eating scenes, both on and in front of the television, can offer us points of connection across the screen and between bodies, and in this chapter I reflect on my own choice of dining companions (Adam Richman in *Man v. Food* and Mads Mikkelsen in *Hannibal*) to examine experiences of both vicarious consumption and the sociality of the shared meal. The accompaniment, however, can equally marry with or mar the flavors of a meal, and it is important to recognize how both viewing and eating have the potential to mobilize, inflect, or activate a series of affects, senses, and feelings to produce a set of shared *and* divergent texts, tastes, and textures. At the heart of this chapter is an understanding of both television and eating as "patterned activities,"[17] and I endeavor to illuminate them by seeing one through the lens of the other. Whether we consume one course at a time or binge in a frenzy, even as our practices of television consumption evolve and change, what emerges is a continued overlapping of textualities and temporalities, metaphors and materialities, that stress the ongoing significance of television within our everyday lives.

From Metaphor to Matter

The synergies between television and eating can initially be emphasized through a set of shared metaphors that reveal continuing cultural anxieties about what is "good" and "bad" for our minds and bodies while also pointing toward a tradition of critical inquiry within television scholarship that is caught between questions of metaphor and matter. In an evocative essay on reality television and dirt, Amy West identifies the ways in which both anti-television discourses and the intellectual pursuits of media scholars have utilized metaphors of contamination: television "as both a conduit of filth and something inherently filthy in itself."[18] For example, on the one hand, television has been famously condemned as a "vast wasteland"; on the other hand, it has been and continues to be theorized, including in this book, via notions of leakiness, pollution, porosity, and messiness. West cites the work of John Hartley and Hamid Naficy, who use such terms in their accounts of the openness and boundlessness of a medium that blurs and muddies the distinctions between "inside and out, text and reader."[19] These metaphors draw on a deep-seated social, cultural, and psychological unease with such border crossings that are also found in anthropological accounts of food and eating. In Mary Douglas's *Purity and Danger*, for example, the risks of pollution and contamination are associated with, according to Anna Meigs, ideas of form and formlessness: "Pollution is, in other words, a negative power attributed to areas of confusion, ambiguity, and disorder within the set of forms or system of classifications."[20] Eating, in relation to television, connects us to a long tradition of thought regarding the ambiguities of food and the unstable borders and boundaries of the body that I will return to later in this chapter, but it also presents us with a series of metaphorical associations that open up a series of critical inquiries. These associations, for instance, remain entangled with the kinds of value judgments that continue to circulate about both the television text and the act of viewing. As acts of consumption and incorporation,[21] the metaphors that align the two practices are often concerned with bad kinds of nutrition or an absence of nourishment (in relation to both food and the notion of a cultural good). This is clearly apparent within the figure of the couch potato, the labeling of "junk food TV," or the reference to television as "chewing gum for the eyes." While they remain twinned with notions of contamination, these metaphors also evoke specific anxieties within Western culture whereby "nutrition is mapped onto moral concerns about food and the body" and are especially heightened around the figure of the child.[22] Here the moral regulation of television is mapped onto emblems of mostly poor nutrition: metaphors that refer to ready and accessible modes of consumption—like the ready-made processed TV dinner—that are easy and immediate and require limited cognitive effort, physical exertion, or skill.

Another metaphor has emerged in the last ten years, popularized with the advent of the DVD box set. It is captured in a term that refers to a specific practice of television viewing—a term that found its way into online dictionaries from Oxford and Collins in 2013 and 2014, respectively. The word "binge-watching" describes the practice of viewing "multiple episodes of (a television programme) consecutively or in rapid succession, typically on DVD or through a digital streaming service."[23] As a phenomenon enabled by more recent technological developments and promoted by the television industries, it has prompted much discussion in the popular press and academic scholarship.[24] But it also returns us to familiar metaphors of addiction (television as, in Marie Winn's terms, the "plug-in drug")[25] that are here invoked through the practice of bingeing. "Bingeing" refers to addictive, compulsive, and repetitive forms of consumption, such as binge-eating and binge-drinking, that are more often than not associated with self-destructive and dangerous forms of behavior. Charlotte Brunsdon observes that the use of this particular metaphor might be seen as sitting uncomfortably with the types of "quality," "prestige," and "prized" television with which it is commonly associated.[26] However, Tryon's analysis of the branding and marketing of Netflix reveals the ways in which bingeing is requalified as a superior, even prestigious, form of viewing, "not as a passive activity but as one aligned with active viewing practices, as a way of managing one's time in front of the television rather than succumbing to a television schedule."[27] Anyone who has emerged bleary-eyed from a lengthy TV binge or lazily submitted to autoplay will recognize that this kind of self-management is easier said than done. These are, however, the logics of choice, autonomy, and self-governance that characterize the neoliberal consumer of a range of lifestyle products, including both food and television.

In this context the practices of binge-watching and platform mobility have, as I suggested earlier, been imagined to result in the removal of television from the times and spaces of the domestic and its characteristic experiences of distraction and interruption. The notion that television has risen above the noise or pollution of both the flow of the everyday and the flow of a traditional broadcast schedule is one that sits uneasily with some television scholars. This is due partly to the implied forms of judgment and evaluation that accompany this discourse, but also to the shift to individualized and privatized forms of viewing that are seen to dilute the nation-binding projects and potentials of earlier models of public service broadcasting.[28] The metaphors of eating associated with television remind us of the kinds of value judgments that are made about different types of television and different models of consumption. But they also present us with an opportunity to examine other ways in which the connections and disconnections that are forged between those oppositions of public and private, inside and outside, self and other, have captivated theorists of both eating and television.

Here I want to note other forms of incorporation that have been associated with the practice of binge-watching and that attest to the continued relevance of television within our everyday lives and social relations. Netflix in particular, as the dominant streaming video company in the 2010s, has emerged as a locus for a set of memes and practices associated with binge-watching. For example, in an article from February 2014, the women's magazine *Redbook* coined the term "breast-flixing," with bingeable television described as a "nursing resource" that allows one to mindlessly zone out while a baby feeds.[29] Maggie Kilgour describes breastfeeding as the first and the most infantile in the positioning of inside and outside, and the same article carries with it those perennial anxieties of cross-contamination as it worries over whether too much violent TV or "non-stop hating on King Joffrey" will be unhealthily transmitted to the baby. A second form of incorporation, closely related to eating, appears in the popular euphemism for casual sex as "Netflix and Chill."[30] The company even conducted a survey to better understand the impact of the service on users' dating and romantic relationship habits. According to Netflix's study, 75 percent of participants believed that watching the streaming service is acceptable for a casual date, 51 percent saw password sharing as a milestone in their relationship, and 58 percent felt that binge-watching a show together was a great way to bond with a significant other.[31]

In a case of meme-come-true, a New York apartment advertised on Airbnb was themed as a "Netflix and Chill" room, complete with branded bedding, condoms, a large flat-screen TV facing the bed, and a minibar.[32] These metaphors and memes are interesting as contemporary expressions of television's continued relationship to the everyday, and like the Bedtime Hour, they illuminate its uses and its usefulness as a tool, a resource, and a social technology. They also highlight the kind of everyday and intimate behaviors and relations that are often overlooked in the promotion of new models of television consumption and spectatorship. For those who watch alone, however, the advertised benefits of binge-viewing for personal relationships has been countered by the reporting of other recent studies that emphasize "feelings of loneliness and depression linked to binge-watching television."[33] Yet whether we use a service such as Netflix as a nursing resource, a relationship facilitator, or an (un)happy substitute for human connection, these examples speak to television's continued role within our social relations and our domestic scenes of care, and as that relational device it works to illuminate both the presence and absence of the others in our lives.

Amy West's and Misha Kavka's writing on reality television has emphasized the possibilities of making a conceptual shift from the metaphors we use to think about television to questions of matter and materiality.[34] In line with this approach, I also want to make the move from metaphor to matter while acknowledging that, in the case of eating, the two can potentially remain intertwined (bingeing on biscuits *while* bingeing on Netflix, for example). The practice of eating *with* television illustrates these ongoing relations and the entanglement of television within our domestic worlds. Moving through the looking glass, and partly inspired by what David Morley has termed a non-media-centric approach to media studies, what might our investigations look like if we placed eating rather than television as the central activity in our concerns?[35] Research on eating with television in health and social science traditions, for example, has focused on television viewing, food intake, and eating habits and behaviors; recently, more research has concentrated on the potential correlation between television viewing and a so-called obesity epidemic. In one such study from 2003, television viewing was linked with a decrease in physical activity and was seen to directly influence eating behaviors, such as snacking, that result in increased calorie consumption: here we have our archetypal couch potato.[36] In a 2012 study titled "ObesiTV," the authors argue, "It is common to eat while watching television. . . . Such a distraction can lead to 'mindless eating' or a lack of attention paid to consumption due to external cues in the environment."[37] What is also clear from this alternative disciplinary vantage point is how the dynamics of distraction and attention continue to preoccupy studies of television. Television is seen as distracting the viewer from monitoring the amount of food eaten, acting as a trigger for snacking behaviors and operating as a *cue* for both when to eat and when to stop eating: "It is hypothesized that the allocation of attention to tasks such as watching television may disrupt the ability of individuals to adequately respond to normal internal hunger and satiety cues, and instead lead to a greater reliance on external cues, such as the end of a television show, to signal the completion of a meal."[38]

What such studies also reveal is an entanglement of cues, rhythms, and temporalities between eating and viewing that invite us to turn inside out the relationships between the screen, the context of viewing, and the body of the viewer. Calling attention to the relationship between television and eating asks us to think about the ways in which, as practices of consumption, they are nestled within one another, not just through metaphor but also in their materialities and temporalities. Sebastian Abrahamsson writes, for example, of how "food produces rhythms, patterns, and temporalities, punctuating everyday life through practices of cooking, eating and digesting."[39] And here I want to suggest how the idea of the "eating scene" as an activity that takes place in front of the television (as well as frequently on the television) presents a site through which we can unravel some of the patterns and processes involved in eating with television and that point toward a continuity of concerns with the "situatedness, the materiality and the multiplicity of relations" that occur between television and daily life.[40]

The Eating Scene

At the center of Alison Waller's *Rereading Childhood Books* is the analysis of what she refers to as the "reading scene." This she describes as "a conceptual and narrative space, shaped and defined by remembering, in which individual's encounters with texts take place."[41] Waller draws on ideas of reader-response theory to investigate the production of meaning within that "virtual space between text and reader."[42] I have drawn on this approach at different stages in this book to illuminate aspects of the relationships between text and context that are pivotal to an experience of television. Remaining attentive to the acts of remembering that are mobilized within the reading scene, I also wish to insert the practice of eating into what Waller describes as this "dynamic fulcrum" and to consider how it inflects the act of viewing.[43] The relationship of food and its sensuous realm to memory has been widely discussed: Proust's tale of tasting a madeleine that involuntarily transports him back to a childhood scene still stands as perhaps the most famous example. The relationships among food, drink, and ritual—religious and secular, spectacular or banal—have also been a central concern for a range of disciplines. Certainly, there are particular foods, smells, and tastes that I associate with my own past and present television rituals: the comfort of a cheese and onion pasty with baked beans while watching afternoon movies with my sisters, our ritual snack nights that accompanied eviction episodes of *Big Brother* (and in which the cat was also included), or the family treat of a takeaway pizza with Saturday night TV and my mum's insistence on making a salad to go with it. Not all my memories are so warm and cozy. Food, and more specifically the risk of contamination, has been a recurring source of anxiety for me. I can trace this back to a number of events, one of which was an illicit childhood viewing of *Monty Python's The Meaning of Life* (1983). Watching it on a VHS tape recorded off the telly, I recall being thoroughly disturbed by the scene where a greedy, engorged, and grotesque Mr. Creosote explodes in a fancy restaurant. Arriving at my grandparents for Sunday dinner shortly after this viewing, I can still feel the panic that the "homely" smells in the kitchen evoked as I began to worry about the repercussions of eating. For a long time the very idea of a "wafer-thin mint" (the final morsel that triggers the eruption) and the memory of the dining room drenched in effluence would strike fear into my body: my stomach would clench, my heart would race, bile would rise in my throat. As an adult living with IBS, I still often worry about the effect food might have on my body.

As a patterned activity, the cues and sequences of food preparation, consumption, and digestion can potentially rhyme with those of television. Writing the majority of this book from home, I fell into a particular lunchtime pattern, breaking at noon to have something to eat accompanied by two episodes of a sitcom on Netflix. Across my lifetime I have probably shared more meals with television than with anyone else, and historically, the television schedule has operated as a cue for cooking and preparation times, as I would aim to have a meal ready in time for the start of a particular program. While on-demand services have allowed me to schedule a more flexible lunch hour, these kinds of cues are still in operation. I dart between kitchen and living room, firing up the streaming stick plugged into the TV (then back to stir the pan), scrolling through the onscreen menus (then back to boil the kettle), forwarding through the ads (then back to plate up). When the meal's ready I hit Play as I sit down, and the sofa makes its familiar squeak under my weight. Eating with television requires choices to be made and potential risks to be avoided. The choice of food, for example. Some foods are easier to eat with television—crisps, sweets, snack foods, finger foods that don't require the skilled use of cutlery or the balancing of hot plates on limbs or laps. Foods that encourage "mindless" eating and the kinds of disappointment this might entail (of putting your hand in the crisp bag and realizing they've all gone). Choices of program are also important. First, no subtitles: eating, viewing, and reading are one step too far for me to be able to do all relatively effectively. Second, no programs that I suspect will make me squirm, cringe, feel sick or revolted, or put me off my food (no zombies and no plastic surgery). But television's contingent character means these program choices are not always reliable. In my lunch break from writing, I sit down with a bowl of vegetable soup balanced on a plate (already a risky choice) to watch a couple of episodes of the sitcom I am working through. I am on episode 2 of the third series of GLOW (Netflix, 2017–), and our gorgeous ladies of wrestling are taking a rare day off from their Las Vegas residency. Getting into the car with her new husband and the show's producer, Bash, an unusually quiet Rhonda suddenly vomits down the side of the vehicle. The unexpected interruption curtails their day plans and, prompting me to look away, immediately puts me off my bowl of soup.

This might seem like a banal scene in both the program and my own daily life. But it illuminates the significance of eating within television's ordinary affects and the microdistractions and interruptions that characterize our experiences of the medium and technology, whether in the bored slip of the glance between screens that characterize the ephemeral and unforgettable activities of second-screen viewing or in the snag of memory and reflection that produce, in Lynn Pearce's terms, a series of "parallel texts."[44] Where the moment of disgust mobilizes my look away and the cessation of eating, similar head-turns and brief losses of appetite can also be brought about by instances of shame or guilt, such as encountering a famine relief campaign as you tuck into a hearty meal. Silvan Tomkins has described shame as an "experience of the self by the self,"[45] and in this reflexivity it has been seen by others to awaken a sense of our selves as social beings and bodies.[46] Of course, the capacity of these feelings to linger will depend on the spectator and whether they are swept back into television's flow or find themselves acting on this potential awakening.

The point I want to emphasize is the mutual shaping of experience that occurs within the eating scene. In understanding television as an accompaniment to eating and vice versa, the relationship between text and reader, or text and eater, might be seen to function together to produce a "composite" product.[47] Writing on the possibilities of eating and *cinema* spectatorship, Amelie Hastie argues that "the things that we eat help to enable our bodies to engage in an aesthetic, material, social experience at the movies" as she remembers the what, where, and with whom of eating in the cinema.[48] The embeddedness of television in domestic space and routines, though, presents a different regime of consumption. The geography of the home and the often close proximity of viewing to dining and food preparation areas (made even closer through open-plan living trends) presents a whole host of sensory stimulations, such as steamed-up windows or cooking smells that permeate the thresholds between rooms. The range of what and how you can and can't eat or drink is also massively extended as the relatively private space of the home and public space of the cinema are governed by different sets of behaviors and expectations: sneaking a Happy Meal or fish supper into the local multiplex, for example, can feel like a transgressive act both in terms of bringing in food purchased off the property and in terms of the potential cacophony of smells that might be unleashed on fellow cinemagoers. However, we might learn from Hastie's attention to "the ways that different textual forms, spaces, and experiences intersect and coalesce, as each informs the other."[49] Interdisciplinary scholarship has also explored the coconsumption of viewing images of food with eating to understand the ways in which both hunger and satiety can be stimulated.[50] The work of medical anthropologist Anna Lavis, for example, focuses on the seemingly contradictory use of food porn imagery on pro-anorexia websites. Through this dialectic of excess and abstention, she considers how eating can involve acts of "imagined consumption." Eating, Lavis writes, "is an act that may comprise tasting without swallowing, viewing without chewing, ingesting without incorporating food. Each one of these moments is, itself, an act of eating, as this becomes multiple, and is shared across many eating bodies and virtual and actual spaces."[51]

In an attempt to avoid risky program choices with my dinner, I'll often resort to watching professional chefs competing in formats such as *MasterChef: The Professionals* (BBC, 1990–) or *Great British Menu* (BBC, 2006–). Such programs might be recognized as offering a form of "vicarious consumption,"[52] though the aspirational dishes and skillful techniques on show vary widely from the limited delights of my own repertoire of meals. Writing on food television has tended to focus on its more pleasurable affective register. Cheri Ketchum, for example, considers moments of tasting on the Food Network and the "requisite 'ooohs' and 'aaahs'" that are performed in order to communicate to the viewer something they cannot taste themselves.[53] These formats often favor expressive modes of presentation. Joanne Hollows, for example, emphasizes the sensual and sexual presentation and performance of Nigella Lawson as "the camera lingers on her face as she eats and groans with satisfaction."[54] In *Masterchef: The Professionals*, former South London greengrocer Greg Wallace "coos" and "corrs" over successful dishes as his eyes bulge and his smile widens with an infectious enthusiasm. His fellow professional judges (Marcus Wareing and Monica Galetti) are more restrained but still communicate a range of responses through their facial reactions; the more unaccomplished chefs in the competition, for example, prompt frowns, raised eyebrows, and wide eyes, this time with an entertaining incredulity.

These are programs that seek to create an interconnection between the food and performer onscreen and the viewer at home. In the absence of the viewer's ability to taste and smell the food for themselves, sights and sounds are emphasized in the preparation of the food, and the body of the performer offers a vicarious point of connection. Misha Kavka has provocatively written of models of contagion within affect theory and how these might be applied to think through the possible transference of affective states between participants and viewers. She argues that "televisual transmission enhances the capacity of bodies to enter into intimacies through affect, closing the distance between them like joining together the ends of a string."[55] Forms of vicarious consumption on offer in a program such as *MasterChef* or through the figure of Nigella Lawson presume an alignment between our tastes and desires in order for a pleasurable affective response to be transmitted. Yet our responses to food and eating on television are historically and culturally specific—a delicacy in one culture, for example, may prompt disgust in another. While my own experiences of eating with television are local and specific, it is important to remain aware of the global flows and networks, the cultures of taste, and the politics of production and consumption that are crystallized in the act of eating.[56] The potential for both alignments and misalignments between what we see onscreen and what sits on our plate prompts a wide assortment of composite texts and affective responses, ranging from the unfortunate alignment in my viewing of *GLOW* between the textures of vegetable soup and those of vomit to the broad sense of camaraderie to be found in *30 Rock* and a bag of cheesy Wotsits.[57] Our eating scenes open up to view a range of sensory dimensions and a set of social, cognitive, and material concerns that take place within these practices of consumption. The ambivalences of eating require the potential for intimacy and proximity that Kavka regards, in television, as situated alongside the possibilities of distance, since in eating with television we are as likely to be pushed away from the text as pulled toward it.

A few years ago my accompaniment of choice to my evening meal was the short-lived but infamous series *Man v. Food* (Travel Channel, 2008–10): I stored it up on my TiVo as a daily treat. The series was perhaps, for me, one of the most deliberate program choices I have made to fulfill that sense of vicarious food consumption. I have been a vegetarian for the past fifteen years, and while my friends and students, in line with critics of the series, are often disgusted by the displays of gluttony and excess, I remained captivated by the virtual possibility of eating a cheeseburger once again: a prospect that thrills and appalls in equal measure.[58] In the three seasons of *Man v. Food*, host Adam Richman toured across the cities and states of the United States to sample culinary delights and local favorites, with an emphasis on American-style barbecued meats, fried things, and fast food. Each episode was framed around a specific eating challenge at a local diner or restaurant to be faced by Richman himself. These notorious challenges included a range of time-based competitions and the testing of endurance, stamina, and digestive capacity as Richman took on a variety of food challenges: super-hot chili chicken (suicide six wings challenge, Brooklyn), mountains of seafood (fifteen dozen oysters challenge, New Orleans), giant pizzas and burgers (eleven-pound carnivore pizza challenge, Atlanta), sugar and fat overloads (twenty-four-ounce malted milkshake challenge, St. Louis). The eating challenge has emerged as a common "game frame" in various competitive formats of reality television, often taking the form of gross-out scenarios of gustatory abjection. In such shows, personalities and contestants are challenged to consume a range of revolting concoctions: for example, a vomit omelet in *Jackass* (MTV, 2000–2007), gruel made from rat carcasses in *Fear Factor* (NBC, 2001–6), or fish-gut milkshakes in *Big Brother* (Channel 4, 2000–2010; Channel 5, 2011–18). Richman's challenges certainly chime with this spectacular presentation of food and eating, but it is also situated within the context of a homegrown, local, and everyday version of America (that equally has global appeal). These are also challenges that emphasize the ambivalent terrain of food and eating—neither outright disgusting nor entirely pleasurable.

Whether he won or failed, in each episode Richman was invariably cheered on by restaurants full of local fans and patrons acting as his own personal pep squad and accompanied by a series of visual and aural motifs more familiar from boxing or wrestling coverage than from food television. For example, the show's logo featured an animated graphic of a masked wrestler thumping a chicken leg, and the ding of the boxing ring bell and thwack of a gloved punch accompanied each cut between scenes. This playful macho aesthetic, complete with bass riff and rock guitar flourishes, ran throughout the series and set the scene each time for the challenge Richman faced as he squared up to his opponent in the "timeless battle" of man versus food. This aesthetic produced a particular soundscape that accompanied the images of food, the sizzle of steak on the grill or the thump of meat landing on a countertop, and each mediated by Richman's boyish enthusiasm for an all-American cuisine. While such examples were clearly part of the strategies that program makers use to communicate and share a sensory realm with the viewer at home, the presentation of food within these challenges also communicated something about the ambiguities and ambivalences of eating.

In episode 8 of season 2, Richman visits Philadelphia to "duke it out" with the ultimate cheesesteak at Tony Luke's restaurant. He is joined in battle by Tony Luke himself and their challenger—five pounds of cheese, meat, and bread and half a pound of fried onions to be eaten within one hour. As the camera pores over the sandwich in close-up, this is less the spectacle of skill and expertise or the tempting of taste buds familiar from cookery competitions such as *MasterChef* than an exercise in demonstrating the scale, weight, and density of the challenge. For example, an insert of the sandwich crashing into the frame is synchronized with the pounding sound of a dropped heavy weight. Despite their momentous task, the men set about with bravado. Tony Luke, a large man with bald head and goatee, meanly stares into the camera while aggressively ripping a bite out of the sandwich. Large bites of bread and meat protrude from Richman's cheek as he chews with gusto. At eleven minutes in, Richman has already eaten three pounds, the atmosphere is positive, the crowd is still chanting, and Richman is dancing and chomping in his seat as he remarks to Tony Luke, "This is sooo good!" Those familiar with the series know that man's battle against food is never easy, and Richman's voiceover signals the shift in the drama—"I'm plugging along, feeling no pain, and then my opponent pops me with a surprise upper right cut to the kisser." The once delicious and gooey cheese has turned into congealed glue, morphing the former delight into "the hardest swallow ever." A sequence of performative gestures mirrors the knockout blow—Richman, eyes bleary, shakes his head clear; his fists thump the Formica table as he visibly forces himself to chew and swallow. Tony Luke isn't faring any better than Richman: he mops his clammy brow and, hunched over the sandwich, similarly struggles to chew. While Tony Luke eventually gives up, Richman, with the aid of some hot sauce, goes on to finish the challenge. "In this battle of man versus food, man won." The cheesesteak is defeated.

The challenge provokes a range of responses from this vegetarian viewer. I can still recall the combined taste of cheese, onion, pickles, and meat from the burger vans I frequented as a student (often at the end of a night in the pub with friends) and the way we would eat with ravenous, drunken abandon. Yet the images of excess and discomfort, the thought of eating animal flesh, and the inevitable pain of indigestion also constitutes a revolting spectacle: the ghost of Mr. Creosote is never far from mind. The ambivalent affects that my viewing of *Man v. Food* produces is entirely embedded in my own anxious history with food. In this particular eating scene, the parallel texts of the program and the autobiography of the viewer are joined by a series of affects that converge and depart and the memories of tastes and textures that have both accrued and been lost over time. What transpires for me is a cacophony of remembered thoughts and feelings that revolve around the material, aesthetic, cognitive, social, and ethical transactions of the eating body. *Man v. Food* is just one example of the ways in which television draws on the ambivalent affective registers associated with food and eating. Food as a source of pleasure and comfort is as likely to be activated as feelings and forms of disgust and shame, the latter often mobilized as ways to control and discipline the reality television participant.[59] But the eating scene, both on and with television, illuminates some of the characteristic features of television's affective economy: its messiness and contradictions, its violent mood swings and protean character, its cruelties and its charms. Within these affective and moral economies, forms of imagined and vicarious consumption make visible the cohabitation of our on- and offscreen worlds and point toward the kinds of connections and disconnections that can be provoked or prompted by our eating encounters.

Serial Pleasures and Patterned Activities

The act of eating has been theorized as one that simultaneously reinforces and dissolves those boundary lines between the self and the world. As Kilgour reminds us, "The idea of incorporation . . . depends upon and enforces an absolute division between inside and outside; but in the act itself that opposition disappears, dissolving the structure it appears to produce."[60] In this context, one particular television series of recent years stands out as offering an intellectual and artistic rendering of these conceptual slippages. NBC's *Hannibal* is an adaptation of the books by Thomas Harris featuring his most notorious character, the cannibal and gastronome Hannibal Lecter. The show revolves around the relationship between Hannibal (Mads Mikkelsen) and FBI profiler Will Graham (Hugh Dancy), who become locked in a psychological battle as, over the course of three seasons, their relationship takes on different dynamics: doctor and patient, hunted and hunter, criminal and accomplice, master and student, colleagues, coparents, tentative friends, and subtextual lovers. The series itself is soaked in symbols, motifs, and tropes of both the incorporation and the transgression of boundaries as characters' identities are stolen, manipulated, and morphed in the game of cat and mouse. Hannibal's crimes, alongside those of a host of other budding serial killers around Baltimore, Maryland, offer a bizarre list of brutal violence and murders dressed up as acts of metamorphosis and transformation that work to invert, transgress, or explode the boundaries between life and death, decay and sustenance: a drugged victim slices off portions of his own face and feeds them to a pack of dogs (season 2, episode 12), a live bird is discovered inside the body of a woman found sown within the uterus of a horse (season 2, episode 8), a pig acts as the surrogate for a human fetus (season 3, episode 7), a victim is found staged within a cherry tree with the cavity of his chest blooming with belladonnas (season 2, episode 6), corpses are repurposed as mushroom gardens (season 1, episode 2) or apiaries (season 2, episode 4), flayed skin is transformed into angel wings (season 1, episode 5), and an offending cellist is turned into his instrument, the cello's neck emerging from his dissected throat, complete with vocal cords for strings (season 1, episode 8). While dynamics of power and mastery are still prevalent in *Hannibal*'s depiction of cannibalism, the series also adheres to more recent theoretical revisions of the concept. As Kristen Guest outlines in the introduction to her edited collection on cannibalism in literature: "The cannibal, long a figure associated with absolute alterity and used to enforce boundaries between a civilized 'us' and savage 'them,' may in fact be more productively read as a symbol of the permeability, or instability, of such boundaries."[61] The fluctuations between extreme violence and high culture, the artistic rendering of savage brutality and the simultaneity of both the "raw" and the "cooked," within the show captures the ambiguity of this reading of the cannibal. As Angelica Michelis argues in her study of the representation of food within a series of crime novels: "The ambivalences and ambiguities that underlie cannibalism inform and inflect social and cultural discourses of food and eating. Representations of the preparation as well as the consumption of food are implicated in the construction of binary oppositions: civilization vs. barbarism; inside vs. outside; pleasurable vs. abject, but at the same time reveal that these apparently separate spheres inhabit each other. Acts of consumption are moments of transgression as well as acts of sustenance."[62] This reading of the "possibilities" of cannibalism once again foregrounds the ambiguities and ambivalences of eating and how, similar to the theorization of television, they work to disturb the "straightforward differentiation between inside and outside."[63] As a text, *Hannibal* has been celebrated for its self-reflexivity and its theatricality in the design and staging of Hannibal's crimes and culinary creations.[64] But beyond the spectacularization of food and violence, the series invites us to think about eating as a patterned activity that exists alongside the serial pleasures of television (and in the context of *Hannibal*, the serial pleasures of killing).

In her essay "Deciphering a Meal," anthropologist Mary Douglas opens with an anecdote of her family rejecting the idea that a bowl of soup would suffice as a "proper meal." Anyone whose parents offered them a disappointing piece of fruit when the request was for pudding should be aware of the codes and conventions that govern our ideas of what constitutes a meal and its constituent parts. While historically and culturally specific—Douglas's own tale is from a mid-twentieth-century middle-class London—her work deciphers the meanings of food as constituted by their position within a series.[65] "Between breakfast and the last night-cap, the food of the day comes in an ordered pattern. Between Monday and Sunday, the food of the week is patterned again. Then there is the sequence of holidays and fast days through the year, to say nothing of life cycle feasts, birthdays and weddings."[66] It is in this ordered pattern, or schedule, that eating and television have arguably made such successful partners. But Douglas also describes the syntagmatic relations within this pattern whereby "the chain which links them together gives each element some of its meaning" and produces, for Douglas, an analogy with linguistic form. Citing Michael Halliday, she writes, "Eating, like talking, is a patterned activity."[67] This book has concerned itself with the relationships between television and other forms of patterned activity that occur within the home, such as caring and sleeping, but Douglas's essay also provides us with an analogy between eating and televisual form. The segmented aesthetics of television, perhaps most visible in the beats and arcs of its series and serial forms,[68] might be seen to find a common structure with the units and sequences that constitute our patterns of eating: the daily menu, the meal, the course, the helping, the mouthful or the daily schedule, the program or episode, the sequence, the scene, the shot. Breaking down a scene from *Hannibal* reveals the potential synchronicity of these analogous patterns.

In a dining scene from episode 11 of the second season, Hannibal guides his protégé, Will, through a gastronomic rite of passage (see figures 3.2–7).[69] The sequence opens with an ortolan bird fluttering in its cage, accompanied by the genteel piano of Bach's "Goldberg Variations." A short montage goes on to reveal the fate of the songbird: transferred to a glass jar, drowned in an amber liquid, then roasted en flambé.[70] Hannibal presents this "rare but debauched delicacy," still flaming, to Will, who is sitting opposite him at the dining table. As he prepares to eat, Hannibal informs his dining companion of the ritual that accompanies the consumption of the bird, where shrouds are traditionally worn to "hide our faces from God." Hannibal, however, confident in his mastery and control over both nature and culture, brazenly proclaims: "I don't hide from God!" Each meal in *Hannibal* (and there are many) is often about the manipulation of and mastery over both the food, created from his victims and realized through its spectacular display, and his dining companions. Generic and narrative expectations and the drama of discovery and capture inform much of the choreography of this particular dining scene as Will and Hannibal flirt around what is known (Hannibal's identity as both killer and cannibal) but remains unsaid. For instance, Hannibal's ultimate desire to kill and consume Will is acknowledged in Will's reply to Hannibal's description of the dish's preparation—"I haven't been gorged, drowned, plucked, and roasted. Not yet."

Hannibal picks up the tiny roasted carcass and holds it out. Will follows his lead, pausing to ask, "Bones and all?," which Hannibal then repeats as confirmation. As the dialogue pauses and the ritual commences, what follows is a patterning of shots that detail in close-up the eating of the ortolan. From a head-and-shoulder shot of Will gently raising the bird toward his mouth, the edit cuts on action to an extreme close-up of his open mouth as he inserts the whole bird before closing his lips around it. Cutting back to the first angle, Will looks up to the left corner of the frame as he chews thoughtfully on the miniroast, and he slowly drops his hand away as he pensively furrows his brow, lost in his contemplation of the experience. The continued soft tones of Bach's aria are now accompanied by the crunch of tiny bones. Will looks up and over to Hannibal, and, in a reverse shot at the same scale, Hannibal's actions mirror Will's. In silence the pair keep chewing, and the repeated pattern of shots and gestures continues. In midshot Hannibal closes his eyes and sighs. An extreme close-up of Will's eyes, also closed, is followed by one of his throat, and his Adam's apple bobs as he swallows the masticated bird. The cut to the reverse shot of Hannibal sees him open his eyes to watch Will, then finally we return to a low-angle close-up of Will as he slowly opens his eyes to the light. The scene offers us a sequence of shots that slowly and sensuously detail the activity of eating (biting, chewing, swallowing) that are repeated between the characters.

But what makes this specifically televisual rather than simply a pattern of editing that is based on the principles of film form? If we return to those syntagmatic relations of eating whereby "each meal carries something of the

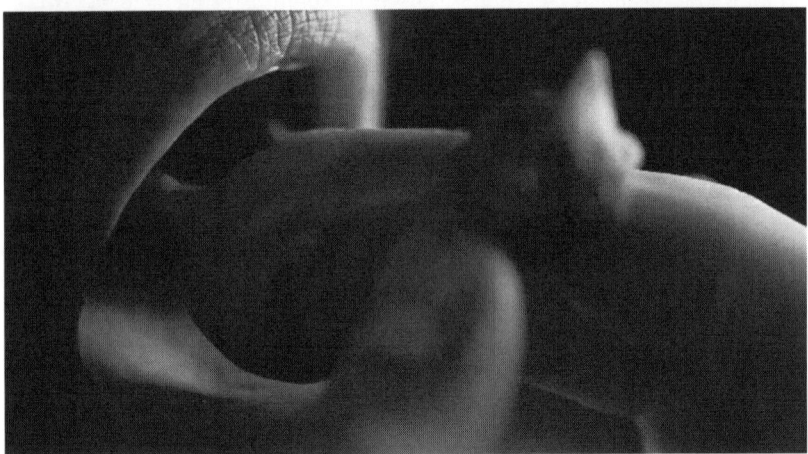

FIGURES 3.2–7 (*above and following pages*) Will and Hannibal perform the ortolan ritual in *Hannibal* (NBC, 2013–5), season 2, episode 11.

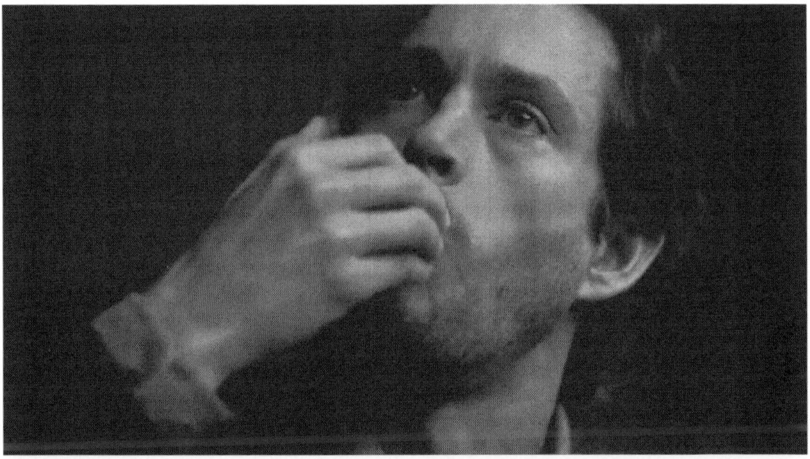

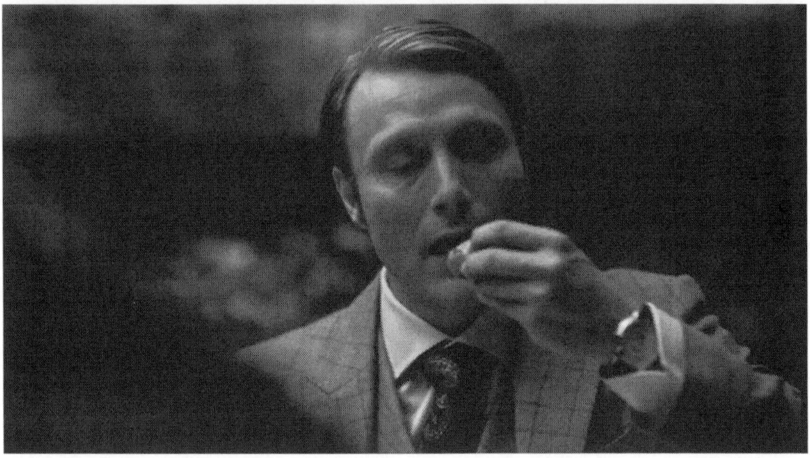

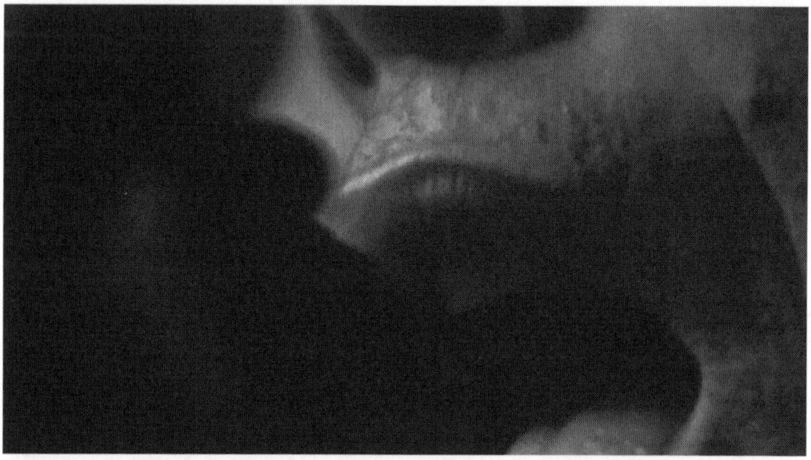
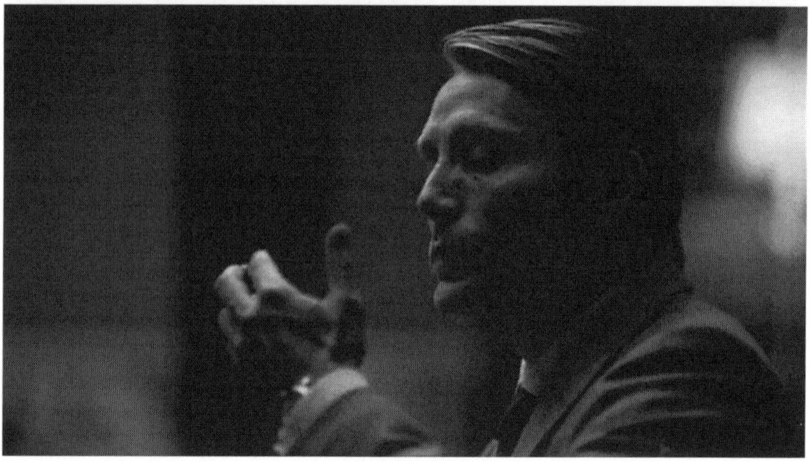

meaning of the other meals," then this one dining scene, as memorable as it is, sits among the many scenes of eating that are repeated across the life of the series.[71] From the convivial sharing of a preprepared lunch between the new acquaintances in the show's first episode (and Will's first unknown taste of human flesh), scenes of shared drinks and meals punctuate the dance between Hannibal and Will, our readings of which accrue both in and over time alongside the building intimacy and intensity of their relationship. In the reciprocity of the ortolan ritual their relationship reaches a momentary climax in which the pattern of looks, the insertion of objects, and the sensuality of the swallow act as, in series creator Bryan Fuller's words, "the equivalent of cinematic fellatio."[72]

TV Bites

When I started thinking about the different synergies between eating and television, I knew that I wanted to write about *Hannibal*. As suggested above, in this show the representation and performance of eating is central. The ritual of the ortolan, for instance, demonstrates the ways in which eating is at the heart of the twisted social relations and power play between characters. Likewise, in another episode from season 2, Hannibal serves his captive companion Dr. Abel Gideon, a rival serial killer played by Eddie Izzard, his own clay-baked limb. Hannibal watches with restrained delight as Gideon rises to the challenge and samples his own cooked flesh. What interested me about *Hannibal* was less the spectacle and stylization of food in the series than *how* it is consumed and the performance of the bite, chew, and swallow. Douglas describes the bite or mouthful as the "gastronomic morpheme," and what I want to suggest is how, as a unit of analysis, the bite allows us to consider another way in which acts or performances of eating on television might be framed and understood: as both the *ingested* and the *digested* text. The TV bite is twofold: first, as a patterned performance or a repertoire of gestures that is repeated across a series by a performer; and second, as a "bite" which is itself "bitten" from the text to be digested and regurgitated as part of the morsels and nibbles (GIFs, Tumblrs) on offer via a digital and dispersed screen media culture.

Eating, in the context of *Hannibal*, is emphasized as a ritualistic and iterative behavior that might be thought of as, and in relation, to performance. Performance itself is described by Diana Taylor as a "*reiterated* act" or "process" and by Richard Schechner, famously, as "twice-behaved behavior."[73] For the eating performer, repetitive processes of ingestion, mastication, swallowing, and digestion are then multiplied by the reiterative processes of performance. The consequences of the cumulative effects of the performance of eating are, for example, humorously represented in an Alka-Seltzer commercial-within-a-commercial from 1969. Due to constant contingencies and interruptions, an Italian American actor is forced to perform multiple takes in which he tastes and then praises "Mama's spicy meatballs." By take 59 the actor is struggling to continue, and Alka-Seltzer, for those times when "you eat more than you should," saves the day. The ad comically calls attention to the alignment of the digesting body and the performing body within the cumulative demands of a repetitive mode or regime of production.

Though Taylor writes on performance theory, historical reenactment, and cultural memory, her work on the archive and the repertoire might be fruitfully applied to the context of the serialized and routinized forms of performance on television. In relation to the "repertoire" (as an embodied form of knowledge), for example, she writes that "performances replicate themselves through their own structures and codes."[74] Through the continual recurrence of scenarios in television series and serials (e.g., the dining scene in *Hannibal*), we begin to see particular patterns at play. Here, I argue, the act of eating presents us with a particular scenario that makes visible distinctive frames of performance and the repertoires of performers. But it is also through the repetitive forms of television (the serialized dinner scene) and their digital dispersal (the GIF of the bite or swallow) that these repertoires can be seen to (re)produce points of familiarity and connection.

In rewatching (or bingeing on) all three seasons of *Hannibal* as preparation for writing this chapter, I became obsessed with Mads Mikkelsen's mouth: the width of his smile, the perennial pout, the curve and bow of his top lip, the curl of his chin in profile. The centrality of both eating and drinking within the text itself continually draws attention to this part of his face. But he never scoffs or gorges, licks, gnaws, or suckles his food. He never slurps, gulps, or necks his drink. He samples and tastes, considers and contemplates. He is expert, gourmet, and connoisseur. While recognizing that taste itself is a "performing activity,"[75] this performance of tasting is fundamental to the construction of his character as part of a social elite. The cultural capital accumulated through the ritual of wine tasting, for example, is embodied in the pause in the conversation or scene as he takes time to sniff, taste, then momentarily contemplate what sensations and flavors burst onto his palate (the reaction to which is always muted; see figures 3.8–10). Each decorous sip is formed from a pattern or a repertoire of gestures that are repeated across the many dining scenes within the series.

FIGURES 3.8–10 Hannibal tastes and contemplates a fine vintage: he sniffs . . . he sips . . . he studies. GIF set taken from a Tumblr called "Hannibalcrackers."

This repeated scenario, the moment of performance ritualized by the series, feeds my obsession. I begin to mimic the performance. I buy a bottle of red wine and try it on for size. This is not about identifying with the character or internalizing the text through its literal re-creation and ingestion, a process other scholars have discussed: Rebecca Williams, for example, has written on the forms of embodied fandom associated with *Hannibal* in which viewers re-create the dishes Hannibal serves (with human meat substitutes) to consume them in tandem with the character.[76] Rather, it is something closer to a kinesthetic mode of learning or engaging with the world—aligning and connecting with another body to see what the performance feels like and to revel in its construction.

Historian and theorist of visual culture Anna McCarthy has shared with me her own childhood memories of mimicking with her sister the performance of TV chef Graham Kerr in *The Galloping Gourmet* (CJOH-DT, 1969–71). At the end of each episode Kerr would taste the dish he had prepared in front of the studio audience. Taking a mouthful, he would close his eyes as he smiled, swooned, and fawned over the delicious food, appearing to be lost momentarily in a state of pleasure. And each time the audience would chuckle, pulling Kerr, comically, from his brief reverie. This moment became both a repertoire and a routine repeated each episode by Kerr and each dinnertime by the McCarthy sisters. Taylor refers to performance as a "constant state of againness,"[77] and for me this expression captures a sense of how television texts perform and relate to daily routines and affective experiences such as eating, sleeping, and caring for children, activities that can, like television, be mundane, tiring, frustrating, and boring (perhaps even nightmarish), but also a source of comfort, familiarity, conciliation, connection, and pleasure. This "constant state of againness" captures another and a newer form of television. Sure that I couldn't be the only one preoccupied with Hannibal eating, I took to Google and quickly found a series of GIFs that captured and isolated Mikkelsen's patterned performance of tasting. That others had taken the time to make and circulate these characteristic bites seemed to validate my own obsession.[78]

As individual looped fragments, these GIFs of eating might be understood as the (un)digested text. Insatiability is written into their infinite cycles and their constant state of againness: the bite that is never chewed, the mouthful that is never swallowed, the gulp that is never digested. Anna McCarthy, however, invokes a more complex temporality. "On the one hand," she observes, "we encounter them in the miniaturized durationality of the looped fragment. On the other, we encounter them unexpectedly, in the indeterminate *durée* that is the flow of social media."[79] While the GIF takes on different styles and shapes, uses and functions, as a "souvenir of viewership"[80] the looping fragments of television programs are also suggestive of the digested text, their molecular or morphemic structure like the particles of food absorbed by the body (or perhaps the waste that remains). They are moments that condense and capture a performance, a feeling, or a sentiment and that accrue other meanings and resonances in their circulation. As McCarthy explains, "GIFs create new meanings in the process of exchange. Their layers accrue, bearing traces of where they have been."[81] Looping *in* and *over* time, as an iterative form, the GIF, like Taylor's reading of the scenario, "bears the weight of accumulative repeats [and] makes visible, yet again, what is already there: the ghosts, the images, the stereotypes."[82]

Early studies of television audiences often took an anthropological approach that focused on the symbolic and ritual significance of domestic objects.[83] Analyses of ritual, by way of performance studies, emphasize the way we might understand the repetitions, routines, and habits of everyday life as offering a point of connection with others. "Performances function," Taylor argues, "as vital acts of transfer, transmitting social knowledge, memory and a sense of identity."[84] The connections forged through the rituals and performances of eating, then, might be seen to act as a particularly effective form of transfer. The TV bite in its various iterative forms is also layered with traces of where I have been (and the ghosts of who I've been with). It is also indicative of the ways in which television generates connections and associations through familiarity and its ongoing relationship to the familial. As the lone viewer, watching *MasterChef* and dining from the tray balanced on my knees, I take comfort from Maud Ellmann's thoughts on the relationality of eating: "From the beginning one eats for the other, from the other, with the other: and for this reason eating comes to represent the prototype of all transactions with the other, and food the prototype of every object of exchange." And as Hannibal well knows, "every mouthful testifies to the seduction and annihilation of the other. It is impossible to eat alone."[85] In paying attention to the routinized ways in which characters and personalities eat on television, I am reminded of the bodily tics or habits of my own family members and the ways they eat that irritate, annoy, or amuse: my mum clutching the cup in two hands, staring into the distance as she takes tiny slurps of hot tea; my dad breathing heavily through his nose as he tucks into his dinner; the surprising speed and accuracy of Alice's hand (more often characterized by poor motor skills) as she grabbed at a chocolate éclair. Whether familiarity breeds contempt or fascination, the attention to eating speaks to the sociability and communality of the medium. These bites and performances, both ritualized and mimicked, remind us of the iterative pattern of eating and of television. Looping in and over time, they speak to our intimacies and familiarities with television characters, texts, and technologies as our dining companions.

Perhaps I was never alone after all.

In her treatise on the practice of feminist auto/biography, Liz Stanley writes, "Social life, lives, and the writing of lives, are all intertextually complex and that to every statement about them should be appended another beginning 'And also. . . .'"[1] For me, Stanley's statement chimes with what media scholars have remarked on as the endlessness of television, and in doing so it illuminates the suitability of life-writing as a critical tool for thinking about the multiplicities of this particular medium and technology. The "and also" of her approach to auto/biography points toward the cumulative impact of the iterations within both television and our everyday lives but recognizes both as incomplete and partial. So while this book has been framed by an understanding of the situatedness of the scholar within a particular time and place, it also recognizes the significance of the changes and transitions that take place for the viewer across the life journey.

I've been writing this book over the last eight years and living it for a lifetime, and in preparing this final chapter I've come to realize quite how important the relatively lengthy gestation of the project has been, as it has required me to reflect on the durational experiences of both writing and watching television, and the changes in my own life that have occurred in the interim. While plotting and planning this chapter I turned forty, and my own domestic situation has changed quite substantially. I've been in the midst of finding, buying, moving, and making a new home. A coincidence, perhaps, but the idea of home has been very much on my mind. At points it has been overwhelming, and I've not particularly wanted to tackle the rich tapestry of scholarship devoted to *home* while also wrestling with solicitors, banks, newly discovered leaks, and faulty showers. Moving into a semidetached house and garden in the suburbs of Glasgow, I've also distracted myself with newly discovered pleasures that have emerged after fifteen years of living in second-floor apartments: hanging washing out on the line, having my own recycling bins, weeding the garden paths, and watching the family of suburban foxes that live in the small wood at the bottom of our modest plot. This move has also been something of a homecoming. I grew up in houses, and though my new home looks very different from the one I grew up in, and the relatively flat suburbs that stretch for miles beyond the city are a sharp contrast to the peaks and troughs of the valleys that cut through West Yorkshire, I had definitely missed having stairs and a front door. As I reorient myself to this new home, a whole host of memories and behaviors resurface. I find myself heading upstairs when I need the bathroom, then turning around halfway up when I remember it is on the ground floor underneath the stairs. I remember being taught by my mother how to hang the washing out, how to overlap the individual items to double up on pegs. In many ways I feel like I'm playing at being at home, the work of socialization enacted on the young girl finally coming to fruition. This new reality often feels more like a performance than a chore—a "restored behavior," in Richard Schechner's terms, and one that highlights the performative aspects of everyday life, the "years of training and practice . . . of adjusting and performing one's life roles in relation to social and personal circumstances."[2]

I've been experiencing a strange overlap between my new life as a homeowner and the ideas of home I've encountered both in the critical literature and on television. There are connections I'd never quite made before, but as I shuttle back and forth on seemingly endless trips to DIY stores, I begin to feel a particular affinity, once again, with the work of social anthropologist Mary Douglas and her idea of home. "Home," she writes, "starts by bringing some space under control."[3] This space requires ordering, planning, and the anticipation of needs. My hurried unpacking of the kitchen on moving day involved the ordering of food and equipment and a quick assessment of the best place to store them: putting the cutlery drawer next to the cooker, tea bags in the cupboard over the kettle, and cleaning products under the sink; pinning a grocery list to the refrigerator. Douglas observes how "each kind of building has a distinctive capacity for memory or anticipation,"[4] looking back to what has gone before but also toward future needs. The grocery list, in a most banal way, is an emblem of that dynamic of loss and recuperation that is continually manifest in the home. The iterative movement that this book has preoccupied itself with also emerges in relation to this idea of home, and the temporal logic of the loops between past, present, and future finds resonance with understandings of home and its associated forms of labor. Douglas is certainly not the only feminist scholar to recognize that cyclicality and repetition are the cornerstones of the domestic sphere. The "pattern of regular doings" that Douglas recognized—dishes that are cleaned, put away, taken out, dirtied, cleaned, put away, taken out, dirtied (ad infinitum)—was central to the early theorizations of television as a domestic and a feminized medium that opened this book and that have formed the basis for the collected essays on practices of care, sleep, and eating.

Television has also heavily invested in the ordering and reordering of home. From the instructional features and programs that documented DIY techniques in the mid-twentieth century,[5] through a "makeover takeover" and the boom in lifestyle formats toward the turn of the millennium,[6] television found itself adapting to a new age of austerity in the aftermath of the global financial crash of 2008.[7] As Helen Powell has written, "Since its inception television has informed how we visualize our homes" by manufacturing particular dreams and anxieties associated with homemaking.[8] Property programming in the UK and beyond often revolves around this particular idea or fantasy of home, with its emphasis on order, coordination, and planning: the "forever homes" sought in *Location, Location, Location* (Channel 4, 2000–) are often envisaged as future-proof, offering the idealized family room to grow in both familial and financial terms. Such lifestyle programming asserts a particular vision of home that remains in line with the "modernist rationalization of space" brought about by Victorian reformers in the nineteenth century.[9] Here the rules and rooms of the British home became organized and segregated by status and function, enforcing clearer separations between "the private and the public, home and work, and between feminine and masculine spheres."[10] For example, while an aspirational series such as *George Clarke's Amazing Spaces* (Channel 4, 2012–) works to rationalize and compartmentalize small-scale domestic spaces, formats such as DIY SOS: *The Big Build* (BBC, 1999–) focus on recovering these patterns of space for families whose lives have been disrupted by illness or disability. While these programs point toward "better" futures and lifestyle solutions for their participants, the duplication of formats and the endless cycles of repetition on networks such as HGTV in the United States and Home in the UK present a more complex temporality. Those loops of memory and anticipation or loss and recuperation are emphasized through repeated narratives of makeovers and transformations and the continual articulation of dreams and anxieties about home.

Home, then, with its associated dreams and anxieties, is at the heart of this chapter, though my focus moves away from the kinds of programming mentioned above to interrogate instead the multiplications and meanings of home within my own life—past, present, and future. In moving to my own new home I've found myself living with ghosts. I think a lot about my late grandparents, since many of my new neighbors are of their generation and have lived on the street for the past fifty years or so. The snatches of inheritance I received helped to fund this new beginning, and a photograph of my grandmother as a young woman sits on the landing windowsill overlooking a garden I know she would have loved. I also no longer live on my own. I've been settling into new routines and rituals not always of my own choosing, surrounded by colors, fabrics, tastes, and sounds I've not personally curated. I've been learning to compromise after two decades of relative independence. I've been getting used to sharing a bed every night and no longer having free rein over the television. There is so much that is new and so much that is familiar, as old ways of being "at home" and absent kin take up residence alongside new occupants and plans for the future. These new and remembered experiences and the benign ghosts I live alongside point back to the uncanny doubling that exists within the home. Here the overlapping of experiences and presences continually reminds me that home is an intertextual site that weaves together multiple times and spaces, memories and identities. As I've attempted to argue across this book, television occupies a central place in this rich tapestry, but it also acts as an ideal vehicle through which it is woven.

This final chapter returns to where this book began and to the comings and goings that have characterized much of my academic life so far as I reflect on the experience of living between Glasgow and West Yorkshire and the repeated journeys made between two particular versions of home. These comings and goings, I argue, find a parallel in the television series *Last Tango in Halifax* (BBC, 2012–) and are underpinned by both a pattern of movement that recurs across the drama and a history of representations of northern England.[11] Within these images, stories, and movements I look to explore the ways I find my own autobiography both located in and dislocated from the North. If *Last Tango in Halifax* opens up a space in which to consider relationships between past and present, then through my concluding example I move toward some imagined futures both for myself and for television. Through an encounter with the midlife terrain of the sitcom *Catastrophe* (Channel 4, 2015–19), I examine those loops between memory and anticipation—the previously on and the coming up—that characterize both television storytelling and the "and also . . ." of life-writing.

Between Homes

I have now been a Glasgow resident for the last eleven years: two hundred miles and sometimes a world away from my family and my childhood in the county of West Yorkshire in the north of England. This last decade has been characterized by a repeated journey up and down the main motorways that connect the central belt of Scotland to England's northern cities. I have been pivoting on an "axis of departure and return"[12] between where I live and where I am from, always, yet never quite, at home. This movement, both transitory and continuous, has much in common with the contributions to Lynne Pearce's edited collection *Devolved Identities*. While responding to a particular moment in time marked by the devolution of the United Kingdom, each essay in her collection speaks to a not uncommon experience for university teachers and researchers: living *between* homes. In Pearce's words, each of her contributors has been "haunted by the difficulty, if not the impossibility, of 'return,' if only on economic grounds."[13] The scarcity of academic posts often requires the scholar to make difficult choices between employment and location. I was lucky to get my first full-time post at Leeds Metropolitan University in 2008 before the consequences of the global financial crash took its toll on the job market in UK higher education.[14] With my foot in the door and the security that has followed, I recognize that the journeys I have made and continue to repeat are of a planned and privileged form of mobility. They might be described, in essayist James Wood's words, as a kind of "secular homelessness," a term that he uses to describe the experience of having grown up in England but having lived for the last eighteen years in the United States.

For Wood, his adult life has been lived "without the finality of exile, but also without the familiarity of home."[15] But I've found myself thinking that perhaps the *less* of Wood's homelessness is actually *more* and that there are, in fact, too many coordinates in time and space that I have called home. Growing up we moved often, though within the same three-mile circumference, to accommodate both Alice's changing needs and my mother's itchy feet. As an undergraduate and postgraduate student I seemed to live in a different dwelling every year, and my flat in Glasgow marked the longest time I'd resided in a single property. I often dream about returning to these various homes. In a recurring variation on a theme I find myself breaking back in to reclaim a place that is rightfully mine. Caron Lipman and Catherine Nash have written of the practice of domestic genealogy and the ways people seek out the histories of their homes' former inhabitants.[16] My own dreams enact a reversal of this genealogical imagination, as I want to know who lives there now, what they are doing, and whether they feel our continued presence. It seems we all live *with* and *as* ghosts.

In her response to a reader's letter in the *Paris Review* about the experience of living in between homes, the poet Claire Schwartz (drawing on the poetry of Natasha Trethewey) writes, "When we say *home* we are also naming a moment; when we point to a memory and say *then*, we also mean 'there.' To be inbetween is to hold complexity. To hold complexity is to have many possible sites of connection."[17] Pearce similarly sees this cross section of time and place as fundamental to the experience of traveling home. In her own contribution to *Devolved Identities*, she reflects on her experiences of journeying between her home in Scotland, her work in Lancaster, and her childhood home in Cornwall. "Travelling 'back home,'" she writes, "is always, of necessity, a journey through time as well as space."[18] For Pearce, the coordinates of home are both sited and shifting, "a destination so fixed in place, but so floating in time. . . . Home is there to pull any number of carpets from under our feet."[19] This sense of disorientation is evident not only in our movement between homes but in the very idea of home. For example, in an evocative editorial to an issue of *New Formations* dedicated to "the question of home," Angelika Bammer writes of home as existing in "a virtual space between loss and recuperation."[20] For Bammer, "home" is occupied by a sense of indeterminacy that unsettles the affective dimensions and assumptions of home as a fixed, stable, and secure site. Instead, the home itself is read as a site of disorientation: "Semantically, 'home' has always occupied a particularly indeterminate space: it can mean, almost simultaneously, both the place I have left and the place I am going to, the place I have lost and the new place I have taken up, even if only temporarily."²¹ This disorientation is characterized by that historical link between "home" and "sickness" and understandings of the home as both *heimlich* and *unheimlich:* a potential space of both welcome safety and dark secrets.²² This sense of disorientation is further compounded by the multiplicity of times and spaces that point toward the copresence or uncanny doubling that is often evoked in discussions of home. As Rachel Bowlby writes, "The house . . . is irredeemably driven by the presence of ghosts, its comforting appearance of womblike unity, doubled from the start by intruding forces . . . untimely and dislocated hauntings of other times and places and other presences."²³

It is unsurprising, then, that television's own uncanny presence within the home has offered a rich seam for storytellers and scholars to mine. Broadcast television's sense of liveness and the accompanying characteristics of copresence, immediacy, and simultaneity—of times and places connected via the screen and signal—have been central to an understanding of television as, in Jeffrey Sconce's terms, a "haunted medium."²⁴ For the purposes of this chapter, I want to remove the gothic undertones and think simultaneously about the locations and dislocations of television in relation to our ideas of home and the journeys we make between them. As Mimi White suggests, our encounters with television are many and have always been "a relation between at least two places or identities, and often more."²⁵ White's comments are a response to the Eurocentric ethnographic encounters with other television cultures that underpinned early television theory, most notably in British academic Raymond Williams's formulation of the concept of "flow" while watching US television in a Miami hotel room.²⁶ What I want to assert, in line with the approach taken by this book, is the possibility for our autoethnographic or autobiographical encounters with television to be similarly characterized by a set of shifting coordinates that continually align and misalign the times, places, and identities we have occupied across our own lives. These are encounters through and with television that call into being where we are, where we've been, and even where we are heading, the affect of which can be comforting, reaffirming, jarring, and disorienting.

By way of illustration of this ambivalent affective terrain, I want to briefly draw on an alternative transatlantic encounter with hotel television. In season 4, episode 23 of the US sitcom *Friends* (NBC, 1994–2004), two-thirds of the gang travel to London for Ross's wedding to his English bride-to-be, Emily. Following a day of sightseeing and Great British celebrity cameos, Joey lies on his hotel bed and phones home to discover that a heavily pregnant Phoebe and lovelorn Rachel have just ordered the "Joey special" from his favorite pizza restaurant in New York. A disgruntled Joey puts down the phone and switches on the TV. He is greeted by the theme tune and opening credits of *Cheers* (NBC, 1992–83) and its familiar refrain: "Where everybody knows your name and they're always glad you came." Joey's face lights up with recognition, he rubs his feet together and strokes his own arm as an expression of comfort (figure 4.1). As the theme tune proceeds, the camera locks in on a close-up of Joey: his expression morphs, his eyebrows upturn, and his bottom lip begins to quiver (figure 4.2). The audience laughs. The initial shot of comfort and familiarity is followed by longing and homesickness: television can make home feel so very close and so very far away. The nostalgic gestures of the opening of *Cheers*, with its clear lyrical allusions to a sense of both longing ("Sometimes you just want to be") and belonging ("where everybody knows your name"), make manifest Joey's homesickness. What Joey yearns for is arguably not a specific place, but the Boston-based sitcom operates as a stand-in for the US and for the regularity and familiarity offered both by a tight-knit community of friends and drinking companions and by the sitcom form.[27] The moment pivots around a series of coordinates as, from the comfort of his London hotel room, Joey's longing for his actual home is located in his virtual or televisual home of the *Cheers* bar.

Though *Friends* occupies a curious space within popular culture, I should note that the US sitcom has never been a locus for my own affections or nostalgia.[28] I use it here to illustrate the shifting alignment between times and places that can occur in the act of watching television. In that dual experience of both stasis and movement and the distant lands traveled to from the comfort of home (or vice versa for Joey), others have drawn interesting parallels with the practice of driving. For example, in Margaret Morse's classic essay on television and its analogues, the freeway and the mall, she considers how an experience of distraction, or the "partial loss of touch with the here and now,"[29] becomes a central characteristic of each of these spaces. In her argument she draws on Roland Barthes's description in *Mythologies* of the "practice of driving as an alternation between two objects of attention":[30] the scenery through the car window and the window itself.[31] In this scene, driving produces a viewpoint that oscillates between an awareness of the here and now (the inside of the car) and an elsewhere (the landscape beyond). Morse takes Barthes's formulation one step further to consider the impact of traveling through the "derealised space" of the freeway in a move that speaks to a particular time and geography of the urban and suburban United States in the late 1980s and a postmodern moment in cultural criticism. I'm writing from

FIGURES 4.1 AND 4.2 The ambivalence of homesickness: Joey catches the opening of *Cheers* in his London hotel room. *Friends* (NBC, 1994–2004), season 4, episode 23, "The One with Ross's Wedding, part 1."

a different set of coordinates, of course, but the metaphor of driving remains a useful one through which to think about television. It foregrounds the relationship between the here and now, and not only an elsewhere but also an elsewhen, that can project us backward and forward in time: as Lynne Pearce writes, "For anyone who drives a lot and covers the same stretches of road over a period of years, it is no exaggeration to say that the past lurks around every corner."[32]

In their study *Locating Television*, Anna Cristina Pertierra and Graeme Turner discuss the impact of the "digital turn" on television studies, arguing "that the emphasis upon studying new platforms for delivery, on the one hand, and recent transnational trends in programming and formats, on the other, has resulted in a certain de-contextualization, perhaps even a de-territorialization, of television."[33] While I agree with their claim that television "can only ever be studied as located," the forms and affects of dislocation it can produce remain of equal merit in our discussions. Also writing in response to a "digital turn," this time in the context of memory studies, Susannah Radstone has also insisted on the continuing significance of location and locatedness for "meaning-making and the affective dimensions of life in the present."[34] But these are affective dimensions that are, once again, characterized by disorientation. Radstone writes: "Far from a loved one, we find ourselves neither where we, or they, are. These disorientating experiences demonstrate the competing material and psychical realisms of location. Where we are, and where we feel we are, may not coincide."[35] Here Radstone draws a parallel between the dizzying experiences of location and memory with the experience of leaving the cinema, where "our surroundings, even when familiar, may take on a strangeness lent to them by the continuing presence of the cinema's imaginary spaces and places."[36] These lingering cinematic worlds might bleed out beyond the screen before dissolving into the hubbub of the city or the reality of trying to remember where you parked. For television, however, this dizzying experience is underpinned by that axis of departure and return that remains both transitory and continuous, characterized by that constant alternation between here and there, now and then. It is in this capacity that television's richness can capitalize on, or play with, our understandings of and feelings associated with the indeterminacy of home.[37] And it is in the experience of journeying between homes that my own relationship to location and place comes into view.

All Points North
While living alone in Glasgow in the early 2010s, Sally Wainwright's family drama *Last Tango in Halifax* emerged as a focal point for my homesickness.[38] The show offered me a way to return home and to feel proximate to a landscape I grew up in, all the while calling into focus the realization that, to repeat Radstone's words, "where we are, and where we feel we are, may not coincide."[39] But it was in the scenario that the series enacted that I also found a(n) (e)motional rhythm that resonated with me, one that revolved around a constant and all-too-familiar axis of retreat and return across times and places I associated with my family home in the North of England. I am not from Halifax, but I was born and raised, following Yorkshire poet Simon Armitage, in the "True North" of West Yorkshire.[40] This is something my Scottish friends would probably contest, but as chronicler of the north Peter Davidson writes, "everyone carries their own idea of north within them."[41] Set in the same county, *Last Tango in Halifax* is a drama about two childhood sweethearts, Alan and Celia (played by Derek Jacobi and Anne Reid), who reunite through Facebook as widows in their twilight years and impulsively decide to get married. This relationship is set against those of their respective adult daughters, who are both working single parents but from very different walks of life. Alan's daughter, Gillian (Nicola Walker), lives in a ramshackle farmhouse on the windswept moors above Ripponden in the Calder Valley. A hard-working sheep farmer, she also works part-time at a supermarket to make ends meet. Celia's daughter, Caroline (Sarah Lancashire), is an Oxbridge-educated principal of a private school and lives in a large Victorian property in leafy and affluent Harrogate. It is a drama that revolves around the tension and the movement between the past, present, and futures of lovers, families, and places. Alan and Celia's memories of, and nostalgia for, their youthful romance are set against the subsequent life choices made by themselves and their daughters, the consequences of which continually challenge both their reignited romance and the idealized image they hold of one another. For example, when Caroline's decision to come out to her family is met with bigotry by her mother, Alan is confounded by Celia's response, which, to him, seems mismatched against the kind and caring woman he loves.

What we see in *Last Tango in Halifax* are characters living with the legacies of choices and accidents, and storylines that are patterned by forms of loss and recuperation: betrayals eventually met with forgiveness, deaths followed by births, trauma giving way to healing. For instance, as the drama proceeds we learn how the young Alan and Celia came to part, as a strategically lost letter written by a teenage Alan to Celia on the eve of her move to Sheffield diverts the course of the young couple. It is the woman tasked with the letter's delivery who instead becomes Alan's first wife and Gillian's mother. As they reconnect with each other decades later, Alan and Celia's romance finds its way back on track, yet the revelation of this letter leads Gillian to recriminations and reassessments of her late mother. As scholars of the soap opera have taught us, endings are often also beginnings, and while the recuperations on offer are tentative and hopeful, they keep open the possibility that the pattern will repeat and that the paths taken may derail or loop in different directions.

The patterns produced through the machinations of plot and character are foregrounded in the opening credit sequence, which remains unchanged across the show's life. Given its title, the significance of movement within the series shouldn't come as a surprise. The opening credits explicitly reference the classic Latin ballroom dance through both the use of graphics and the musical theme of an impassioned solo violin with percussive accents provided by the iconic sound of the castanets. The graphics combine the notations of the choreographer (blue dotted lines and arrows) with the branches of the family tree (black connective lines). As the dance evolves, romantic and familial relationships are mapped out, with the body of the dancer-character replaced by the name of the actor. The camera moves with increasing pace around the notations, animating the sequence, and eventually pulling back to reveal the show's title. The cultural misalignment between the passion of the tango and the setting of a postindustrial northern town sets the comic tone for the series, but the sequence also works to emphasize the significance of the dance, the tangled web of the family drama, and the careful plotting of the celebrated dramatist: here the screenwriter becomes choreographer.

Given the scenario at the center of *Last Tango in Halifax*, the drama is also built around continual departures and returns, both in the reunions and separation of relationships and in the shuttling to and fro between Gillian and Caroline's homes (Alan and Celia live with their respective daughters in the first season). The drama is punctuated by aerial shots of cars traversing country roads, traveling down motorways that carve through the hills, negotiating narrow moor lanes and the steep climb to and from the farm and its hilltop location (see figures 4.3 and 4.4). As Faye Woods suggests, the driveway of Gillian's farm becomes a key site for the drama "as a narrative built around a middle distance romance, arrivals and departures focus much narrative action on this driveway, set against the spectacular view that surrounds it."[42] Warm welcomes, furious departures, surprise visitors, and sad farewells are reacted to against repeated shots of the house from the drive, and of the view

FIGURES 4.3 AND 4.4 Gillian's Land Rover and Caroline's car journeying through the Yorkshire landscape. *Last Tango in Halifax* (BBC, 2012–20), season 1, episode 4.

from the driveway down the valley that emphasize both its remoteness and its relation to the town below (see figures 4.5 and 4.6).

Watching the series for the first time, I was struck by the deep sense of homesickness that it prompted. I was living on my own in Glasgow but still returning to West Yorkshire every other weekend to visit family and to help out with my young niece and nephew. I was still reeling from the challenge of moving to a new city and the exhaustion that can come from navigating an unfamiliar place. *Last Tango in Halifax* felt like a balm, a comfort text for sure, making home feel close, tangible, and deeply longed for. I recognized the landscapes, the accents, and the microregional politics and references that informed the tensions within the drama:[43] a place where "everybody knows your name" and where life, despite the drama, was known and easy. This response to the series could certainly be framed by a notion of "cultural proximity" that has been used "to explain (even in the age of globalization) the preference for national or regional programs that are closer to one's own culture."[44] As Milly Buonanno writes: "People expect and are pleased to recognise themselves, their own social, individual and collective world, their customs and lifestyles, accents, faces, landscapes and everything else that they perceive as close and familiar."[45] Notions of proximity, familiarity, and recognition are central to how we imagine forms of televisual spectatorship. Certainly, the extent to which we do or don't identify with television characters or how we recognize ourselves or our own absence on the screen has been central to existing autoethnographic writing on television and popular culture.[46] However, what I've sought to establish across this book is the processual and contingent nature of our identities as they are activated by television and its domestic setting. Proximity, familiarity, and recognition are always open to distance, unfamiliarity, and misrecognition and are underpinned by instabilities that emerge, for example, in the oscillating dynamics of anxiety and security, the multiplications of times and spaces or the ambivalences associated with the home. The relevance of the journey for this approach also chimes with Zoë Shacklock's writing on the kinesthetics of television as a way to emphasize the embodied experience of the viewer. Shacklock places at the center of her inquiry an understanding of the viewer as an "entity in motion" rather than a "static object for consumption."[47] As that "entity in motion," I have found myself in recent years wavering on the border between past and present, home and work, Scotland and Yorkshire. *Last Tango in Halifax* marked a point of oscillation between different ideas and experiences of home, but it also captured, in its setting and its themes, something about our past and present expectations of both the people and places and the contin-

FIGURES 4.5 AND 4.6 Views of and from the farm. *Last Tango in Halifax* (BBC, 2012–20), season 1, episode 3.

ual push and pull of home. In their introduction to *Writing Otherwise*, Jackie Stacey and Janet Wolff describe their collection's preoccupation with "places we couldn't wait to leave but to which we have returned; places by which we have always been haunted. Places we travel between, when belonging is primarily found in the sense of journeying."[48] For me the resonance of the series was generated by not only that distant proximity to a familiar landscape and culture but also the centrality and pattern of movement *through* a particular geography that mirrored my own journeying between times and places, across dales and moors, and that spoke to the very indeterminacy of home.

As you drive over Cringles moor between Silsden (where my sister now lives) and Addingham (where we grew up), there is a view where the latter village can be seen nestled alongside the weaving course of the River Wharfe at the bottom of the wide valley. Beamsley Beacon stands framed against the sky, with the rolling Yorkshire dales following the line of the river as they rise up and down before fading into the distance on the left. On the right, farther east and down the valley, the famous profile of Ilkley Moor leans over the Victorian spa town below, and the sky sweeps beyond over the heads of Leeds and Bradford. The view is so familiar to me, like my reflection in the mirror or the back of my hand. This is where I grew up, where I went to school, where I dreamed of escaping, where I left, and where I return. This is also the landscape of *Last Tango in Halifax*: the combination of rugged moor and softer dale, the remnants of agricultural and industrial heritage, the land as site of labor and leisure, the "ragged edges" of town and country.[49] While Ripponden and Harrogate, the two Yorkshire towns that form the central axis of the drama, are only forty miles apart, the distance between them is visually bridged by moorlands, where the bleak landscapes of Gillian's Ripponden farm, closer to the "masculine grimness"[50] of Ted Hughes's poetry in *Remains of Elmet*,[51] are set in stark contrast to the well-to-do Yorkshire Tea Room formality of Caroline's Victorian spa town.[52] There are several traditions of representation in which these views of the north might be positioned. Wainwright's drama, alongside the critically acclaimed *Happy Valley* (BBC, 2014–), could certainly be read as an example of a northern pastoral: that "interpenetration of northern town and country," as Peter Davidson argues, "that is a constant theme in the work of northern British writers."[53] It is also central to an iconography of the North repeatedly referenced in the tradition of social realist drama crystallized by British New Wave cinema of the late 1950s and early 1960s. Films such as *Saturday Night and Sunday Morning* (dir. Karel Reisz, 1960) foregrounded male anxieties of entrapment and the desire for escape, with mothers and girlfriends imagined as the anchors holding them back. It is here that my own view evokes a classic trope within this cycle of films and one that has recurred in depictions of the North ever since.[54] "That Long Shot from That Hill of Our Town" has been understood by scholars of the British New Wave to capture a sense of the specificity of northern landscapes and geographies and tied them to the trials and tribulations of the white male psyche, the protagonist desiring escape caught on those ragged edges between town and country.[55]

Taking back the land, the work of Sally Wainwright has been positioned by several female scholars as a way of wrestling critical territory from the academic and popular preoccupation with "difficult men" in both US "quality" and "complex" drama and in relation to the gendered representational traditions of the north of England.[56] Wainwright's work has also been utilized to explore a renewed interest in melodrama and the emotional lives of women, alongside interest in the representation and function of place and landscape on television. As Faye Woods writes, Wainwright is particularly adept at "interweaving an investment in the emotional dynamics of Northern women's lives with an investment in Northern landscapes."[57] For Woods, Wainwright's dramas are infused by the "echoes of female voices and views which frame the region, from the Brontë sisters and their film and televisual adaptations, to the poetry of [Sylvia] Plath, and the landscape photography of Fay Godwin."[58]

In these family dramas and their landscapes I hear my own echoes and vividly recall my own dreams of escape. Those times when I bunked off school to go and sit on the edge of Ilkley Moor, where the look back over the town was preoccupied by teenage unhappiness and family anxieties: the worry of Alice's increasingly frequent hospital stays and my grandparents' encroaching dementia. With my older sister away at university and my parents seemingly fraying at the edges, I was desperate to leave and terrified to go. I left for the first time in the late 1990s to study at the University of Warwick, bouncing between Yorkshire and the Midlands until the end of my degree. I came home to a world on the edge of catastrophe: the Twin Towers fell that September, and my sister died a few months later. Still submerged in grief, I returned to Warwick in the mid-2000s to undertake a PhD, and all the while I dreamed of returning home and, having had enough of student living, a place where I could settle.

I did, for a short while, taking up a full-time post in Leeds. But home didn't seem to fit anymore, friends had left, family dynamics had changed, and I felt more unsettled than ever. So I left, again, to a future pointing farther north. Longing for home doesn't necessarily equate with belonging there, though, and as Svetlana Boym has observed, "Homecoming does not signify a recovery of identity; it does not end the journey in the virtual space of imagination. A modern nostalgic can be homesick and sick of home at once."[59] Actually returning to Yorkshire presented a different reality than the one I'd imagined and often felt like that carpet being pulled out from under my feet.[60] Though I was, in Simon Armitage's words, always "half expecting flags and bunting," the welcome was warm but often preoccupied, as family life had carried on in my absence, and I was reminded of my continued position on the periphery. At these moments I now longed for Scotland and the excitements of my new city life (like a regular bus service). I sought out the images and sounds of Glasgow to educate my Yorkshire family. This was where I had proudly pinned my flag and where I now belonged. At least until I returned north of the border.

In writing on the north there is a continual tension between the past and present representations and expectations of place that is part of a tradition established by northern authors. Davidson, for instance, identifies the themes of departure and return as central to the work of writers who traveled south in the immediate postwar period and returned in the latter half of the twentieth century to a north that had dramatically changed.[61] Wainwright's own biography offers a similar trajectory, with the dramatist born and bred in the region but now living in Oxfordshire (one of the Home Counties surrounding London in the South of England). Yet she consistently returns to the towns and landscapes of the Calder and Aire Valleys with a perspective that positions her both inside and outside the region, occupying a place both "without and within the North."[62] In *Last Tango in Halifax* we see a drama that is underpinned by a pattern of movement that has been associated with a particular place across a history of images and stories. It is there in both the biography of its author and rippling through my own experience as a viewer caught on both the inside and outside of an image of home.

I've wanted to use this experience of living in between to illuminate the kinds of unsettled feelings that television can both respond to and provoke. It is in thinking through these experiences, ideas, and images of the different norths I have inhabited that I am drawn to an additional use of television. Peter Davidson's idea of the north is similarly unsettled. Characterized by a "succession of clouds, seasons and weathers," his writing revolves around an appreciation of its "mutability."[63] At the center of his book *Distance and Memory* is a captivating study of what he describes as a northern aesthetic of fugacity (a scientific term used to capture a sense of the evanescent or transitory character of the north).[64] Davidson's idea of north as transient and changeable also emerges in its connection with the compass: as he reminds us, the compass is "always pointing to a further north."[65] In this sense, north has to be understood as "a shifting idea, always relative, always going away from us. . . . north moves always out of reach."[66] In the shuttling between homes, the north, my north, is both tangible and tantalizing, both where I am and where I long to be. And it is in its capacity to hold those points of connection together that television also acts as a compass: as a means through which to locate ourselves in the here and now while continually reaching out to times and spaces beyond the screen.

Imagined Futures
Reaching out or pointing forward, the future tense of television has always been a part of its promise. For example, in chapter 2 the medium's emphasis on continuity was a central dynamic of the child's bedtime ritual. At the time of writing a fifth season of *Last Tango in Halifax* is due to air, with the trailers promising the arrival of new challenges and the resurfacing of old tensions. Television fills our homes with endless speculation and anticipation—the spoilers, recaps, and cliff-hangers that hook the viewer into its serial pleasures; the twenty-four-hour commentary, analysis, vox pops, and polls that populate the television news cycles; the hype and the buzz, the reminders and notifications, the alerts and amber weather warnings: be ready, winter is coming. The future tense of television is there to both fill time and keep the audience tuning in, but it also continually loops us between what has occurred and what may be coming next, like the compass, providing a link between where we are and where we are heading. It is through this iterative temporality that television remains folded into the dynamics of memory and anticipation that have been seen, by writers such as Kathleen Stewart and Mary Douglas, to characterize our domestic lives. This is perhaps no better illustrated than in the "previously on" sequences of serialized drama (see figures 4.7 and 4.8), where the story and the viewer pivot between past and future. In such sequences the strategic selection of scenes and sound bites work to remind the viewer of key elements of the story so far while pointing toward those plotlines and character developments that will be most pertinent to the upcoming episode. While streaming video on a platform like Netflix offers viewers bingeing on content the option of skipping the recap, presuming that ongoing events will still be fresh in their minds, I still like to sit through these interludes, searching for clues as to where the story will take me next.

 Sharing a home and a TV, I have become much less of an autonomous viewer, the kind that is imagined in promotions for contemporary television

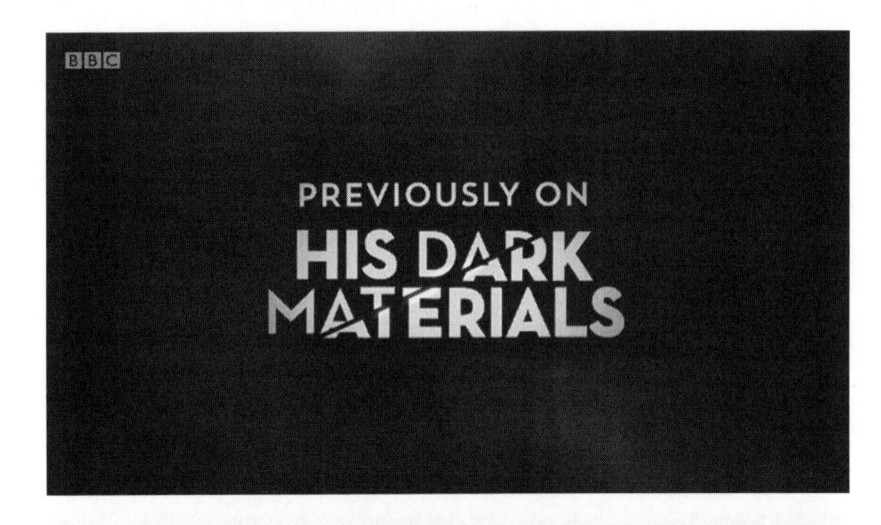

FIGURES 4.7 AND 4.8 Where we were and where we are heading. *His Dark Materials* (BBC, 2019–), season 1, episode 3.

technologies. The focus and pace of my viewing now has to take into account the schedule and preferences of someone else. If we are watching a series, I can't go ahead on my own without the possibility of conflict, and with increased control over our viewing comes responsibility for program choices, which can often lead to squabbles and recriminations. Quite often I'm more than happy to relinquish the power of the remote and decline from making yet another decision. Instead, we often take up "old" ways of viewing and submit to the pull of the broadcast schedule—flicking through the channels for the most amenable option or until something catches our attention. We've settled into a weekly routine of viewing that has become part of that pattern of "regular doings" performed within the home and that can offer an important sense of security and familiarity. However, the idea and experience of domesticity within this book has been characterized by the tension between control and disruption in its material (the clean and the dirty), social (familial comfort and conflict), and psychical dimensions: these regular doings are forever accompanied by their continual undoings. As we navigate through the "mess" of the contemporary television landscape, these patterns of doing and undoing emerge quite clearly in the explosion of the streaming-video-on-demand market. My levels of life admin have recently multiplied as I shop around for content: canceling, pausing, and renewing subscriptions while trying to find the right balance between the levels of access I desire and, like the true Yorkshire woman, how much I am willing to pay.

This pattern of doing and undoing keeps the home at the center of this book, the principal site of the kinds of television I have written about, in a vital state: to repeat Stewart's words, "open, emergent, vulnerable, jumpy."[67] I am still alarmed if the phone rings late at night or the "breaking news" banner crosses the television screen. I worry too much, though. I always have. The cognitive behavioral therapist I am sent to see refers to it as "catastrophizing." To catastrophize is to "imagine the worst possible outcome of an action or event," and it is a pattern of thinking that I've been practicing for most of my life. It is also one that constantly projects me into an imagined future.

Now I am grown up (apparently) and settled with a partner and a home. I am of an age that has been populated with questions from the concerned or curious regarding my reproductive status. The school friends I grew up with are now all mothers, and while I'm happy to share in the loves and labors of child rearing, I'm keenly aware of my place, once again, on the periphery. It's the space I occupied in our teens when my caring responsibilities for Alice could curtail the freedoms my friends seemed to enjoy. In thinking about where we were then and who we are now, I feel like I might be growing backward or at least in a different kind of loop. But this book has been concerned with challenging the cultural scripts that can dictate the life journey and models of chrononormativity, "reprofuturism," growth, and development that have been met with stringent critique from feminist, queer, and disability studies scholars. Certainly the decisions I have made, or perhaps more accurately delayed, about my own reproductive future have been informed by my caring history alongside my ability to imagine the worst possible scenario. In relation to my own life journey, these are possible futures that I have steered my way around; or, perhaps less strategically, I've dallied along the way so as to avoid having to select a particular path.

Many television shows—perhaps *Sex and the City* (HBO, 1998–2004) is the most (in)famous—have charted this midlife terrain and the continued pressures on women of those milestones of growth and maturity. In the UK there has recently been a cluster of sitcoms written by women that chart the contemporary experiences of (a predominantly white and middle-class) femininity.[68] Occupying such territory is *Catastrophe*, created and written by Sharon Horgan and Rob Delaney. The first season of the sitcom revolves around the blossoming relationship between anxious and analytical "Sharon" and the caring, laid-back "Rob," who accidently conceive a child during an anonymous fling. Across the show's four seasons Sharon and Rob encounter various trials and tests of their relationship, including premature birth, a second baby, house moves, sexual harassment charges, potential infidelities, unemployment, alcoholism, car accidents, and the illness and death of parents. Given these circumstances, Sharon's own ability to catastrophize throughout the series seems entirely justified. In episode 4 of the first season, Sharon is five months pregnant and Rob has moved from Boston to make a go of their relationship. Her "geriatric pregnancy" (as the comically cold and clinical doctor with a penchant for alcohol rub refers to it) has not been going well. First, precancerous cells are detected in her cervix, and now, at a follow-up appointment with her doctor, she is told to prepare for a "substantially different child-rearing experience." Because of her age (she is in her early to mid-forties) she is told she has a 1 in 50 chance of having a baby with Down syndrome. Within the doctor's statements about the "difficulties of having a disabled child" is the implicit suggestion that she could choose to terminate the pregnancy. Unable to face that particular horror, Sharon, still clad in a hospital gown, walks out of the consultation room (briefly returning to collect her underwear).

This scene, specifically the doctor's attitude, clearly chimes with Alison Kafer's account of the prevailing "belief that disability destroys the future or that a future with disability must be avoided at all costs."[69] This she blames on an ableist failure of imagination and the limitations within our dominant models of vertical relationships. "Reproduction, generation and inheritance," she writes, "are shot through with anxiety. These sites of reproductive futurity demand a child that both resembles the parents and exceeds them. . . . The child through whom legacies are passed down is without doubt, able-bodied/able-minded."[70] Such failures of imagination are further reinforced as the episode continues. Sharon voices many concerns, stereotypes, and assumptions about raising a child with disabilities: she worries she's not a "good enough person" and recalls a family friend who had a son with Down syndrome only ever looking "old and tired." Reluctantly and anxiously she goes ahead with an amniocentesis test despite fears that the test itself could harm the fetus. When the clinic eventually calls her with the results, she is out shopping, but she doesn't meet the eventual all-clear with delight or celebration. She simply sits down in the supermarket aisle: relieved, deflated, shell-shocked. In the final scene of the episode, having just dropped her parents off at the airport, she waits in line for a taxi back to the city. Glancing to the end of the queue, she sees a young girl with long blond hair, blue eyes, and Down syndrome (figure 4.9). Catching Sharon looking (figure 4.10), the girl smiles at her and waves. Her mother, a pretty young woman with the same blond hair, looks across to Sharon and offers back a dimpled smile. Momentarily embarrassed for having been caught staring, Sharon smiles back—"Sorry," she calls across and then pauses before adding, "She's gorgeous." The young mother chuckles as she strokes the hair out of her daughter's eyes. "She is, isn't she."

In her study of the human stare, Rosemarie Garland-Thomson writes, "An encounter between a starer and a staree sets in motion an interpersonal relationship, however momentary, that has consequences. This intense visual engagement creates a circuit of communication and meaning-making."[71] Arguably, the consequences of this stare are charted in a remarkable twenty-two-second shot as the camera returns to focus on Sharon. Filmed in close-up, it gently hovers in front of her as, alone again with her own thoughts after this brief encounter, different emotions flood across her face. Her eyes held on the mother and daughter, her smile, there to put others at ease, quickly fades. Her eyes fill with tears, but she does not cry.[72] She looks away. As the wind blows her hair around, she brushes it back from her face, then glances over once again to the mother and daughter. Given the events of the episode, we read Sharon's emotions as complex and multiple in this moment. There are traces of guilt (for missing out on having such a "gorgeous" child), of shame (for the assumptions made about having and raising a child with disabilities), and of relief (that the anxiety is over, for now) (figures 4.11 and 4.12).

FIGURES 4.9 AND 4.10 Sharon's encounter with a lost possible future. *Catastrophe* (Channel 4, 2015–19), season 1, episode 4.

FIGURES 4.11 AND 4.12 Caught in a stare: Sharon's knotted response. *Catastrophe* (Channel 4, 2015–19), season 1, episode 4.

This moment, within the context of the episode, plays out the "cultural dialectic between perfectibility and inclusion" that arises in the competing ideologies of reproductive technologies and prenatal screening and of more inclusive discourses of disability.[73] The moral and ethical decisions faced by Sharon are highlighted by her coming face to face with her own ignorance of what caring for a child with disabilities looks and feels like.[74] She is caught in this moment, isolated from the world through the use of the close-up and the shift to the nondiegetic musical score (as the ambient sound fades, the musical soundtrack, a melancholic pop-folk track, takes precedence). But she is also framed by a sequence of looks, or perhaps more accurately stares, that enact, in Garland-Thomson's words, a "circuit of communication and meaning-making" between Sharon, the daughter and mother, and the viewer. It is this encounter and the forms of self- and social recognition it prompts that trigger Sharon's knotted emotional response.

In his essay on audience-oriented criticism, Robert C. Allen draws on Wolfgang Isher's theory of reading to unpack the relationship between serial narratives and their viewers. For Isher and Allen this relationship is characterized by a continual tension or connection between what the reader/viewer has learned and what they anticipate will happen next. This alternation between retrospection and expectation produces a viewpoint that "constantly 'wanders' backward and forward across the text."[75] The reader's or viewer's "work" is in making these connections through the gaps and silences of the text. The above scene offers an example of such a gap, with both Sharon and the viewer looking back and forth to connect a complex web of desires, motivations, resonances, and recognitions set in play by the series. Feminist scholars of the soap opera have also taught us that the richness of the serial viewing experience comes from what the viewer brings to the text—not just in terms of narrative comprehension but in understanding the viewer as embodied and situated, their own lives unfolding in parallel to the stories onscreen. In this sense, television produces and responds to a relational form of memory as it shares in the work of making our pasts meaningful. Feminist philosopher Sue Campbell, for instance, considers how the experience of our own and others' pasts are layered into multiple worlds brought into being by co-performance.[76] The performative texture of memory and remembering draws attention to its relational qualities as emergent, embodied, and contingent. The unrequited gaze of television viewing might seem to run counter to the conversations and interactions that Campbell describes as central to the work of reminiscence and recollection, but television's interactions with memory shuttle across the screen, both thickening the text and bringing into being, welcome or not, a layering of on- and offscreen worlds. Here Lynne Pearce's intertextual autobiographical approach proves illuminating in the ways it can bring together cultural texts with self-texts to "articulate what neither textual reading not autobiographical reading could achieve on their own."[77]

In Sharon's knotted emotional response I can't help but find myself entangled. Not in a position of identification, despite our mutual catastrophizing, but caught by the snag of the stare and the encounter that the scene enacts and from which a mesh of memories and associations unravel. I recall a conversation I was once on the periphery of, and I remember not really getting it at the time (I must have been about ten years old), but the conversation clicked into place years later. After Alice's diagnosis, my dad had asked the doctor whether Rett syndrome was an inherited genetic disorder. He was worrying about our possible futures and the kinds of "child-rearing experience" that my sister and I might inherit. I think back to that conversation and then back to my own future as my thoughts alternate between the reality of that experience for my own parents and what I think I would do or what I think I would never do in Sharon's situation.

Another fragment quickly follows. I'm in a café. I'm not sure where or who I'm with. A family of women come into the room and sit at the table across from me. Among them is a young woman in a wheelchair. She has long mousy brown hair and a round face, her body is curved to one side, and her hands are clasped together. My stomach flips. Here she is again. I say nothing to the company I'm with, because they all entered my life after Alice. I'm alone for a moment, in the moment, before one of the women at the table catches me in a stare. Like Sharon, I look away; unlike Sharon, I say nothing. Feeling ashamed, I remain on the outside looking in on the world of disability and a group of strangers who feel like family.

Or was it a pub? As in a dream, one familiar place substitutes for another. I'm definitely in a pub. It is the period between Christmas and New Year's, and my friend Mel is visiting from London. Both of my sisters are sitting opposite me. Alice is sixteen. In a few weeks she will be back in the hospital with another chest infection, and that one will be her last. We decide it is about time for her to try a beer. Jess holds the pint to her lips, and with her arms folded across her body, Alice's eyes light up as she tastes the unfamiliar drink and we all laugh together. "It was just a sip!" we tell my disapproving dad when we get home.

The scene from *Catastrophe* finds both me and Sharon caught in a stare and the connections and disconnections it forges. The moment weaves itself into the memory of an encounter where the familiar triggered the familial, but it also illuminates my own position on both the inside and outside of a kinship and identity informed by disability. For example, the sense of kinship emerging in the encounter in the café came from the recognition of a series of idiosyncratic behaviors and physical characteristics common to girls and women with Rett syndrome: the twisting and clasping of hands, the curvature of the spine, and a jaw that juts slightly forward. Each tic and trait, born of a genetic anomaly, offers a point of horizontal identification across those with the syndrome and between their families and communities (my mum tells me that Alice's own eventual diagnosis was prompted by a chance encounter with a stranger who recognized her own daughter in Alice). This horizontal identity is also tied to a vertical one that situates these girls and women as sisters, daughters, cousins, and aunts and in relation to the physical and behavioral inheritances that run down families.[78] The crossing of these horizontal and vertical lines opens up a series of resonances where physical resemblance, for instance, has the power to evoke familial association among strangers, potentially tying those individuals and families, willingly or not, to a specific and sometimes unspoken community. The scene from *Catastrophe* catches me in a sequence of looks and recollections that point backward and forward but that also gesture sideways to other ways of being as it silently confronts the assumptions and ignorance surrounding disabled children and their families.[79]

Writing about this moment in *Catastrophe* has been an attempt to untie a series of knots in order to reveal something about the complexity of our everyday encounters with the world (and the strangers in it) and with television. The modes of recognition that operate within these encounters can be both political and personal, forging and reiterating our sense of self and our models of kinship. The work of this chapter, and indeed this book, has been part of an endeavor to think again about television's characteristics of intimacy, familiarity, repetition, and duration and how these qualities are activated in relation to our ideas of home and the families we build within them.

Partial Lives

This book has explored an experience of living with television both in and over time, and through practices and performances of the everyday I have sought to reimagine the repetitive and iterative movements and patterns that are associated with the forms and feelings generated by television. Through the lens of everyday practices of caring, sleeping, eating, and journeying, I have attempted to chart some of the continuities and changes in the ways I have used and experienced television over time, as both a broadcast medium and as an on-demand service. These uses have varied across the years, becoming more or less important as the circumstances of my life have changed, and have been made most visible to me in relation to my own family history and the cycles of care and inheritance. A central aim of this book was to develop an understanding of how television has functioned in different ways at different points within my own life, never simply moving forward in a linear or teleological sense but looping in and across a multitude of times and places. I hope to have thereby highlighted the possibilities of forms of life-writing for our critical analyses of television and to have argued for a more heterogeneous understanding of the viewer, and the television scholar, as traveling in and over time.

It is here that I recognize the partiality of my own life with television and that pull to speculate on both our futures. Perhaps the question I should be asking is, Do we really know what television is in the here and now, never mind what it might be in the future? But this is a question that has already generated plenty of discussion and provoked much anxiety. If, as Patricia Mellencamp wrote, "anxiety is television's affect,"[80] it is also its dominant critical mode. From the "worrying responsibly" of the early feminist scholar[81] to the "anxious love" of television by the film studies intellectual,[82] patterns of anxiety have consistently haunted the discipline and continue to recur alongside more apocalyptic pronouncements. As an industry, technology, and cultural form, it remains vibrant, messy, and precarious: it is not without its losses, but neither is it over just yet.

In writing this final chapter I have found myself returning to that pivot somewhere in the middle: the middle child with a love for her technological equivalent, living between homes, between lifestyles, between ages and generations. Perhaps this is a consequence of reaching middle age, but I have found myself in an apperceptive mood informed by the relationships I both observe and inhabit.[83] Those who find themselves simultaneously caring for younger children and elderly parents have sometimes been referred to as the "sandwich generation." It is something I watched my own mother do as she returned to the care work she perhaps thought she had left behind but instead found herself helping to look after two young grandchildren while attending to the needs of her own mother and stepfather living with dementia. In many ways it is watching the pragmatism and compassion of my mother's work that has inspired my own thoughts on giving and receiving care, and its consequences for how we imagine and value human experience and subjectivity. Her experience has been central to the futures I imagine for myself as a daughter rather than as a mother. This book has concerned itself with the ways in which television is open to the contingencies of the domestic and the everyday, and it remains folded into these imagined futures. Contingency is understood here as the condition of being dependent on chance but also as a possibility that must be prepared for. Perhaps it is a desire to seek order in what is inherently messy, whether this is everyday life in the home or a vast and multiplying televisual landscape. For instance, beyond the messiness of the general everyday, dementia can introduce a radical kind of disorder in the home and family. In their final years, each of my grandparents lived and died with dementia. I remember my maternal grandmother, Muriel, a fastidious homemaker, attempting to make tea in the electric kettle or unpacking her food shopping into the washing machine. Those regular doings of homemaking became regular undoings until she couldn't live independently at home anymore. In a powerful essay on her relationship with her mother, who had Alzheimer's, the anthropologist Janelle Taylor describes a series of "firsts" experienced in relation to her mother's encroaching dementia and suggests how they might be compared with the milestones society sets for the very young child. These first gains, such as learning to walk, talk, read, and write, became first losses: forgetting names or which cupboard the cups live in; losing language, speech, and comprehension. Yet Taylor resists a simple narrative of growth and decline to foreground an additional set of firsts that are intimate and cherished: tucking her mother in at night or holding her hand during a walk around the park.[84] These are moments that speak to both a reversal and a continuity of caring relations between mother and daughter. In relation to those firsts that are still to come, I sometimes find myself searching for signs or clues as to what is coming next: a too-often-repeated question from one of my parents or a misplaced name somersaults me through that recent past and into an imagined future.

In response to this anxiety and in moments of crisis and transition, I imagine that television will still be there for me. To return to Joey's encounter in *Friends*, the scene speaks to a certain serendipity of the television experience as it can work with or against our everyday affects, and simply turning the television on can produce such accidental encounters. The notion of television "on demand" speaks to a more strategic and planned form of viewing that might be seen to minimize such risks, disruptions, or even opportunities, and this certainly has implications for our exposure to different voices, images, stories, questions, and answers that once characterized the medium's ability to act as a cultural forum. However, given television's place within the home and family, it continues to sit within an everyday realm of leisure and labor, loss and love. It is perhaps in our capacity to manage our own viewing that television can arguably respond more effectively to these domestic conditions and can be instrumentalized for a range of purposes, chosen to fulfill specific needs, desires, tasks, and identities. And as that technology of care, it continues to act as cradle, companion, and compass, although the places it leads may not always be along paths we wish to follow.

This might be a happy ending of sorts, but it is one that still swings, for me, between security and anxiety. Too solipsistic, too self-indulgent, too parochial, too happy, too sad, too middle class, too neurotic, too subjective, too domestic, too fractured, too partial. The terms used to criticize the work of autoethnography ring in my ears alongside an uneasy sense of both illegitimacy and privilege. In writing this last chapter these voices have gotten louder, calling into existence multiple boundaries to the approach I have taken. In *Doing Time*, Rita Felski writes of the need to explore the various social conditions that may affect the desire to speak or remain silent about the self.[85] The boundaries faced are political, cultural, methodological, ethical, and psychological, and as Liz Stanley notes, "the boundaries within each self may be as great as those between one self and another."[86] I'm acutely aware of the things that remain unsaid, the conversations with my loved ones I haven't been able to have, and how the ethics of writing about the family informs the things we can and cannot say: my brother Joseph's short story, for instance, is one I've yet to raise or to write. These, I suggest, are further complicated by the ethics of representation and, in the context of my own family history, the ways we talk about disability and about "vulnerable" subjects. Yet the approach I've taken is also one that "makes *us* vulnerable,"[87] and as Liz Stanley and Sue Wise have suggested in their work on feminist ontologies and epistemologies, "to locate oneself within research and writing is a hazardous and frightening business."[88]

To locate oneself is also to recognize the necessary incompleteness of the task at hand, for both the life-writer and the television scholar, as our object of study continues to evolve and expand. "Unfinished" and "incomplete," though, are terms that can make a writer more than a little nervous, especially as she draws nearer to the end. So, instead, I want to emphasize an additional form of movement and an experience of time that respects the "and also" of this particular autobiography of television. The value of stillness is one recognized in the earliest feminist writings on television spectatorship: the pause in the day's occupations offered by the afternoon serial enables a point of both emancipation and reflection. As Carol Lopate observed, "Everyday life, which often induces boredom and restlessness when taken in its own time, becomes filled with poignancy when the moment can be languished upon."[89]

There is a moment in the first season of *Last Tango in Halifax* that resonates with me more than any other. In many ways it is similar to the final image of Lance in *Cucumber* or Sharon's stare in *Catastrophe* as it pulls us into a close-up, filled with poignancy and caught in between pasts and futures, life and death. In episode 4, after a long and anxious night in which Caroline and Gillian wait at the farm for news of a missing Alan and Celia, Caroline travels back to Harrogate early the next morning. From an aerial shot of the motorway carving its way through the hills, the image cuts to a service station café. Halfway home, a weary Caroline sits down at a table, coffee in hand. She looks out through the glass-paned walls to see a family reunited in the car park. The camera returns to a close-up of Caroline, whose frown begins to lift as the early morning light floods the interior. It is, for Caroline, a moment of epiphany, before she returns to Harrogate, tired and emotional but clear as to what her next steps will be. The break at the service station café offers a point of clarity and reflection, but it is also a moment of respite from familial cares and concerns and the worry her mother has induced. It is a pause rather than a full stop, a brief moment of time out of time and a space between places. If television has taught us anything, it is that stories never end and that what we might value most of all, as the medium and the technology evolves, is the option of pressing pause.

EPILOGUE   (UN)PAUSE

FEBRUARY 2020. I've just delivered the revised manuscript of the book to my editor at the press. The bottle of budget champagne I received for Christmas is still sitting on the shelf in the office: I'm waiting for the right time, the all-clear, the green light, before I can celebrate. The news from the other side of the world is looking increasingly grim as a new virus has emerged and taken hold in Wuhan, China. In the UK, the stops, starts, stalls, and reboots of the Brexit agenda continue to dominate the news cycle, though *Channel 4 News*, our viewing of choice during a winter's evening meal, seems to have abandoned their "countdown to Brexit" and are instead focusing on the climate crisis—the devastating wildfires in Australia and the flooding that now appears to be an annual occurrence in the UK. Catastrophe seems to lurk on every horizon. I am, however, preoccupied by other events. We've just adopted a rescue cat, and I've discovered a new love of veterinary television. I binge-watch the CBBC series *The Pets Factor* (2017–) with my niece and nephew, and we squirm together on the sofa at the surgery scenes. We're also on strike again, with the latest round of industrial action by the Universities and Colleges Union. On the picket line I discuss the merits of reality television with my friends from elsewhere in the College of Arts (a medievalist and a modernist): since we have more time on our hands than usual, recaps of the dating antics on *Love Island* (ITV2, 2015–) and *Love Is Blind* (Netflix, 2020–) keep us going through the cold Scottish mornings.

March 2020. The UK is finally in lockdown. Over the past few weeks we've watched the virus spread through Europe and take hold in Italy, Spain, and France. Televised images of shoppers stockpiling toilet paper and hand sanitizer translate to a palpable sense of panic in the supermarket aisles. For a brief moment I'm grateful to be a lifelong catastrophizer: I have an emergency stash put away in anticipation of a no-deal Brexit, and bottles of alcohol gel already litter the house. I've already spent the last two weeks at home due to a final and full week of industrial action followed by the preemptive closure of the university campus in Glasgow. The shift to online teaching comes as a steep learning curve as I quickly learn first of Zoom's existence, and then how to operate it. The platform hastens the collapse of the personal and professional into one another as the classes I deliver via Zoom are followed by a flurry of virtual meet-ups: after-work drinks, pub quizzes, catch-ups with old friends ("Why haven't we been doing this all along?" we proclaim, reaching for a silver lining). Behind the brave face, however, I have been inconsolable about the forced exile from my family, which disrupts the rhythms and patterns that I've grown to live by. The familiar rawness and exhaustion of both grief and high anxiety have nestled in to take their place. Zoom fatigue also quickly begins to take its toll on the body: I seem to have a permanent headache, and my ears buzz while I'm connected. When not on Zoom I remain hooked up to screens, tracking the news and the statistics, the numbers and fatalities creeping skyward, the local, national, and global league tables through which the UK keeps moving up. The news checking is compulsive and habitual, and, like the experience of many others, it feeds my anxiety. The worry about my health and the health of my loved ones, which is constant, is becoming overwhelming. My body reverberates with them, and my fingertips tingle from the constant bleaching of surfaces. Those repetitive behaviors and practices that occur in the home—the doings and undoings described in this book—take on a pathological edge as hypervigilance sets in. I wash my hands regularly for at least thirty seconds (just to be on the safe side). I decontaminate everything that comes into the house. I police my partner's touches and movements (much to his annoyance) and hesitate at his every cough. At the slightest flush I take my temperature (though according to the thermometer I seem to be perpetually on the verge of hypothermia). I do the best I can to control my space and my body—it's draining but offers some sense of reassurance. Then my sister rings from Yorkshire to tell me that she's not feeling very well.

April 2020. I'm on a complete news and social media ban. I've decontaminated my media use and replaced the early evening news with the ontological securities that broadcasting can provide instead. The gentle humor, bonhomie, and repetitive pleasures of the quiz shows *Pointless* (BBC, 2009–) and *Richard Osman's House of Games* (BBC, 2017–) now break my working day. When the weather is good, and it has been unusually so, we listen to Craig Charles's radio show in the garden. Aside from my government-sanctioned exercise, I haven't yet left the house, having taken to heart the mantra "Stay home. Protect the NHS. Save lives." At work and in conversation with family and friends, discussion quickly turns to our consumption of television, which has emerged as something close to a renewed civic duty. In an era of "peak TV" and the explosion of online video-streaming services, the television industry might seem to be primed to cater to this much-reported "new normal" as viewers turn to television content to fill the time vacated by work (for some) and travel, leisure, and face-to-face socializing (for many). The medievalist and the modernist joke that as a TV scholar "my time has come." However, while a certain class of viewers and commentators binge on the new Netflix offering *Tiger King*, I seem to have lost my appetite.

The shift to streaming television online and the cancelation of cable and satellite packages is often referred to in the US as "cord cutting." As a term, it fits well with the rhetorics of choice, empowerment, and autonomy that certain media industries favor. But its allusions to our primary point of connection and the umbilical cord are not lost on me, especially at times like these. Recent days have highlighted the existence of the ties that bind us to television in both its broadcast and online variants—ties that are numerous and that can be simultaneously social, familial, psychological, emotional, affective, habitual, financial, and epistemological. I've not been watching much television, but I have a distinct preference for scheduled broadcast experiences, ones that can hold me in place, a cradle amid the fear and uncertainty. The daily structures of broadcasting—both television and radio—have, for me, quickly replaced the catch-ups and check-ins lost to the lockdown, providing a sense of continuity, social relations, and care.

In the context and history of public service broadcasting in the UK, our television cultures provide an important set of duties and affordances that are both enshrined in law (to educate, inform, and entertain) and amorphous and quotidian (its structures of feeling). Often framed as the cultural equivalent to or the sister institution of the NHS, the BBC, for example, has played a key role in, to quote its own lockdown tagline, "bringing us closer" during the current period and our enforced distance from others. While many productions, including flagship soap opera *EastEnders*, have necessarily been halted, the BBC's response to the crisis—making rapid changes to production, increasing educational and religious programming, renewing its archival offering—have arguably reinvigorated its public service status. Its central role within the cultural life of the nation feels suddenly undisputed as it rallies to offer programming that can supplement, support, or replace often new domestic practices such as homeschooling or religious worship. I am quickly sucked up into the affective communities and communications that are mobilized by the response of our public service broadcasters to the pandemic. Trailers, station identifications, and PSAs fill the gaps between programs and circulate via social media, gently yet insistently reminding us to stay home while offering the continued promise of connection to a national community. Montages of households—together in separation—become a dominant aesthetic, and the screens-within-screens of the video conference call are quickly operationalized for advertisements for financial services and utility companies that offer reassuring messages of continued customer support. The BBC, in its own take on the "stay at home" order, mobilizes a series of pertinent clips from "much-loved" sitcoms on the themes of isolation or staying home, lightening the mood while simultaneously reasserting the role and reliability of television, both past and present, in our time of need. In this context the comforting appeals of the sitcom form take on renewed therapeutic dimensions. For those of us on a coronavirus news ban, however, the broadcast experience is not without its risks and can rapidly produce a seesaw of emotions, illustrated by the slightly panicked rush to the radio dial or TV remote to quickly change the channel or press mute when the news comes on. Occasionally I'll squeeze my eyes shut, stick my fingers in my ears, and hum a tune like a belligerent child until the threat has passed. It is perhaps akin to the new experience of holding my breath when I pass someone, anyone, in the street. Television, in this instance, is neither object of attention nor distraction but something to actively avoid or strategically ignore for risk of affective contamination.

Alongside our new lockdown routines and behaviors, I've also been getting used to a series of textual shifts that have occurred on television and the different configurations of bodies in (televised) space. Beyond its news and current affairs programming, television testifies to the pandemic in a number of ways. The scholar in me remains intrigued by the impact of these changes on our emotional and affective engagements with television as they work to defamiliarize the long-standing codes and conventions of a set of forms, formats, and performances. The absence of the studio audience, for instance, is keenly felt in long-running chat and panel shows such as *Have I Got News for You* (BBC, 1990–) or *The Graham Norton Show* (BBC, 2007–). These programs now take place via home video setups and Zoom-style interviews from the TV studio, further blurring those disintegrating lines between home and work. Previously the reactions of the studio audience would work to anchor the responses of audiences at home and manage and shape the televised performance, and without this we are left floundering: cues are harder to read, performers and their interactions become unsynced, and we are all more exposed to the potential failures and breakdowns of communication and intention. The glimpses backstage, however, and the ever-present mise-en-scène of our home lives (including the comical interruption of animals and children) quickly become naturalized for us in our roles as television viewers, home office workers, and socially distanced family members. Occasionally it is heartening to see our own awkward and clunky conversations mirrored in the exchanges onscreen. Everyone, it seems, is feeling the effects of this strange new world, though not all are feeling it equally.

May 2020. The weather has stayed good and we've embarked on a number of projects around the house. We're clearly not the only ones, as many of the front gardens, yards, and driveways in the neighborhood are looking spruced, tidy, and bright. Whatever free time I have I spend in the garden, making the most of the sun. I chat with my octogenarian neighbor out on her daily walk—she lives alone and is increasingly fed up, but her sense of humor remains razor-sharp as she points to a patch of weeds I've missed. After a brief natter she's "away to watch my shows" as she heads in for her lunchtime viewing of the talk show *Loose Women* (ITV, 1999–). Her viewing habits have not necessarily changed, but they've become increasingly important as a way to connect to the world, structure the day (though the days of the week are becoming increasingly hard to distinguish), and pass the time during the long hours of lockdown. We are all getting a taste of what life might be like for people living with chronic illnesses or disabilities, whose old normal looks a lot like our new normal: a daily reminder of the ambivalences at the very heart of the idea and experience of home.

With the urgency of the peak abating in the UK, conversations on television and online turn to the inequalities that the pandemic has magnified. For instance, the first reported fatalities of health and social care workers in the UK made visible both the contribution of Black, Asian, and Minority Ethic communities across these sectors (though daily news briefings predominantly feature a parade of white medical experts) and the specific impact that the virus is having on different demographics within society. Preexisting and newly revealed inequalities have also been amplified by the Black Lives Matter protests, swelling first in the United States and then across the UK and Europe, ignited by the death of George Floyd, yet another victim of police brutality, this time in Minneapolis. Our bodies, the spaces between them, and the meanings they produce feel more visible than ever, and not just in the distance between screens or presenters on *The One Show* sofa. Whether classed, raced, or gendered, the value society places on a life seems perversely captured in the phrase "underlying health conditions," which has been prominent since the emergence of the virus. An intended point of reassurance for the ideal (healthy) bio-citizen, it hastens the marginalization of the elderly, disabled, and chronically ill. Momentarily I inhabit the terror I would feel if Alice were still here and the relief that she isn't. Switching on *Channel 4 News* one evening (I'm now on a carefully moderated diet), I see the actor Rory Kinnear interviewed about the loss of his disabled sister to the coronavirus. With eloquence, love, and pride he defends the meaning and value of her life. It pours through the screen and I am engulfed with tears and shame, shame and guilt for the fleeting sense of relief I felt that Alice is gone.

August 2020. Tentatively we have pressed unpause over the last couple of months, as the lockdown measures in Scotland have been gradually easing. The weather has also returned to the rainy norm. The cost to life and the livings of UK citizens has been disastrous: the UK has recorded both the highest tally of deaths and the largest economic contraction in Europe. At last, in prime minister Boris Johnson's words, we are truly "world-beating." As we cautiously emerge from our homes, the UK's Office of Communications reports on the unsurprising uptake of television during the earlier months of the year: adults have spent 40 percent of their time watching television (both broadcast and online). Traditional broadcasters achieved a record share (the highest for six years) in the early lockdown period, led by the demand for trusted news programming and illustrated by audiences of over 14 million viewers tuning in to watch the national addresses of both the prime minister and the Queen.

Before the pandemic the BBC was seeking to identify and legitimate its existence in the new digital era following a number of high-profile attacks on the organization from would-be cord cutters that questioned its purpose and funding model. The pandemic has revealed, however, that public service broadcasting remains a powerful communicator. Yet questions and uncertainties remain: Who is the "us" that the BBC purports to "bring closer"? How will the voice that speaks of and to the nation manage the divisions and diversities that the pandemic and the Black Lives Matter protests have highlighted? What is its future among the increasing uptake of streaming services that also soared during lockdown among both younger and older viewers? These are debates that will continue for the time being and that remain significant for understanding the place of television in the UK. However, this book has necessarily drawn on a wider frame of reference while detailing a set of experiences that are local and specific.

Favorable reviews from the press have come in, and I'm finally given the green light. I started this book project around eight years ago and had originally intended chapter 4 to act as its conclusion—a new set of living arrangements, a milestone birthday, a pause rather than a full stop. From February to August the apparent certainties of that world have been overtaken, necessitating this epilogue. But my original conclusions remain much the same and, as my friends suggested, may have become even more pertinent. The preoccupations of this book have perhaps become differently vivid to viewers who were less self-conscious about their television viewing than I was: the entanglement of television within various domestic and familial routines and practices; the relationships between inside and outside and the crossing of thresholds; the patterns of feeling; and the ambivalences of television's affective terrain have all been illuminated by the pandemic and expressed within a number of commentaries and op-eds written in response to lockdown viewing. In this new normal, television offers a distinctive and familiar set of affordances—as placeholder, caretaker, lifesaver—but also, for myself, a continued source of profound anxiety and fascination.

With the easing of the lockdown and as yet without a vaccine, virus cases are beginning to rise once again. Of course, it never went away and continues to circulate the globe in fits and starts—emerging in one nation just as another appears to be descending from the peak. At present the focus is on a much-feared second wave across Europe and a set of local lockdowns in the UK have been implemented to tackle clusters and spikes in specific areas. As

I watch, the numbers relayed by television news begin to creep up again. This is not the shock of the catastrophic moment (such as the *Challenger* disaster or the attacks on the Twin Towers) but a drama (or perhaps a nightmarish soap opera or apocalyptic serial, to be more precise) that creeps and builds, peaks then falls away, loops and repeats, with no end in sight. In this sense, and in the context of this book, it feels particularly televisual.

REUNITED WITH MY SISTER, niece, and nephew for the first time in four months, in August we take our annual Scottish holiday on the Isle of Arran. On the beach at Lamlash I finally drink that bottle of champagne—it's now or never. On our way back to Glasgow we receive the news that the Bradford district, where my sister lives, has been put back on lockdown. There are no dates in the diary to meet again—"We'll take it as it comes," I say, ever hesitant but also, this time, accepting and grateful for the time we've had. Amid the uncertainty I write down a list of the shows I need to catch up on and those I've been meaning to revisit—all five seasons of *Line of Duty* (BBC, 2012–) are on the iPlayer, and *Buffy the Vampire Slayer* (WB/UPN, 1997–2003) has landed on Amazon Prime. I can't hang around. I have places to go and old friends to meet. A consolation, perhaps, but when the nights draw in and our social worlds shrink again, television will still be there for me. I take a breath, and press resume.

NOTES

INTRODUCTION
1. Silverstone, *Television and Everyday Life*, 3.
2. Caughie, "Telephilia and Distraction," 5.
3. The autobiographical voice has been invoked in a number of recent books that consider lifelong relationships with and durational experiences of television. Elana Levine, for instance, opens her study of US daytime soaps with an account of the layering of time experienced by a longtime soap viewer alongside her own memories of excitedly following a major *General Hospital* (ABC, 1963–) storyline on a radio in the schoolyard. Amy Villarejo's phenomenological claim in *Ethereal Queer* that "we live as and on television" is partly informed by an account of her childhood in West Los Angeles growing up in proximity to sites of television production. In an approach more firmly embedded in literary criticism, Ann duCille's *Technicolored* employs a sustained use of family history and memoir to examine changing representations of African Americans on US television screens. See Levine, *Her Stories*, 1–3; Villarejo, *Ethereal Queer*, 11; and DuCille, *Technicolored*.
4. Roth, "Auto/Biography and Auto/Ethnography," 13.
5. Waller, *Rereading Childhood Books*, 14.
6. Haraway, *Simians, Cyborgs, and Women*, 183–201.
7. Stanley, *Auto/Biographical I*, 14.
8. Stanley, *Auto/Biographical I*, 61.
9. See Tryon, "TV Got Better."
10. Frolova, "'We Pretty Much Just Watched It All Back to Back!,'" 245.
11. For a useful overview of writing in this area and a discussion of autoethnography as method for cultural studies scholars, see Manning and Adams, "Popular Culture Studies and Autoethnography."
12. Roth, "Auto/Biography and Auto/Ethnography," 3–4.
13. Uotinen, "Digital Television and the Machine That Goes 'PING!,'" 166–67.
14. Freeman, *Time Binds*, 4–5.
15. Freeman, *Time Binds*, 5.

16 Stacey and Wolff, *Writing Otherwise*, 7.
17 Newman and Levine, *Legitimating Television*, 163–64.
18 Schwartz, "Poetry Rx."
19 Felski, *Doing Time*, 82.
20 Felski, *Doing Time*, 79.
21 Part of Felski's project is to unpick an approach to ideas of time that is "preoccupied with establishing the differences between epochs" rather than the differences *within* them (*Doing Time*, 14). Felski begins to achieve this internal complexity by demarcating three specific "scales" of time that she sees as existing concurrently—everyday time, life time, and large-scale time—and this approach allows her to combine characteristics of the linear and the cyclical. Felski, *Doing Time*, 14–19.
22 Felski, *Doing Time*, 20.
23 Felski, *Doing Time*, 85.
24 Amanda Ann Klein and R. Barton Palmer refer to these textual loops as "multiplicities" in a collection that covers a range of case studies from across film and television. See Klein and Palmer, *Cycles, Sequels, Spin-Offs, Remakes, and Reboots*.
25 *Oxford English Dictionary*, s.v. "iteration (*n*.)," accessed February 15, 2021, https://www.oed.com/view/Entry/100312.
26 *Oxford English Dictionary*, s.v. "iteration (*n*.)," accessed February 15, 2021, https://www.oed.com/view/Entry/100312.
27 Helen Piper offers a useful discussion of this as a logic of the serial in her essay "'How Long Since You Were Last Alive?,'" 248.
28 Freeman, *Time Binds*, 5.
29 Villarejo, *Ethereal Queer*, 10.
30 Johnson, *Online TV*, 18.
31 Joyrich, "Queer Television Studies," 135. Gary Needham similarly argues for an understanding of the temporal experience of television as a "significant location for queerness" in his essay "Scheduling Normativity," 157.
32 Joyrich, "Queer Television Studies," 135.
33 Joyrich, "Queer Television Studies," 135–36.
34 Felski, *Doing Time*, 84.
35 Intersectional scholars such as Alison Kafer and Robert McRuer have already created an alliance between disability and queer theories and activisms as ways to understand and challenge cultures of compulsory ablebodiedness and heterosexuality. The intersection between notions of "queer time" and "crip time" has also been a particularly productive line of inquiry. See Kafer, *Feminist, Queer, Crip*; and McRuer, *Crip Theory*.
36 Mills, "What Does It Mean to Call Television 'Cinematic'?"
37 Mittell, *Complex TV*, 35.
38 Lotz, *The Television Will Be Revolutionized*, 13.
39 Schwaab, "'Unreading' Contemporary Television," 21.
40 Moseley, Wheatley, and Wood, "Introduction: Television in the Afternoon," 1.
41 Jacobs, "Television, Interrupted," 258.
42 The work of Shaun Moores, for instance, offers some compelling insights into these digital arrangements within everyday life. See Moores, *Digital Orientations*.

43 Mellencamp, *High Anxiety*, 5.
44 Ethnographic accounts and cultural histories of television are often situated within or upon this terrain, and the resulting scholarship has formed important foundations for both the discipline and for this particular project. These areas of scholarship are extensive and cover different national contexts and historical periods. Key early texts include Lull, "The Social Uses of Television"; Morley, *Family Television*; Fachel Leal, "Popular Taste and Erudite Repertoire"; O'Sullivan, "Television Memories and Cultures of Viewing, 1950–1965"; Spigel, *Make Room for TV*; Mankekar, "National Texts and Gendered Lives."
45 Felski, *Doing Time*, 93; Silverstone, *Television and Everyday Life*, 7.
46 Stewart, *Ordinary Affects*.
47 Stewart, *Ordinary Affects*, 2.
48 Stewart, *Ordinary Affects*, 55.
49 Mellencamp, *High Anxiety*, 80.
50 Stewart, *Ordinary Affects*, 56.
51 Stewart, *Ordinary Affects*, 56.
52 Stewart, *Ordinary Affects*, 56.
53 Lury, "A Response to John Corner," 372.
54 For a recent exploration of the threshold of television, see Josie Torres Barth's essay "Sitting Closer to the Screen."
55 Vanessa Feltz is a journalist, broadcaster, and television personality who has been working in British television and radio for a number of decades. She is perhaps most famous for her daytime talk show in the 1990s and for her public meltdown in the first UK series of *Celebrity Big Brother* in 2001.
56 Lance's death is situated by the drama in the context of a history of homophobia and hate crime experienced by the queer community in Manchester. In a nostalgic gesture to Davies's earlier series set in the same community, Lance encounters the character of Hazel as he leaves the bar on Canal Street. Hazel's presence is itself marked as ghostly, while she warns Lance of the danger he is in, ambiguity remains as it whether his encounter with her is real or imagined.
57 Holdsworth, "Televisual Memory," 131.
58 Highmore, "Bitter after Taste," 123.
59 Freeman, *Time Binds*, xvii.
60 Brunsdon, *The Feminist, the Housewife, and the Soap Opera*, 55.
61 Lopate, "Daytime Television."
62 Modleski, *Loving with a Vengeance*.
63 Modleski, *Loving with a Vengeance*, 89.
64 Modleski, *Loving with a Vengeance*, 87.
65 Spigel, "Detours in the Search for Tomorrow," 225.
66 Ellis, Adams, and Bochner, "Autoethnography," 283.
67 Waller, *Rereading Childhood Books*, 25.
68 Pearce, "Introduction: Devolution and the Politics of Re/location," 28.
69 Pearce, *Feminism and the Politics of Reading*, 9.
70 See, for example, Allen, "Audience-Orientated Criticism and Television"; and Geraghty,

"Continuous Serial." See also the work of C. Lee Harrington and Denise D. Bielby, which employs a life course approach and perspectives from cultural gerontology to examine the lives of soap opera fans. Harrington and Bielby, "A Life Course Perspective on Fandom."
71 Mellencamp, *High Anxiety*, 5.
72 Brunsdon, *The Feminist, the Housewife, and the Soap Opera*, 68.
73 Mol, "I Eat an Apple," 30.
74 White, "Flows and Other Close Encounters with Television," 106.

1. TO (NOT) GROW UP WITH TELEVISION

1 Kuhn, *Family Secrets*.
2 Spigel's images, she argues, are of "people staging their own visual responses to television" that run parallel to the official manuals and guides for how to incorporate TV into the home in the mid-twentieth century. For Spigel, with television providing a setting rather than a focal point, the technology "becomes a backdrop for the presentation of family, self and gender." Spigel, "TV Snapshots."
3 Kittay, *Love's Labor*.
4 Barnes et al., "Introduction," 17.
5 Titchkosky and Michalko, "Body as the Problem of Individuality," 140.
6 Brown and Reavey, "Turning Around on Experience," 146.
7 Kittay, "The Personal Is Philosophical Is Political," 406.
8 Pallant, *Demystifying Disney*, 89.
9 Newman, *Video Revolutions*, 43.
10 Meltzer and Kramer, "Siblinghood through Disability Studies Perspectives," 19.
11 See Ryan, *Crippled*.
12 Eakin, *How Our Lives Become Stories*, 57.
13 Couser, *Vulnerable Subjects*.
14 See, for example, Torrell, "Plural Singularities."
15 Eakin, *How Our Lives Become Stories*, 169.
16 Ward, "Reciprocity and Mutuality," 166.
17 Schormans, "People with Intellectual Disabilities (Visually) Reimagine Care," 180.
18 Schormans, "People with Intellectual Disabilities (Visually) Reimagine Care," 181.
19 Ward, "Reciprocity and Mutuality," 167.
20 Rueschmann, *Sisters on Screen*, 12.
21 Stockton, *Queer Child*, 10.
22 Mitchell, *Siblings*, 1.
23 Newman, *Video Revolutions*, 44.
24 Mitchell, *Siblings*, 10.
25 I am indebted to Hannah Andrews for this observation on the sibling-like relationships among TV, film, and new media.
26 Mitchell, *Siblings*, 4.
27 Sigafoos et al., "Communication Intervention in Rett Syndrome," 305.
28 A wealth of literature from a range of disciplines has troubled the assumed temporalities

of childhood and child development. See, for example, Hockey and James, *Growing Up and Growing Old*; James and Prout, "Re-presenting Childhood"; Lee, *Childhood and Society*; Burman, *Deconstructing Developmental Psychology*; Uprichard, "Children as 'Being and Becomings'"; and Solomon, *Far from the Tree*.

29 Kafer, *Feminist, Queer, Crip*, 27.
30 Kafer, *Feminist, Queer, Crip*, 25.
31 Forgacs, "Disney Animation and the Business of Childhood," 374.
32 Recent live-action remakes include *Cinderella* (2015), *The Jungle Book* (2016), *Beauty and the Beast* (2017), *Aladdin* (2019), *Dumbo* (2019), and *The Lion King* (2019). *The Little Mermaid*, *Snow White*, and *The Hunchback of Notre Dame* are scheduled for production in the next few years.
33 Forgacs, "Disney Animation and the Business of Childhood," 368.
34 Forgacs's account of the disturbing disablism evidenced in the production archive of *Snow White and the Seven Dwarfs* offers one such example of the association of disability with infantilization. These archives record, for example, the reference to adult male dwarves in terms like "childlike" and "piglike" that consistently infantilized, desexualized, and dehumanized. Forgacs, "Disney Animation and the Business of Childhood," 370.
35 Runswick-Cole and Goodley, "The Learning Disabled Child."
36 Suskind, *Life Animated*, 41.
37 Numerous parallels are drawn within the film by both Owen and the filmmakers. Further examples include the morning of Owen's graduation, when as he dresses in his gown he watches *The Little Mermaid* and recites the words the royal adviser, Sebastian the crab, speaks to King Triton: "Children got to be free to live their own lives." When dumped by his girlfriend, he watches the Little Mermaid, Ariel, crying into the sea, and as he refers to the importance of social acceptance during his speech to a university audience, he draws a parallel with the exclusion and eventual social inclusion of the Hunchback of Notre Dame.
38 Mattingly, "Becoming Buzz Lightyear," 4.
39 Mattingly, "Becoming Buzz Lightyear," 4.
40 As Richard Dyer famously argues in his essay "Entertainment and Utopia": "Entertainment offers the image of something better to escape into, or something we want deeply that our day-to-day lives don't provide. Alternatives, hopes, wishes . . . the sense that things could be better, that something other than what is could be imagined and maybe realized." Dyer, *Only Entertainment*, 20.
41 Disney's "sing-along" videos were compilations of musical numbers from both animated and live features drawn from across the Disney archive. Lyrics would appear on the bottom of the screen with an icon of Mickey Mouse acting as "bouncing ball." The videos were often either themed and tied to specific holidays (e.g., Christmas) or synergized with the VHS release of key animated feature films during the Disney renaissance period.
42 See, for example, Gorbman, *Unheard Melodies*.
43 Elefanta and Wigramb, "Learning Ability in Children with Rett Syndrome," 100.
44 For a useful discussion of what is at stake in disabled children's play, see Goodley and Runswick-Cole, "Emancipating Play."
45 Kittay, "Personal Is Philosophical Is Political," 398.

46 Barnes, "Beyond the Dyad," 34.
47 Runswick-Cole, "Living with Dying and Disabilism," 814.
48 Ginsburg and Rapp, "Enabling Disability," 545.
49 For further discussion on children's television and forms (and formats) of generational transmission, see Messenger-Davies, "Heirlooms in the Living Room"; and Gorton and Hansen, "Caring for Past Television."
50 M. Davidson, *Concerto for the Left Hand*, xxiii.
51 Kafer, *Feminist, Queer, Crip*, 23.

2. BEDTIME STORIES

1 Tatar, *Enchanted Hunters*.
2 Albert and Jones, "Temporal Transition from Being Together to Being Alone," 131.
3 A transitional object is something that "represents the infant's transition from a state of being merged with the mother to a state of being in relation to the mother as something outside and separate." Winnicott, *Playing and Reality*, 10.
4 Silverstone, *Television and Everyday Life*, 15.
5 Silverstone, *Television and Everyday Life*, 3.
6 Silverstone, *Television and Everyday Life*, 16. This emotional dynamic identified by Silverstone draws on Patricia Mellencamp's *High Anxiety* and is reimagined in John Ellis's paradigm of witness and working through, *Seeing Things*.
7 Villarejo, *Ethereal Queer*, 154.
8 As David Oswell has argued, writing on early BBC children's television, "Programme forms and the scheduling of programmes were oriented to their domestic child audiences in such a way as to encourage an intimacy between children's television and the conditions of its reception." Oswell, *Television, Childhood, and the Home*, 47.
9 Launched on February 11, 2002, CBeebies is the BBC's brand aimed at preschool children from zero to six years old, with programming for older children provided by the separate but related brand CBBC. In Britain the channel is free to air, but it also has a presence (supported through subscription, advertising, or both) in a number of other television territories, including the Republic of Ireland, Singapore, Poland, Indonesia, Australia, and the United States.
10 When CBeebies attempted to remove *In the Night Garden* from this programming block in 2008, it was met with uproar by a group of parents. One such parent wrote in a petition on Facebook: "CBeebies are having a laugh. . . . My four-year-old refused to believe it was bedtime because *ITNG* hadn't been on and it was daylight outside." Reynolds, "Anger as BBC Moves *In the Night Garden*."
11 Scannell, *Radio, Television and Modern Life*, 149.
12 Silverstone, *Television and Everyday Life*, 11.
13 *Wogan* was a thirty-minute chat show broadcast at seven o'clock every weeknight on BBC One from 1985 to 1992 and hosted by Irish broadcaster and television personality Terry Wogan. As I grew up I learned to appreciate Sir Terry and his dry sense of humor.
14 Scannell, *Radio, Television and Modern Life*, 144.
15 This "sense of care," David Oswell writes (albeit skeptically), is not unique to public ser-

vice broadcasters but is apparent in the educational promises of a range of children's media producers. Oswell, *Television, Childhood, and the Home*, 21.
16 Oswell, *Television, Childhood, and the Home*, 26.
17 Oswell, *Television, Childhood, and the Home*, 4.
18 In contrast to this, Mol instates the value of a "logic of care." See Mol, *Logic of Care*.
19 Tronto, *Moral Boundaries*, 106.
20 Tronto, *Moral Boundaries*, 107.
21 This sense of television's potential usefulness as part of a process of care is drawn from Scannell's argument in *Radio, Television and Modern Life*. In a footnote to his discussion, Scannell embellishes on his particular use of Heidegger's *Being and Time*. He writes: "The meaningfulness of the background of everyday existence is discussed as manifest in the ways in which *equipment* (Heidegger's famous example is a hammer—here we understand radio and television in this way) is *ready-to-hand* and thereby meaningfully *available*. That is to say, everyday (humanly produced) things present themselves as useful and useable. We understand (we grasp) everyday things by knowing what to do with them and how to use them. Everyday objects are self-disclosing. They show themselves precisely as such things (as unremarkable, obvious, self-evidently that they are *for* anyone and everyone) by virtue of their being made in such ways as to be found as usefully usable by anyone." Here Heidegger's hammer is reimagined as a hairbrush. Scannell, *Radio, Television and Modern Life*, 145.
22 Brown, "Where CBeebies Toddles Next."
23 Briggs, "Meaning, Play and Experience."
24 Bignell, "Familiar Aliens," 376.
25 See Holdsworth, "Something Special"; and Moseley, *Stop-Motion Animation for Children*.
26 Griffiths, "CBeebies Bedtime Hour Changes."
27 Ashby, "*Pajanimals* Review."
28 Mol, *Logic of Care*, 46.
29 Oswell, *Television, Childhood, and the Home*, 25.
30 Longfellow, "The Children's Hour."
31 The "Toddler's Truce" was eventually abolished in 1957. While the BBC governors voted to maintain this "closed period" on television, its opening was eventually enforced after a petition by ITV companies. This only applied Monday through Saturday, though; the "God Slot" on Sunday stayed closed. The postmaster general of the time, Lord Charles Hill, wrote in his memoirs: "This restriction seemed to me to be absurd, and I said so. It was the responsibility of parents, not the State, to put their children to bed at the right time. Many people get home from work between 5 and 6 P.M. and it was unreasonable to deny them the opportunity of watching television." Quoted in Sendall, *Independent Television in Britain*, 245.
32 McGown, "Watch with Mother."
33 Steemers, *Creating Preschool Television*, 21.
34 Oswell, *Television, Childhood, and the Home*, 21. Oswell acknowledges the "idealized" image of parenting created by the BBC in this context and argues that "whether or not mothers actually did watch with their children what emerges is that the BBC had been

NOTES TO CHAPTER TWO   153

successful at creating a 'loving' and 'caring' relationship between mother, child and television as a specifically discursive space." *Television, Childhood, and the Home*, 69.
35 Tatar, *Enchanted Hunters*, 39.
36 Interview on BBC *Breakfast*, May 25, 2015.
37 Lynn Spigel charts similar strategies and concerns that emerged in relation to the use of television by children in the postwar American context in her essay "Seducing the Innocents: Childhood and Television in Postwar America" in *Welcome to the Dreamhouse*.
38 See, for example, Cardiff and Scannell, "Broadcasting and National Unity."
39 Lury, "Halfway down the Stairs," 273.
40 Tatar, *Enchanted Hunters*, 16.
41 For a further account of the relationship between literary and media texts, see Helen Bromley's essay "Pandora's Box or the Box of Delights."
42 Interviewed in the *Telegraph* to mark the series launch in 2007, Anne Wood commented on the impetus behind *In the Night Garden*: "There is so much anxiety around looking after children and so on, and especially around bedtime—a time when we need children to be happy and relaxed. . . . I wondered if there was anything we could make to alleviate that." Carter, "They Come in Peace."
43 Lury, *Interpreting Television*, 89.
44 BBC, "From Tot to Toddler to Tearaway."
45 Tatar, *Enchanted Hunters*, 9.
46 This rhyme is also danced to by the character "Teddy" in *Andy Pandy* (a much-beloved puppet series that formed part of the *Watch with Mother* strand and was originally produced in 1950).
47 David Buckingham, for instance, observes how writers like Marie Winn and Neil Postman "explicitly draw on one of the most seductive post-Romantic fantasies of childhood: the notion of a pre-industrial Golden Age, an idyllic Garden of Eden in which children could play freely, untainted by corruption." Buckingham, *After the Death of Childhood*, 35. Stephen Kline's study of children's media, *Out of the Garden*, similarly positions pretelevision childhoods and children's culture as an "innocent garden world." Commenting on the children's picture books of the Victorian era, he laments the images of "children who communed with one another and the things they found in the garden (animals, butterflies, sticks, rivers) through pretending. They did not rely upon toys as a tool for projecting their imagination or on television narratives to script their imaginary adventures." Kline, *Out of the Garden*, 144.
48 It is interesting to note that the etymology for the word "green" (meaning inexperienced) comes from the Old English "growan," meaning "to grow."
49 Natov, *Poetics of Childhood*, 92.
50 The seasonal rituals and routines of the real-world garden present a space that is both constant yet ever changing. This is a key feature of many of the essays in Francis and Hester, *The Meaning of Gardens*. The sense of security provided by these seasonal rhythms is also a prominent feature of preschool television, specifically in interstitial songs and imagery.
51 See, for example, Tom Chivers's comic list of the shows most "unsettling" elements, "*In the Night Garden* Is a Surrealist Orgy of Sex and Death," on the popular culture commentary website *Buzzfeed*.

52 Jones, "'Endlessly Revisited and Forever Gone,'" 33.
53 Jones, "'Endlessly Revisited and Forever Gone,'" 33–34.
54 Felski, *Doing Time*, 85.
55 Natov, *The Poetics of Childhood*, 91.
56 Nikolajeva and Taylor, "'Must We to Bed Indeed?,'" 148–49.
57 Nikolajeva and Taylor, "'Must We to Bed Indeed?,'" 160.
58 Nikolajeva and Taylor, "'Must We to Bed Indeed?,'" 159.
59 The relationship between adult and child in processes of learning and remembering has been much explored by psychologists. See, for example, research on "instructional scaffolding" by social psychologists David Wood, Joseph Bruner, Gail Ross, and David Middleton, which draws on the work of psychologist Lev Vygotsky (this research is outlined in D. J. Wood, "Teaching the Young Child"). See also Derek Edwards and David Middleton's study of the use of family photographs within this relationship: Edwards and Middleton, "Conversational Remembering and Family Relationships."
60 Johnson, "The Continuity of 'Continuity.'"
61 For example, the musical bandstand recalls *The Magic Roundabout* (ORTF, 1963–73; BBC, 1965–77), where episodes would often end with Zebedee's call "time for bed." The wooden Pontipines also evoke the stop-motion figurines of programs such as *Camberwick Green* (BBC, 1966) and an animation style associated with the beloved work of Gordon Murray Puppets Productions and Small Films (see Moseley, *Stop-Motion Animation for Children*).
62 Quoted in Carter, "They Come in Peace."
63 For a discussion of this understanding of childhood, see Katz, "Childhood as Spectacle."
64 Blunt and Varley, "Geographies of Home," 3.

3. TV DINNERS

1 Chuck Tryon describes platform mobility as "the idea that films and television shows can move seamlessly from one device to another with minimal interruption." Tryon, "Make Any Room Your TV Room," 289.
2 Tryon, "Make Any Room Your TV Room," 289–90.
3 Tryon's project builds on the work of Lynn Spigel and her seminal account of the arrival of television in the US postwar home to consider the discourses of family and domestic life that accompany the introduction of new television technologies, in particular the notion of "togetherness in separation," whereby multiple sets or devices can produce domestic harmony by individualizing consumption while maintaining the family unit. Spigel, *Make Room for TV*.
4 The full chorus lyrics are as follows: "I'll go it alone, that's how it must be/ I can't be right for somebody else/ If I'm not right for me/ I gotta be free, I gotta be free/ Daring to try, to do it or die/ I gotta be me" (song and lyrics by Walter Marks).
5 Tryon, "Make Any Room Your TV Room," 289.
6 Turner, "Approaching the Cultures of Use," 226.
7 Evans, "Layering Engagement."
8 Evans, "Layering Engagement," 117.

9. Evans, "Layering Engagement," 123.
10. Evans, Coughlan, and Coughlan, "Building Digital Estates," 197.
11. See, for example, Sconce, *Haunted Media*.
12. Lury, Parisi, and Terranova, "Introduction: The Becoming Topological of Culture."
13. Kilgour, *From Communion to Cannibalism*; Probyn, *Carnal Appetites*.
14. Probyn, *Carnal Appetites*, 13.
15. Gauntlett and Hill, *TV Living*, 38.
16. See Benson-Allott, *Remote Control*, 66–69.
17. Douglas, "Deciphering a Meal," 37.
18. West, "Reality Television and the Power of Dirt," 63.
19. West, "Reality Television and the Power of Dirt," 66. Such metaphors recur, for example, in Jason Jacobs's discussion of the role of interruption in accounts of television's textuality and the notion that digital television texts enable such "textual pollutions" to be removed. Jacobs, "Television, Interrupted," 259.
20. Meigs, "Food as a Cultural Construction," 101.
21. Incorporation is a process "in which an external object is taken inside another." Kilgour, *From Communion to Cannibalism*, 4.
22. Coveney, *Food, Morals and Meaning*, 161.
23. *Oxford English Dictionary*, s.v. "binge-watching (n.)," accessed March 11, 2021, https://www.oed.com/view/Entry/64180145?rskey=vWgsNa&result=1&isAdvanced=false#eid.
24. Others have traced the history of the term within popular press commentary, and a flurry of articles on the subject have recently appeared. See Glebatis Perks, *Media Marathoning*; Jenner, "Is It TVIV?"; Jenner, "Binge-Watching"; Tryon, "TV Got Better"; Pittman and Sheehan, "Sprinting a Media Marathon."
25. Winn, *The Plug-In Drug*.
26. Brunsdon, "Bingeing on Box-Sets," 65.
27. Tryon, "TV Got Better," 112.
28. See, for example, Buonanno, *The Age of Television*, 20–26.
29. Le Vine, "The Rise of 'Breast-flixing.'"
30. With respect to television's relationship to forms of incorporation, a tangential study (beyond the scope of this chapter) could be imagined as engaging with existing scholarship on television viewing and sexual activity. See, for example, Bersamin, Bourdeau, and Fisher, "Television Use, Sexual Behavior, and Relationship Status."
31. The company surveyed 1,008 of its 40 million American subscribers aged nineteen to twenty-nine with the findings reported as an advertorial across a number of media outlets. Olson, "'Netflix and Chill' Is Good for Your Relationship, Says Netflix."
32. Reinstein, "This Airbnb Is a 'Netflix and Chill' Utopia."
33. Dovey, "Binge-Watching Television Linked to Loneliness and Depression."
34. Kavka, "A Matter of Feeling."
35. Morley, "For a Materialist, Non–media-centric Media Studies."
36. Gore et al., "Television Viewing and Snacking," 400.
37. Boulos et al., "ObesiTV," 149.
38. Boulos et al., "ObesiTV," 149.
39. Abrahamsson, "Cooking, Eating and Digesting," 288.

40 Bertoni, "Soil and Worm," 64.
41 Waller, *Rereading Childhood Books*, 23.
42 Waller, *Rereading Childhood Books*, 25.
43 Waller, *Rereading Childhood Books*, 23.
44 Pearce, "Introduction: Devolution and the Politics of Re/location," 29.
45 Tomkins, *Shame and Its Sisters*, 136.
46 See Probyn, *Blush*.
47 Pearce, "Introduction: Devolution and the Politics of Re/location," 29.
48 Hastie, "Eating in the Dark," 295.
49 Hastie, "Eating in the Dark," 285.
50 Anna Lavis, for example, considers how recent studies have "suggested that viewing images of food may reduce the desire to eat by engendering a feeling of having eaten." Lavis, "Food Porn, Pro-anorexia and the Viscerality of Virtual Affect," 4. In a similar vein, Charles Spence and colleagues argue that "visual exposure to food has already been shown to exert an essential role in terms of consumption behaviors." Spence et al., "Eating with Our Eyes," 3.
51 Lavis, "Food Porn, Pro-anorexia and the Viscerality of Virtual Affect," 6.
52 Adema, "Vicarious Consumption."
53 Ketchum, "The Essence of Cooking Shows," 227.
54 Hollows, "Feeling Like a Domestic Goddess," 183.
55 Kavka, "A Matter of Feeling," 471.
56 Annemarie Mol's essay on the eating of an apple evocatively explores the numerous lines of inquiry at play in the act of eating. Mol, "I Eat an Apple."
57 The vomitus in the Mr. Creosote scene from *Monty Python's The Meaning of Life* was actually made from large amounts of minestrone soup. Hind, "Lunch with Terry Jones."
58 Critics of the program were particularly appalled by what they saw as a shameless and wasteful celebration of gluttony. See, for example, Brion, "Alton Brown Calls *Man v Food* 'Gluttonous' and 'Disgusting.'"
59 There are a range of formats and genres of food programming that focus on the moral and ethical discourses that surround health, nutrition, and forms of (self-)governance—bad and good, wrong and right, supersize and superskinny. See, for example, Ouellette and Hay, "Makeover Television"; and Leadley, "Supersize vs. Superskinny."
60 Kilgour, *From Communion to Cannibalism*, 4.
61 Guest, *Eating Their Words*, 2.
62 Michelis, "Food and Crime," 144.
63 Michelis, "Rhyming Hunger," 65.
64 See, for example, Nussbaum, "To Serve Man."
65 Douglas places her understanding of the syntagmatic meanings of food in opposition to Claude Lévi-Strauss's famous binary. Lévi-Strauss, *The Raw and the Cooked*.
66 Douglas, "Deciphering a Meal," 37.
67 Douglas, "Deciphering a Meal," 37.
68 See Newman, "From Beats to Arcs."
69 In the second series, having been framed by Hannibal as the much-sought-after "Chesapeake Ripper," Will, now aware that Hannibal is in fact the serial killer, is exonerated by

his former doctor's machinations. Unable to prove what he knows, he sets about an elaborate ruse to convince Hannibal that he is now his willing student and accomplice, all the while hoping to finally catch him in the act.

70 The program's food stylist, Janice Poon, describes the preparation and ritual of the consumption of the ortolan bunting in her online blog: "Ortolans are tiny songbirds no bigger than a man's thumb. Unfortunately for their species they are delicious. Now illegal to sell for the purposes of eating, they are famous as food of gourmands through the ages. They are captured live and force-fed until they are bloated. Not with a feeding horn, as are foie gras geese and ducks, but by taking advantage of their instinct to feed voraciously at night. Romans used to blind the birds so they would think it was night and feed endlessly. Now, they are merely put in covered cages and fed nuts and fruit. When they become so bloated they cannot move, they are quickly drowned in Armagnac, then plucked and roasted whole—they are eaten in one mouthful—bones guts and all. The little head with the brain and the crispy beak is thought to be the best part. Traditionally, one covers one's head with a cloth napkin while eating the bird so God will not see you engaging in such debauched indulgence." Poon, "Episode 11 Ko Ko Mono."

71 Douglas, "Deciphering a Meal," 44.

72 Series creator Bryan Fuller stated in an interview: "We've had dinner scenes where we shoot things so intimately then I'm like, 'OK, we are delivering the equivalent of cinematic fellatio, but they've got their clothes on, and they're sitting at a dinner table.' We definitely don't shy away from it, because I think it's fascinating and it's titillating, but we stop just short of kissing and penetration!" Dibdin, "Bryan Fuller Q&A."

73 D. Taylor, *The Archive and the Repertoire*, 2–4.

74 D. Taylor, *The Archive and the Repertoire*, 21.

75 Teil and Hennion, "Discovering Quality or Performing Taste?," 35.

76 Williams, "On Hannibal, Cooking and Fandom."

77 D. Taylor, *The Archive and the Repertoire*, 21.

78 Another celebration of a distinctive performance of tasting can be found in the Tumblr dedicated to "The Bite of the Berry." The site features a series of screen-grabs of Mary Berry (a judge on *The Great British Bake Off*) tasting the bakes of contestants. Berry's bite is distinctive because of its precarity—holding a biscuit, for example, in her birdlike fingers and almost wincing she bites to the side of her mouth, using her molar teeth to crack into the baked goods. For particular bakes (e.g., hard or dense bakes like biscuits) we sense her anxiety over the safety of her dentures. See http://maryberry bitingintothings.tumblr.com (accessed November 22, 2018).

79 McCarthy, "Visual Pleasure and GIFs," 114.

80 Bianconi, "Gifability."

81 McCarthy, "Visual Pleasure and GIFs," 113.

82 D. Taylor, *The Archive and the Repertoire*, 28.

83 See, for example, David Morley's discussion of the Household Uses of Information and Communication Technologies (HICT) conducted by Morley alongside Roger Silverstone and Eric Hirsch. Morley, *Home Territories*, 92.

84 D. Taylor, *The Archive and the Repertoire*, 2.

85 Ellmann, *The Hunger Artists*, 53.

4. HOMECOMINGS AND GOINGS

1 Stanley, *Auto/Biographical I*, 18.
2 Schechner, *Performance Studies*, 28–29.
3 Douglas, "The Idea of Home," 287.
4 Douglas, "The Idea of Home," 294.
5 See Brunsdon, "Taste and Time on Television."
6 See Moseley, "Makeover Takeover"; and Brunsdon et al., "Factual Entertainment on British Television."
7 See Shimpach, "Realty Reality"; and all essays in "Gender and Property TV after the Financial Crisis," a special issue of the *European Journal of Cultural Studies*.
8 Powell, "Time, Television, and the Decline of DIY," 96.
9 See David Morley's account of the work of British cultural historian David Chaney in *Home Territories*, 22.
10 Morley, *Home Territories*, 22.
11 This analysis of *Last Tango in Halifax* emerged following conversations with my fellow Yorkshire woman Alison Peirse, who was then living between Newcastle and Leeds, and a coauthored paper we presented together on the series at Leeds Beckett University in 2015.
12 J. Wood, "On Not Going Home."
13 Pearce, "Introduction: Devolution and the Politics of Re/location," 24.
14 The accelerated marketization of the higher education sector in the UK was partly brought about by a substantial increase in tuition fees of up to £9,000 per year in 2010. Tuition fees were first introduced in 1999.
15 See Roger Cohen's response to Wood's essay in the *New York Times*: Cohen, "In Search of Home."
16 Lipman and Nash, "Domestic Genealogies."
17 Schwartz, "Poetry Rx."
18 Pearce, "Driving North/Driving South," 162.
19 Pearce, "Driving North/Driving South," 163.
20 Bammer, "Editorial: Question of Home," ix.
21 Bammer, "Editorial: Question of Home," vii.
22 "This historical link between 'home' and 'sickness,' nostalgia and loss, suggests that home, in a sense, has always been 'unheimlich': not just the utopian place of safety and shelter for which we supposedly yearn, but also the place of dark secrets, of fear and danger, that we can sometimes only inhabit furtively." Bammer, "Editorial: Question of Home," xi.
23 Bowlby, "Domestication," 77.
24 Sconce, *Haunted Media*.
25 White, "Flows and Other Close Encounters with Television," 106.
26 As Ethan Thompson writes in the online journal named after Williams's foundational concept: "Williams admits that flow is so typical of TV experience that one isn't likely to notice it—but something about being in that hotel room, out of place, trying to watch a movie, allowed him to see things differently. From his displaced position, Williams recognized 'the facts of flow' which have since been widely accepted as central to the organization and experience of television." Thompson, "Raymond Williams on the Elliptical."

27 In his audience study of comfort television, Kerr Castle argues that the sitcom is "the archetype of a comfort text" in that it "invite[s] laughter, connection, and good feeling." *Friends* itself emerges in the study as a key "comfort text," embodying the qualities that Castle identifies in the studio sitcom—its structures of repetition, presentation of familiar character types and settings, consistency, and warmth of its aesthetics that make it an exemplary "go-to" destination for participants in need to comfort. Castle, "Comfort Television."

28 *Friends* has been consistently available in the UK through syndication on youth channel E4 and then infamously acquired by Netflix for a record sum. The shows access to a new generation has led a contemporary outpouring of nostalgia for the 1990s: *Friends* merchandise is available alongside a range of 1990s-style fashions in clothing stores such as Urban Outfitters. For further discussion of the intergenerational dimensions of the series, see Cobb, Ewan, and Hamad, "*Friends* Reconsidered."

29 Morse, "An Ontology of Everyday Distraction," 193.

30 Morse, "An Ontology of Everyday Distraction," 203.

31 Barthes writes: "At one moment I grasp the presence of the glass and the distance of the landscape; at another, on the contrary, the transparency of the glass and the depth of the landscape; but the result of this alternation is constant: the glass is at once present and empty to me, and the landscape unreal and full." Barthes, *Mythologies*, 123.

32 Pearce, "Autopia," 98.

33 Pertierra and Turner, *Locating Television*, 21.

34 Radstone, "What Place Is This?," 109.

35 Radstone, "What Place Is This?," 109.

36 Radstone, "What Place Is This?," 109.

37 Pertierra and Turner, *Locating Television*, 5.

38 Sally Wainwright has been writing for British television since the mid-1990s, but it is her cluster of most recent dramas, including *Last Tango in Halifax* and *Happy Valley*, that have sparked renewed scholarly interest, particularly among UK-based feminist television scholars. Wainwright's dramas have also found an international audience through Netflix distribution deals.

39 Radstone, "What Place Is This?," 109.

40 Armitage's poem "True North" (originally published in his 1992 collection *Kid*) tells of his "triumphant" return to West Yorkshire at Christmas after his first term at Portsmouth Polytechnic on the southern coast of England. See Armitage, *Selected Poems*, 29.

41 P. Davidson, *The Idea of North*, 8.

42 Woods, "Wainwright's West Yorkshire," 356.

43 The drama is explored through its classed West/North Yorkshire divide, a divide that is often visualized during coverage of local and general elections, with the red Labour heartlands of West Yorkshire juxtaposed against a largely blue Conservative dominance in the market towns and rural communities of North Yorkshire. It is also a divide metaphorically bridged by the twilight romance of Alan and Celia, whose political affinities are emphasized through their contrasting choice of breakfast newspapers (Alan reads the center-left broadsheet the *Guardian*, while Celia opts for the more right-wing tabloid the *Daily Mail*).

44 Dhoest, "The Persistence of National TV," 55.
45 Buonanno, *The Age of Television*, 96.
46 See, for example, Manning and Adams, "Popular Culture Studies and Autoethnography."
47 Shacklock, "The Kinaesthetics of Serial Television," 38.
48 Stacey and Wolff, *Writing Otherwise*, 7.
49 P. Davidson, *The Idea of North*, 207.
50 P. Davidson, *The Idea of North*, 211.
51 Elmet is the ancient name for a part of West Yorkshire that includes the upper Calder Valley and sections of the Pennine moorland. *Remains of Elmet*, first published in 1979, is a compilation of poems written by native Ted Hughes that responded to the black-and-white photography of Fay Godwin.
52 Though locations around the former Victorian spa town of Harrogate feature in the series, Caroline's house is actually located in the market town of Altrincham in Greater Manchester.
53 P. Davidson, *The Idea of North*, 207.
54 In the first episode of the current season of *Doctor Who* (BBC, 1964–), the drama takes place in the Yorkshire city of Sheffield. It is here that we are introduced to the first female "Doctor," played by Jodie Whittaker, who proudly hails from Huddersfield in West Yorkshire, and her new companions. Having joined forces to defeat an alien threat, at the close of the episode the new team stand together on the hillside overlooking the city.
55 See Higson, "Space, Place, Spectacle," 13.
56 Geraghty, "Re-appraising the Television Heroine"; Gorton, "Feeling Northern"; McElroy, "The Feminization of Contemporary British Television Drama"; Piper, "Broadcast Drama and the Problem of Television Aesthetics"; Piper, "*Happy Valley.*"
57 Woods, "Wainwright's West Yorkshire," 347.
58 Woods, "Wainwright's West Yorkshire," 348.
59 Boym, *The Future of Nostalgia*, 50.
60 Pearce, "Driving North/Driving South," 163.
61 "The centres of the northern cities were slow to be developed after the war, and so memories of the 1950s northern childhoods have aspects of the prewar South. Most northern English writers of that generation were compelled by circumstances to go south, so that the northern cities they revisited in the late 1970s were comprehensively rebuilt. This makes for a tradition of writing about departure and return to a place that has altered in the writer's absence." P. Davidson, *The Idea of North*, 206–7.
62 Gorton, "Feeling Northern," 2.
63 See Robert Macfarlane's foreword to Peter Davidson's *Distance and Memory*, xi.
64 In physics, it refers to the tendency of a gas to expand or escape. Within the context of this chapter, it is perhaps worth noting that the word 'fugitive' comes from the same root.
65 P. Davidson, *The Idea of North*, 8.
66 P. Davidson, *The Idea of North*, 8.
67 Stewart, *Ordinary Affects*, 55.
68 See, for example, *Chewing Gum* (E4, 2015–17), *Fleabag* (BBC3, 2016–19), *Game Face* (E4, 2017–), *Motherland* (BBC2, 2016–), *Sally4Ever* (Sky Atlantic, 2018–), *This Way Up* (Channel 4, 2019–), and *Back to Life* (BBC3, 2019–). This cluster of shows written by and

starring women writers and comedians is perhaps a reflection of new avenues of support via established writer/producers such as Sharon Horgan and her company, Merman, but also a recognition of UK broadcasters' address to more diverse (and niche) audiences.
69 Kafer, *Feminist, Queer, Crip*, 31.
70 Kafer, *Feminist, Queer, Crip*, 29.
71 Garland-Thomson, *Staring*, 3.
72 Despite the stream of "bad news," Sharon does not cry at any other point in the episode.
73 Ginsburg and Rapp, "Enabling Disability," 543.
74 As Ginsburg and Rapp argue, "A gap exists between the medical diagnosis of a fetal anomaly and social knowledge about life with a child who bears that condition. In this gap, the use of amniocentesis and selective abortion becomes perfectly rational." Ginsburg and Rapp, "Enabling Disability," 543.
75 Allen, "Audience-Orientated Criticism and Television," 106. It is interesting to note that Allen also uses a metaphor of driving to illustrate his argument as he reflects on this wandering viewpoint as "not that of the driver of a sports car down a superhighway but rather that of the uncertain tourist with a rather sketchy map, who frequently stops to look back where he or she has been, occasionally takes a side road, and constantly tries to glimpse what lies around the next bend." Allen, *Speaking of Soap Operas*, 78.
76 Campbell, "Inside the Frame of the Past."
77 Pearce, "Introduction: Devolution and the Politics of Re/location," 31.
78 These notions of horizontal and vertical identities are taken from Andrew Solomon's study *Far from the Tree*. In this study Solomon describes vertical identities as those passed down from one generation to the next through both genetics and shared cultural norms. However, he writes, often "someone has an inherent or acquired trait that is foreign to his or her parents and must therefore acquire identity from a peer group." These he refers to as "horizontal identities." Solomon, *Far from the Tree*, 2.
79 This storyline and its unusually nuanced delivery is arguably the result of cocreator Rob Delaney's experience as father to a young boy with a life-shortening illness and disability.
80 Mellencamp, *High Anxiety*, 80.
81 Charlotte Brunsdon outlines the ambivalence of attitudes toward forms of domestic and emotional labor within early feminist writing on television, with scholars caught between the valorization of women's culture and work and paranoid readings of soap as a culture of oppression. Brunsdon, *The Feminist, the Housewife, and the Soap Opera*, 39.
82 Caughie, "Telephilia and Distraction," 9.
83 In her reflections on the experience of driving, Lynne Pearce draws on the psychological term "apperception," "commonly understood as the process by which we perceive new experience in relation to past experience." Pearce, "Autopia," 104.
84 J. S. Taylor, "On Recognition, Caring, and Dementia," 316.
85 Felski, *Doing Time*, 34.
86 Stanley, *Auto/Biographical I*, 87.
87 Stanley and Wise, *Breaking Out Again*, 176 (my emphasis).
88 Stanley and Wise, *Breaking Out Again*, 177.
89 Cited in Brunsdon, *The Feminist, the Housewife, and the Soap Opera*, 56.

BIBLIOGRAPHY

Abrahamsson, Sebastian. "Cooking, Eating and Digesting: Notes on the Emergent Normativities of Food and Speeds." *Time and Society* 23, no. 3 (2014): 287–308.

Adema, Pauline. "Vicarious Consumption: Food, Television and the Ambiguity of Modernity." *Journal of American and Comparative Criticism* 23, no. 3 (2000): 113–24.

Albert, Stuart, and William Jones. "The Temporal Transition from Being Together to Being Alone: The Significance and Structure of Children's Bedtime Stories." In *The Personal Experience of Time*, edited by Bernard S. Gorman and Alden E. Wessman, 112–32. New York: Plenum, 1977.

Allen, Robert C. "Audience-Orientated Criticism and Television." In *Channels of Discourse, Reassembled: Television and Contemporary Criticism*, 2nd ed., edited by Robert C. Allen, 77–103. London: Routledge, 1992.

Allen, Robert C. *Speaking of Soap Operas*. Chapel Hill: University of North Carolina Press, 1985.

Armitage, Simon. *Selected Poems*. London: Faber and Faber, 2001.

Ashby, Emily. "*Pajanimals* Review." *Common Sense Media*. Accessed November 12, 2018. https://www.commonsensemedia.org/tv-reviews/pajanimals.

Bammer, Angelika. "Editorial: Question of Home." *New Formations* 17 (1992): vii–xi.

Barnes, Marian. "Beyond the Dyad: Exploring the Multidimensionality of Care." In *Ethics of Care: Critical Advances in International Perspective*, edited by Marian Barnes, Tula Brannelly, Lizzie Ward, and Nicki Ward, 31–44. Bristol, UK: Polity, 2015.

Barnes, Marian, Tula Brannelly, Lizzie Ward, and Nicki Ward, eds. *Ethics of Care: Critical Advances in International Perspective*. Bristol, UK: Polity, 2015.

Barnes, Marian, Tula Brannelly, Lizzie Ward, and Nicki Ward. "Introduction: The Critical Significance of Care." In *Ethics of Care: Critical Advances in International Perspective*, edited by Marian Barnes, Tula Brannelly, Lizzie Ward, and Nicki Ward, 3–20. Bristol, UK: Polity, 2015.

Barth, Josie Torres. "Sitting Closer to the Screen: Early Televisual Address, the Unsettling of the Domestic Sphere, and Close Reading Historical TV." *Camera Obscura* 34, no. 4 (2019): 31–61.

Barthes, Roland. *Mythologies*. Translated by Annette Lavers. New York: Hill and Wang, 1972.
BBC. "From Tot to Toddler to Tearaway, CBeebies Celebrates Its Fifth Birthday." Press release, March 19, 2003. http://www.bbc.co.uk/pressoffice/pressreleases/stories/2007/03_march/19/cbeebies_garden.shtml.
Benson-Allott, Caetlin. *Remote Control*. New York: Bloomsbury, 2015.
Bersamin, Melina, Beth M. Bourdeau, and Deborah A. Fisher. "Television Use, Sexual Behavior, and Relationship Status at Last Oral Sex and Vaginal Intercourse." *Sexuality and Culture* 14, no. 2 (2010): 157–68.
Bertoni, Filippo. "Soil and Worm: On Eating as Relating." *Science as Culture* 22, no. 1 (2013): 61–85.
Bianconi, Giampaolo. "Gifability." *Rhizome* (blog), November 20, 2012. http://rhizome.org/editorial/2012/nov/20/gifability/.
Bignell, Jonathan. "Familiar Aliens: *Teletubbies* and Postmodern Childhood." *Screen* 46, no. 3 (2005): 373–88.
Blunt, Alison, and Ann Varley. "Geographies of Home." *Cultural Geographies* 11, no. 1 (2004): 3–6.
Boulos, Rebecca, Emily Vikre Kuross, Sophie Oppenheimer, Hannah Chang, and Robin B. Kanarek. "ObesiTV: How Television Is Influencing the Obesity Epidemic." *Physiology and Behavior* 107, no. 1 (2012): 146–53.
Bowlby, Rachel. "Domestication." In *Feminism beside Itself*, edited by Diana Elam and Robyn Wiegman, 71–92. London: Routledge, 1995.
Boym, Svetlana. *The Future of Nostalgia*. New York: Basic Books, 2001.
Briggs, Matt. "Meaning, Play and Experience: Audience Activity and the 'Ontological Bias' in Children's Media Research." *Particip@tions* 4, no. 2 (2007). http://www.participations.org/Volume%204/Issue%202/4_02_briggs.htm.
Brion, Raphael. "Alton Brown Calls *Man v Food* 'Gluttonous' and 'Disgusting.'" *Eater*, September 28, 2010. http://www.eater.com/2010/9/28/6717459/alton-brown-calls-man-v-food-gluttonous-and-disgusting.
Bromley, Helen. "Pandora's Box or the Box of Delights: Children's Television and the Power of Story." In *Small Screens: Television for Children*, edited by David Buckingham, 208–26. Leicester: Leicester University Press, 2002.
Brown, Maggie. "Where CBeebies Toddles Next." *Guardian*, August 16, 2010. http://www.theguardian.com/media/2010/aug/16/cbeebies.
Brown, Steven D., and Paula Reavey. "Turning Around on Experience: The 'Expanded' View of Memory within Psychology." *Memory Studies* 8, no. 2 (2005): 131–50.
Bruce, Jean, and Zoe Druick, eds. "Gender and Property Television after the Financial Crisis." Special issue, *European Journal of Cultural Studies* 20, no. 5 (2017).
Brunsdon, Charlotte. "Bingeing on Box-Sets: The National and the Digital in Television Crime Drama." In *Relocating Television: Television in the Digital Context*, edited by Jostein Gripsrud, 63–75. London: Routledge, 2010.
Brunsdon, Charlotte. *The Feminist, the Housewife, and the Soap Opera*. Oxford: Oxford University Press, 2000.
Brunsdon, Charlotte. "Taste and Time on Television." *Screen* 45, no. 2 (2004): 115–29.
Brunsdon, Charlotte, Catherine Johnson, Rachel Moseley, Helen Wheatley, and Helen Wood.

"Factual Entertainment on British Television: The Midlands TV Research Group's '8–9 Project.'" *European Journal of Cultural Studies* 4, no. 1 (2001): 29–62.

Buckingham, David. *After the Death of Childhood: Growing Up in the Age of Electronic Media.* Cambridge: Polity, 2000.

Buonanno, Milly. *The Age of Television: Experiences and Theories.* Bristol, UK: Intellect, 2008.

Burman, Erica. *Deconstructing Developmental Psychology.* 2nd ed. London: Routledge, 2008.

Campbell, Sue. "Inside the Frame of the Past: Memory, Diversity, and Solidarity." In *Embodiment and Agency*, edited by Sue Campbell, Letitia Meynell, and Susan Sherwin, 211–33. University Park: Pennsylvania State University Press, 2009.

Cardiff, David, and Paddy Scannell. "Broadcasting and National Unity." In *Impacts and Influences: Essays on Media Power in the Twentieth Century*, edited by James Curran, Anthony Smith, and Pauline Wingate, 157–73. London: Methuen, 1987.

Carter, Meg. "They Come in Peace." *Telegraph*, March 18, 2007. http://www.telegraph.co.uk/culture/3663893/They-come-in-peace.html.

Castle, Kerr. "Comfort Television: Considering Everyday Television Use as a Mode of Self-Care." PhD diss., University of Glasgow, 2019.

Caughie, John. "Telephilia and Distraction: Terms of Engagement." *Journal of British Cinema and Television* 3, no. 1 (2006): 5–18.

Chivers, Tom. "We Need to Talk about How Unsettling 'In the Night Garden' Is." *Buzzfeed*, February 17, 2015. https://www.buzzfeed.com/tomchivers/in-the-night-garden-is-a-surreal-orgy-of-sex-and-dea.

Cobb, Shelley, Neil Ewan, and Hannah Hamad. "*Friends* Reconsidered: Cultural Politics, Intergenerationality, and Afterlives." *Television and New Media* 19, no. 8 (2018): 683–91.

Cohen, Roger. "In Search of Home." *New York Times*, April 3, 2014. www.nytimes.com/2014/04/04/opinion/cohen-in-search-of-home.html.

Couser, G. Thomas. *Vulnerable Subjects: Ethics and Life-Writing.* Ithaca, NY: Cornell University Press, 2004.

Coveney, John. *Food, Morals and Meaning: The Pleasure and Anxiety of Eating.* London: Routledge, 2000.

Davidson, Michael. *Concerto for the Left Hand: Disability and the Defamiliar Body.* Ann Arbor: University of Michigan Press, 2008.

Davidson, Peter. *Distance and Memory.* Manchester: Carcanet, 2013.

Davidson, Peter. *The Idea of North.* London: Reaktion, 2005.

Dhoest, Alexander. "The Persistence of National TV: Language and Cultural Proximity in Flemish Fiction." In *After the Break: Television Theory Today*, edited by Marijke de Valck and Jan Teurlings, 51–64. Amsterdam: Amsterdam University Press, 2013.

Dibdin, Emma. "Bryan Fuller Q&A: 'Will, Hannibal Subtext Is like Cinematic Fellatio.'" *Digital Spy*, May 2, 2014. http://www.digitalspy.com/tv/hannibal/interviews/a568139/bryan-fuller-qa-will-hannibal-subtext-is-like-cinematic-fellatio/.

Douglas, Mary. "Deciphering a Meal." In *Food and Culture: A Reader*, edited by Carole Counihan and Penny van Esterik, 36–54. New York: Routledge, 1997.

Douglas, Mary. "The Idea of Home: A Kind of Space." *Social Research* 58, no. 1 (1991): 287–307.

Dovey, Dana. "Binge-Watching Television Linked to Loneliness and Depression: Should You

Get Off Your Couch?" *Medical Daily*, January 29, 2015. https://www.medicaldaily.com/binge-watching-television-linked-loneliness-and-depression-should-you-get-your-couch-319736.

DuCille, Ann. *Technicolored: Reflections on Race in the Time of TV*. Durham, NC: Duke University Press, 2018.

Dyer, Richard. *Only Entertainment*. 2nd ed. London: Routledge, 2002.

Eakin, Paul John. *How Our Lives Become Stories: Making Selves*. Ithaca, NY: Cornell University Press, 1997.

Edwards, Derek, and David Middleton. "Conversational Remembering and Family Relationships: How Children Learn to Remember." *Journal of Social and Personal Relationships* 5, no. 1 (1988): 3–25.

Elefanta, Cochavit, and Tony Wigramb. "Learning Ability in Children with Rett Syndrome." *Brain and Development* 27, suppl. 1 (2005): 97–101.

Ellis, Carolyn, Tony E. Adams, and Arthur P. Bochner. "Autoethnography: An Overview." *Historical Social Research* 36, no. 4 (2011): 273–90.

Ellis, John. *Seeing Things: Television in the Age of Uncertainty*. London: I. B. Tauris, 2002.

Ellmann, Maud. *The Hunger Artists: Starving, Writing, and Imprisonment*. Cambridge, MA: Harvard University Press, 1993.

Evans, Elizabeth. "Layering Engagement: The Temporal Dynamics of Transmedia Television." *Storyworlds: A Journal of Narrative Studies* 7, no. 2 (2015): 111–28.

Evans, Elizabeth, Tim Coughlan, and Vicky Coughlan. "Building Digital Estates: Multiscreening, Technology Management and Ephemeral Television." *Critical Studies in Television* 12, no. 2 (2017): 191–205.

Fachel Leal, Ondina. "Popular Taste and Erudite Repertoire: The Place and Space of Television in Brazil." *Cultural Studies* 4, no. 1 (1990): 19–29.

Felski, Rita. *Doing Time: Feminist Theory and Postmodern Culture*. New York: New York University Press, 2000.

Forgacs, David. "Disney Animation and the Business of Childhood." *Screen* 33, no. 4 (1992): 361–74.

Francis, Mark, and Randolph T. Hester Jr., eds. *The Meaning of Gardens: Idea, Place, and Action*. Cambridge, MA: MIT Press, 1990.

Freeman, Elizabeth. *Time Binds: Queer Temporalities, Queer Histories*. Durham, NC: Duke University Press, 2010.

Frolova, Ksenia. "'We Pretty Much Just Watched It All Back to Back!': Parenting, Digital Television Viewing Practices and the Experience of Television Flow." *Critical Studies in Television* 12, no. 3 (2017): 243–55.

Garland-Thomson, Rosemarie. *Staring: How We Look*. Oxford: Oxford University Press, 2009.

Gauntlett, David, and Annette Hill. *TV Living: Television, Culture and Everyday Life*. London: Routledge, 1999.

Geraghty, Christine. "Continuous Serial—A Definition." In *Coronation Street*, edited by Richard Dyer, 9–26. London: BFI, 1981.

Geraghty, Christine. "Re-appraising the Television Heroine." *Critical Studies in Television Online*, September 6, 2013. http://cstonline.tv/re-appraising-the-television-heroine.

Ginsburg, Faye, and Rayna Rapp. "Enabling Disability: Rewriting Kinship, Reimagining Citizenship." *Public Culture* 13, no. 3 (2001): 533–56.

Goodley, Dan, and Katherine Runswick-Cole. "Emancipating Play: Dis/abled Children, Development and Deconstruction." *Disability and Society* 25, no. 4 (2010): 499–512.

Gorbman, Claudia. *Unheard Melodies: Narrative Film Music*. Bloomington: Indiana University Press, 1987.

Gore, Stacy A., Jill A. Foster, Vicki G. DiLillo, Kathy Kirk, and Delia Smith West. "Television Viewing and Snacking." *Eating Behaviors* 4, no. 4 (2003): 399–405.

Gorton, Kristyn. "Feeling Northern: 'Heroic Women' in Sally Wainwright's *Happy Valley* (BBC One, 2014–)." *Journal for Cultural Research* 20, no. 1 (2016): 73–85.

Gorton, Kristyn, and Joanne Garde-Hansen. *Remembering British Television: Audience, Archive and Industry*. London: BFI/Bloomsbury, 2019.

Griffiths, Angela. "CBeebies Bedtime Hour Changes." *CBeebies Grown-Ups* (blog), May 14. http://www.bbc.co.uk/blogs/cbeebiesgrownups/posts/CBeebies-Bedtime-Hour-changes.

Gripsrud, Jostein. "Television, Broadcasting and Flow: Key Metaphors in TV Theory." In *The Television Studies Book*, edited by Christine Geraghty and David Lusted, 17–32. London: Arnold, 1998.

Guest, Kristen, ed. *Eating Their Words: Cannibalism and the Boundaries of Cultural Identity*. New York: State University of New York Press, 2001.

Haraway, Donna J. *Simians, Cyborgs, and Women: The Reinvention of Nature*. New York: Routledge, 1991.

Harrington, C. Lee, and Denise D. Bielby. "A Life Course Perspective on Fandom." *International Journal of Cultural Studies* 13, no. 5 (2010): 429–50.

Hastie, Amelie. "Eating in the Dark: A Theoretical Concession." *Journal of Visual Culture* 6, no. 2 (2007): 283–302.

Highmore, Ben. "Bitter after Taste: Affect, Food, and Social Aesthetics." In *The Affect Theory Reader*, edited by Melissa Gregg and Gregory J. Seigworth, 118–37. Durham, NC: Duke University Press, 2010.

Higson, Andrew. "Space, Place, Spectacle." *Screen* 25, nos. 4–5 (1984): 2–21.

Hind, John. "Lunch with Terry Jones." *Guardian*, May 20, 2012. https://www.theguardian.com/lifeandstyle/2012/may/20/terry-jones-interview-mr-creosote.

Hockey, Jenny, and Allison James. *Growing Up and Growing Old: Ageing and Dependency in the Life Course*. London: Sage, 1993.

Holdsworth, Amy. "Something Special: Care, Pre-school Television and the Dis/abled Child." *Journal of Popular Television* 3, no. 2 (2015): 163–78.

Holdsworth, Amy. "Televisual Memory." *Screen* 51, no. 2 (2010): 129–42.

Hollows, Joanne. "Feeling Like a Domestic Goddess: Postfeminism and Cooking." *European Journal of Cultural Studies* 6, no. 2 (2003): 179–202.

Jacobs, Jason. "Television, Interrupted: Pollution or Aesthetic?" In *Television as Digital Media*, edited by James Bennett and Niki Strange, 255–82. Durham, NC: Duke University Press, 2011.

James, Alison, and Alan Prout. "Re-presenting Childhood: Time and Transition in the Study of Childhood." In *Constructing and Reconstructing Childhood: Contemporary Issues in the Sociological Study of Childhood*, edited by Allison James and Alan Prout, 227–46. London: Falmer, 2015.

Jenner, Mareike. "Binge-Watching: Video-on-Demand, Quality TV and Mainstreaming Fandom." *International Journal of Cultural Studies* 20, no. 3 (2015): 304–20.

Jenner, Mareike. "Is This TVIV? On Netflix, TVIII and Binge-Watching." *New Media and Society* 18, no. 2 (2014): 257–73.

Johnson, Catherine. "The Continuity of 'Continuity': Flow and the Changing Experience of Watching Broadcast Television." *Key Words: A Journal of Cultural Materialism*, no. 11 (2013): 27–43.

Johnson, Catherine. *Online TV*. London: Routledge, 2019.

Jones, Owain. "'Endlessly Revisited and Forever Gone': On Memory, Reverie and Emotional Imagination in Doing Children's Geographies. An 'Addendum' to '"To Go Back up the Side Hill': Memories, Imaginations and Reveries of Childhood' by Chris Philo." *Children's Geographies* 1, no. 1 (2003): 25–36.

Joyrich, Lynn. "Queer Television Studies: Currents, Flows, and (Main)streams." *Cinema Journal* 53, no. 2 (2014): 133–39.

Kafer, Alison. *Feminist, Queer, Crip*. Bloomington: Indiana University Press, 2013.

Katz, Cindi. "Childhood as Spectacle: Relays of Anxiety and the Reconfiguration of the Child." *Cultural Geographies* 15, no. 1 (2008): 5–17.

Kavka, Misha. "A Matter of Feeling: Mediated Affect in Reality Television." In *A Companion to Reality Television*, edited by Laurie Ouellette, 459–77. Malden, MA: Wiley, 2013.

Ketchum, Cheri. "The Essence of Cooking Shows: How the Food Network Constructs Consumer Fantasies." *Journal of Communication Inquiry* 29, no. 3 (2005): 217–43.

Kilgour, Maggie. *From Communion to Cannibalism: An Anatomy of Metaphors of Incorporation*. Princeton, NJ: Princeton University Press, 1990.

Kittay, Eva Feder, ed. *Love's Labor: Essays on Women, Equality and Dependency*. London: Routledge, 1999.

Kittay, Eva Feder. "The Personal Is Philosophical Is Political: A Philosopher and Mother of a Cognitively Disabled Person Sends Notes from the Battlefield." In *Cognitive Disability and Its Challenge to Moral Philosophy*, edited by Eva Feder Kittay and Licia Carlson, 393–413. Malden, MA: Wiley-Blackwell, 2010.

Kittay, Eva Feder. "When Caring Is Just and Justice Is Caring." In *The Subject of Care: Feminist Perspectives on Dependency*, edited by Eva Feder Kittay and Ellen K. Feder, 257–76. London: Rowman and Littlefield, 2002.

Klein, Amanda Ann, and R. Barton Palmer, eds. *Cycles, Sequels, Spin-Offs, Remakes, and Reboots: Multiplicities in Film and Television*. Austin: University of Texas Press, 2016.

Kline, Stephen. *Out of the Garden: Toys and Children's Culture in the Age of TV Marketing*. London: Verso, 1993.

Kuhn, Annette. *Family Secrets: Acts of Memory and Imagination*. London: Verso, 1995.

Lavis, Anna. "Food Porn, Pro-anorexia and the Viscerality of Virtual Affect: Exploring Eating in Cyberspace." *Geoforum* 84 (2017): 198–205.

Leadley, Alison. "Supersize vs. Superskinny: (Re)framing the Freak Show in Contemporary Popular Culture." *Journal of Popular Television* 3, no. 2 (2015): 213–28.

Lee, Nick. *Childhood and Society: Growing Up in an Age of Uncertainty*. Maidenhead, UK: Open University Press, 2001.

Levine, Elana. *Her Stories: Daytime Soap Opera and US Television History*. Durham, NC: Duke University Press, 2020.

Le Vine, Lauren. "The Rise of 'Breast-flixing': The Best Shows to Binge-Watch while Feeding Your New Baby." *Redbook*, February 21, 2014. https://www.redbookmag.com/life/mom-kids/news/a17092/breastfeeding-binge-watching-nursing/.

Lévi-Strauss, Claude. *The Raw and the Cooked: Mythologiques, Volume 1*. Translated by John and Doreen Weightman. Chicago: University of Chicago Press, 1983.

Lipman, Caron, and Catherine Nash. "Domestic Genealogies: How People Relate to Those Who Once Lived in Their Homes." *Cultural Geographies* 26, no. 3 (2019): 273–88.

Longfellow, Henry Wadsworth. "The Children's Hour." *Atlantic Monthly*, September 1860. Accessed November 12, 2018. https://www.poetryfoundation.org/poems/44628/the-childrens-hour-56d223ca55069.

Lopate, Carol. "Daytime Television: You'll Never Want to Leave Home." *Radical America* 11, no. 1 (1977): 33–51.

Lotz, Amanda. *The Television Will Be Revolutionized*. 2nd ed. New York: New York University Press, 2014.

Lull, James. "The Social Uses of Television." *Human Communication Research* 6, no. 3 (1980): 197–209.

Lury, Celia, Luciana Parisi, and Tiziana Terranova. "Introduction: The Becoming Topological of Culture." *Theory, Culture and Society* 29, nos. 4–5 (2012): 3–35.

Lury, Karen. "Halfway down the Stairs: Children's Spaces in Amateur Family Films from the 1930s to the 1960s." *Home Cultures: The Journal of Architecture, Design and Domestic Space* 10, no. 3 (2013): 267–86.

Lury, Karen. *Interpreting Television*. London: Hodder and Arnold, 2005.

Lury, Karen. "A Response to John Corner." *Screen* 48, no. 3 (2007): 371–76.

Macfarlane, Robert. Foreword to *Distance and Memory*, by Peter Davidson, ix–xiii. Manchester: Carcanet, 2013.

Mankekar, Purnima. "National Texts and Gendered Lives: An Ethnography of Television Viewers in a North Indian City." *American Ethnologist* 20, no. 3 (1993): 543–63.

Manning, Jimmy, and Tony E. Adams. "Popular Culture Studies and Autoethnography: An Essay on Method." *Popular Culture Studies Journal* 3, nos. 1–2 (2015): 187–221.

Mattingly, Cheryl. "Becoming Buzz Lightyear and Other Clinical Tales: Indigenizing Disney in a World of Disability." *Folk* 45 (2003): 9–32.

McCarthy, Anna. "Visual Pleasure and GIFS." In *Compact Cinematics: The Moving Image in the Age of Bit-Sized Media*, edited by Pepita Hesselberth and Maria Poulaki, 113–22. New York: Bloomsbury, 2017.

McElroy, Ruth. "The Feminisation of Contemporary British Television Drama: Sally Wainwright and Red Production." In *Television for Women: New Directions*, edited by Rachel Moseley, Helen Wheatley, and Helen Wood, 34–53. London: Routledge, 2017.

McGown, Alistair. "Watch with Mother." *Screen Online*. Accessed June 4, 2015. http://www.screenonline.org.uk/tv/id/445994/.

McRuer, Robert. *Crip Theory: Cultural Signs of Queerness and Disability*. New York: New York University Press, 2006.

Meigs, Anna. "Food as a Cultural Construction." In *Food and Culture: A Reader*, edited by Carole Counihan and Penny Van Esterik, 95–106. London: Routledge, 1997.

Mellencamp, Patricia. *High Anxiety: Catastrophe, Scandal, Age, and Comedy.* Bloomington: Indiana University Press, 1992.

Meltzer, Ariella, and John Kramer. "Siblinghood through Disability Studies Perspectives: Diversifying Discourse and Knowledge about Siblings with and without Disabilities." *Disability and Society* 31, no. 1 (2016): 17–32.

Messenger-Davies, Maire. "Heirlooms in the Living Room: Retrieving Television's Hidden Histories and the Problem of Changing Formats." *Critical Studies in Television* 5, no. 2 (2010): 34–47.

Michelis, Angelica. "Food and Crime: What's Eating the Crime Novel?" *European Journal of English Studies* 14, no. 2 (2010): 143–57.

Michelis, Angelica. "Rhyming Hunger: Poetry, Love and Cannibalism." *Revista Canaria de Estudios Ingleses* 60 (2010): 61–78.

Mills, Brett. "What Does It Mean to Call Television 'Cinematic'?" In *Television Aesthetics and Style*, edited by Jason Jacobs and Steven Peacock, 57–66. London: Bloomsbury, 2013.

Mitchell, Juliet. *Siblings: Sex and Violence.* Cambridge: Polity, 2003.

Mittell, Jason. *Complex TV: The Poetics of Contemporary Television Storytelling.* New York: New York University Press, 2015.

Modleski, Tania. *Loving with a Vengeance: Mass-Produced Fantasies for Women.* New York: Methuen, 1984.

Mol, Annemarie. "I Eat an Apple: On Theorizing Subjectivities." *Subjectivity* 22 (2008): 28–37.

Mol, Annemarie. *The Logic of Care: Health and the Problem of Patient Choice.* London: Routledge, 2008.

Moores, Shaun. *Digital Orientations: Non-media-centric Media Studies and Non-representational Theories of Practice.* Oxford: Peter Lang, 2017.

Morley, David. *Family Television: Cultural Power and Domestic Leisure.* London: Comedia, 1986.

Morley, David. "For a Materialist, Non–media-centric Media Studies." *Television and New Media* 10, no. 1 (2009): 114–16.

Morley, David. *Home Territories: Media, Mobility and Identity.* London: Routledge, 2000.

Morse, Margaret. "An Ontology of Everyday Distraction: The Freeway, the Mall, and Television." In *Logics of Television: Essays in Cultural Criticism*, edited by Patricia Mellencamp, 193–221. Bloomington: Indiana University Press, 1990.

Moseley, Rachel. "Makeover Takeover." *Screen* 31, no. 3 (2000): 299–314.

Moseley, Rachel. *Stop-Motion Animation for Children on British Television, 1958–1975.* Basingstoke, UK: Palgrave, 2016.

Moseley, Rachel, Helen Wheatley, and Helen Wood. "Introduction: Television in the Afternoon." *Critical Studies in Television* 9, no. 2 (2014): 1–19.

Natov, Roni. *The Poetics of Childhood.* London: Routledge, 2006.

Needham, Gary. "Scheduling Normativity: Television, the Family, and Queer Temporality." In *Queer TV*, edited by Glyn Davis and Gary Needham, 143–58. London: Routledge, 2009.

Newman, Michael Z. "From Beats to Arcs: Towards a Poetics of Television Narrative." *Velvet Light Trap* 58, no. 1 (2006): 29–40.

Newman, Michael Z. *Video Revolutions: On the History of a Medium.* New York: Columbia University Press, 2014.

Newman, Michael Z., and Elana Levine. *Legitimating Television: Media Convergence and Cultural Status*. London: Routledge, 2011.

Nikolajeva, Maria, and Liz Taylor. "'Must We to Bed Indeed?': Beds as Cultural Signifiers in Picturebooks for Children." *New Review of Children's Literature and Librarianship* 17, no. 2 (2011): 144–63.

Nussbaum, Emily. "To Serve Man: The Savory Spectacle of 'Hannibal.'" *New Yorker*, June 29, 2015. http://www.newyorker.com/magazine/2015/06/29/to-serve-man.

Olson, Samantha. "'Netflix and Chill' Is Good for Your Relationship, Says Netflix: How TV Shows Enhance Attraction." *Medical Daily*, February 7, 2016. http://www.medicaldaily.com/netflix-and-chill-healthy-relationships-372584.

O'Sullivan, Tim. "Television Memories and Cultures of Viewing, 1950–1965." In *Popular Television in Britain: Studies in Cultural History*, edited by John Corner, 159–81. London: BFI, 1991.

Oswell, David. *Television, Childhood, and the Home*. Oxford: Oxford University Press, 2002.

Ouellette, Laurie, and James Hay. "Makeover Television: Governmentality and the Good Citizen." *Continuum* 22, no. 4 (2008): 471–84.

Pallant, Chris. *Demystifying Disney: A History of Disney Feature Animation*. New York: Bloomsbury, 2011.

Pearce, Lynne. "Autopia: In Search of What We're Thinking When We're Driving." In *Writing Otherwise: Experiments in Cultural Criticism*, edited by Jackie Stacey and Janet Wolff, 92–105. Manchester: Manchester University Press, 2013.

Pearce, Lynne. "Driving North/Driving South: Reflections upon the Spatial/Temporal Coordinates of 'Home.'" In *Devolving Identities: Feminist Readings in Home and Belonging*, edited by Lynne Pearce, 162–78. Aldershot, UK: Ashgate, 2000.

Pearce, Lynne. *Feminism and the Politics of Reading*. London: Arnold, 1997.

Pearce, Lynne. "Introduction: Devolution and the Politics of Re/location." In *Devolving Identities: Feminist Readings in Home and Belonging*, edited by Lynne Pearce, 1–36. Aldershot, UK: Ashgate, 2000.

Perks, Lisa Glebatis. *Media Marathoning: Immersions in Morality*. Lanham, MD: Lexington Books, 2014.

Pertierra, Anna Cristina, and Graeme Turner. *Locating Television: Zones of Consumption*. London: Routledge, 2013.

Piper, Helen. "Broadcast Drama and the Problem of Television Aesthetics: Home, Nation, Universe." *Screen* 57, no. 1 (2017): 163–83.

Piper, Helen. "*Happy Valley*: Compassion, Evil and Exploitation in an Ordinary 'Trouble Town.'" In *Social Class and Television Drama in Contemporary Britain*, edited by Beth Johnson and David Forrest, 181–97. Basingstoke, UK: Palgrave, 2017.

Piper, Helen. "'How Long Since You Were Last Alive?' Fitz and Tennison Ten Years On." *Screen* 50, no. 2 (2009): 233–50.

Pittman, Matthew, and Kim Sheehan. "Sprinting a Media Marathon: Uses and Gratifications of Binge-Watching Television through Netflix." *First Monday* 20, no. 10 (2015). www.ojphi.org/ojs/index.php/fm/article/view/6138.

Poon, Janice. "Episode 11 Ko Ko Mono." *Janice Poon Art*, May 11, 2014. http://janicepoonart.blogspot.com/2014/05/episode-11-ko-ko-monoa-couple-of-extras.html.

Powell, Helen. "Time, Television, and the Decline of DIY." *Home Cultures* 8, no. 1 (2009): 89–107.
Probyn, Elspeth. *Blush: Faces of Shame*. Minneapolis: University of Minnesota Press, 2005.
Probyn, Elspeth. *Carnal Appetites: FoodSexIdentities*. London: Routledge, 2000.
Radstone, Susannah. "What Place Is This? Transcultural Memory and the Locations of Memory Studies." *Parallax* 17, no. 4 (2011): 109–23.
Reinstein, Julia. "This Airbnb Is a 'Netflix and Chill' Utopia." *Buzzfeed*, January 29, 2016. http://www.buzzfeed.com/juliareinstein/this-netflix-and-chill-airbnb-is-either-the-best-or-worst-th#.tqVBVR11.
Reynolds, Nigel. "Anger as BBC Moves *In the Night Garden*." *Telegraph*, April 2, 2008. http://www.telegraph.co.uk/news/uknews/1583589/Anger-as-bbc-moves-In-The-Night-Garden.html.
Roth, Wolff-Michael. "Auto/Biography and Auto/Ethnography: Finding the Generalized Other in the Self." In *Auto/Biography and Auto/Ethnography: Praxis of Research Method*, edited by Wolff-Michael Roth, 3–16. Rotterdam: Sense, 2005.
Rueschmann, Eva. *Sisters on Screen: Siblings in Contemporary Cinema*. Philadelphia: Temple University Press, 2000.
Runswick-Cole, Katherine. "Living with Dying and Disabilism: Death and Disabled Children." *Disability and Society* 25, no. 7 (2010): 813–26.
Runswick-Cole, Katherine, and Dan Goodley. "The Learning Disabled Child." In *Children and Society: Politics, Policies and Interventions*, edited by Craig Newnes. London: PCCS Books, 2015.
Ryan, Frances. *Crippled: Austerity and the Demonization of Disabled People*. London: Verso, 2019.
Scannell, Paddy. *Radio, Television and Modern Life: A Phenomenological Approach*. Oxford: Blackwell, 1996.
Schechner, Richard. *Performance Studies: An Introduction*. London: Routledge, 2002.
Schormans, Ann Fudge. "People with Intellectual Disabilities (Visually) Reimagine Care." In *Ethics of Care: Critical Advances in International Perspective*, edited by Marian Barnes, Tula Brannelly, Lizzie Ward, and Nicki Ward, 179–94. Bristol, UK: Polity, 2015.
Schwaab, Herbert. "'Unreading' Contemporary Television." In *After the Break: Television Theory Today*, edited by Marijke de Valck and Jan Teurlings, 21–33. Amsterdam: Amsterdam University Press, 2013.
Schwartz, Claire. "Poetry Rx: There's No Going Home." *Paris Review*, December 13, 2018. https://www.theparisreview.org/blog/2018/12/13/poetry-rx-theres-no-going-back-home/?utm_source=bloglovin.com&utm_medium=feed&utm_campaign=Feed%3A+TheParisReviewBlog+%28The+Paris+Review+Blog%29.
Sconce, Jeffrey. *Haunted Media: Electronic Presence from Telegraphy to Television*. Durham, NC: Duke University Press, 2000.
Sendall, Bernard. *Independent Television in Britain: Origin and Foundation, 1946–62*. Vol. 1. London: Macmillan, 1982.
Shacklock, Zoe. "The Kinaesthetics of Serial Television." PhD diss., University of Warwick, 2017.
Shimpach, Shaw. "Realty Reality: HGTV and the Subprime Crisis." *American Quarterly* 64, no. 3 (2012): 515–42.

Sigafoos, Jeff, Vanessa A. Green, Ralf Schlosser, Mark F. O'Reilly, Giulio E. Lancioni, Mandy Rispoli, and Russell Lang. "Communication Intervention in Rett Syndrome: A Systematic Review." *Research in Autism Spectrum Disorders* 3, no. 9 (2009): 304–18.

Silverstone, Roger. *Television and Everyday Life*. London: Routledge, 1994.

Solomon, Andrew. *Far from the Tree: Parents, Children and the Search for Identity*. London: Vintage, 2014.

Spence, Charles, Katsunori Okajima, Adrian David Cheok, Olivia Petit, and Charles Michel. "Eating with Our Eyes: From Visual Hunger to Digital Satiation." *Brain and Cognition* 110 (2016): 53–63.

Spigel, Lynn. "Detours in the Search for Tomorrow: Tania Modleski's *Loving with a Vengeance*." *Camera Obscura*, nos. 13–14 (1985): 215–34.

Spigel, Lynn. *Make Room for TV: Television and the Family Ideal in Postwar America*. Chicago: University of Chicago Press, 1992.

Spigel, Lynn. "TV Snapshots: An Archive of Everyday Life." Unpublished manuscript, n.d..

Spigel, Lynn. *Welcome to the Dreamhouse: Popular Media and Postwar Suburbs*. Durham, NC: Duke University Press, 2001.

Stacey, Jackie, and Janet Wolff, eds. *Writing Otherwise: Experiments in Cultural Criticism*. Manchester: Manchester University Press, 2013.

Stanley, Liz. *The Auto/Biographical I: The Theory and Practice of Feminist Auto/Biography*. Manchester: Manchester University Press, 1992.

Stanley, Liz, and Sue Wise. *Breaking Out Again: Feminist Ontology and Epistemology*. New ed. London: Routledge, 1993.

Steemers, Jeanette. *Creating Preschool Television: A Story of Commerce, Creativity and Curriculum*. Basingstoke, UK: Palgrave, 2011.

Stewart, Kathleen. *Ordinary Affects*. Durham, NC: Duke University Press, 2007.

Stockton, Kathryn Bond. *The Queer Child, or Growing Sideways in the Twentieth Century*. Durham, NC: Duke University Press, 2009.

Suskind, Ron. *Life Animated*. Los Angeles: Kingswell, 2014.

Tatar, Maria. *Enchanted Hunters: The Power of Stories in Childhood*. New York: Norton, 2009.

Taylor, Diana. *The Archive and the Repertoire: Performing Cultural Memory in the Americas*. Durham, NC: Duke University Press, 2003.

Taylor, Janelle S. "On Recognition, Caring, and Dementia." *Medical Anthropology Quarterly* 22, no. 4 (2008): 313–35.

Teil, Genevieve, and Antoine Hennion. "Discovering Quality or Performing Taste? A Sociology of the Amateur." In *Qualities of Food*, edited by Mark Harvey, Andrew McMeekin, and Alan Warde, 19–37. Manchester: Manchester University Press, 2004.

Thompson, Ethan. "Raymond Williams on the Elliptical." *Flow*, May 2, 2009. https://www.flowjournal.org/2009/05/raymond-williams-on-the-ellipticalethan-thompson-texas-am-university-corpus-christi/.

Titchkosky, Tanya, and Rod Michalko. "The Body as the Problem of Individuality: A Phenomenological Disability Studies Approach." In *Disability and Social Theory: New Developments and Directions*, edited by Dan Goodley, Bill Hughes, and Lennard Davies, 127–42. Basingstoke, UK: Palgrave, 2012.

Tomkins, Silvan. *Shame and Its Sisters: A Silvan Tomkins Reader*. Edited by Eve K. Sedgwick and Adam Frank. Durham, NC: Duke University Press, 1995.

Torrell, Margaret Rose. "Plural Singularities: The Disability Community in Life-Writing Texts." *Journal of Literary and Cultural Disability Studies* 5, no. 3 (2011): 321–37.

Tronto, Joan. *Moral Boundaries: A Political Argument for an Ethic of Care*. London: Routledge, 1993.

Tryon, Chuck. "Make Any Room Your TV Room: Digital Delivery and Media Mobility." *Screen* 53, no. 3 (2012): 287–300.

Tryon, Chuck. "TV Got Better: Netflix's Original Programming Strategies and Binge Viewing." *Media Industries Journal* 2, no. 2 (2015): 104–16.

Turner, Graeme. "Approaching the Cultures of Use: Netflix, Disruption and the Audience." *Critical Studies in Television* 14, no. 2 (2018): 222–32.

Uotinen, Johanna. "Digital Television and the Machine That Goes 'PING!': Autoethnography as a Method for Cultural Studies of Technology." *Journal of Cultural Research* 14, no. 2 (2010): 161–75.

Uprichard, Emma. "Children as 'Being and Becomings': Children, Childhood and Temporality." *Children and Society* 22, no. 4 (2008): 303–13.

Villarejo, Amy. *Ethereal Queer: Television, Historicity, Desire*. Durham, NC: Duke University Press, 2014.

Waller, Alison. *Rereading Childhood Books: A Poetics*. London: Bloomsbury, 2019.

Ward, Nicki. "Reciprocity and Mutuality: People with Learning Disabilities as Carers." In *Ethics of Care: Critical Advances in International Perspective*, edited by Marian Barnes, Tula Brannelly, Lizzie Ward, and Nicki Ward, 165–78. Bristol, UK: Polity, 2015.

West, Amy. "Reality Television and the Power of Dirt: Metaphor and Matter." *Screen* 52, no. 1 (2011): 63–77.

White, Mimi. "Flows and Other Close Encounters with Television." In *Planet TV: A Global Television Reader*, edited by Lisa Parks and Shanti Kumar, 94–110. New York: New York University Press, 2003.

Williams, Rebecca. "On Hannibal, Cooking and Fandom." *In Media Res*, September 23, 2015. http://mediacommons.futureofthebook.org/imr/2015/09/23/cooking-hannibal-food-fandom-participation.

Winn, Marie. *The Plug-In Drug: Television, Children, and the Family*. London: Viking, 1977.

Winnicott, D. W. *Playing and Reality*. London: Tavistock, 1971.

Wood, David J. "Teaching the Young Child: Some Relationships between Social Interaction, Language and Thought." In *Lev Vygotsky: Critical Assessments*, vol. 3, edited by Peter Lloyd and Charles Fernyhough, 259–73. London: Routledge, 1999.

Wood, James. "On Not Going Home." *London Review of Books* 36, no. 4 (February 20, 2014). www.lrb.co.uk/v36/n04/james-wood/on-not-going-home.

Woods, Faye. "Wainwright's West Yorkshire: Affect and Landscape in the Television Drama of Sally Wainwright." *Journal of British Cinema and Television* 16, no. 3 (2019): 346–66.

INDEX

Page numbers in italics refer to figures.

Abrahamsson, Sebastian, 87
Adams, Tony, 24
addiction, 84
advertising, 27, 77–78, 79, 80, 82, 86, 102, 142
Aladdin (Disney, 1992), 34
Albert, Stuart, 50, 53–54
Allen, Robert C., 24, 132
anxiety, 14, 46, 67–68, 74, 88, 120, 122–23, 135; and bedtimes, 50, 51, 53–54, 60; and children, 27, 43, 55, 57; and eating, 82, 84
app, 80
Armitage, Simon, 117, 124, 160n40
autobiography, 4–7, 147n3; and care, 25–26, 34–35, 37–38
autoethnography, 6–7, 24, 137, 147n4, 147nn11–12, 149n66, 161n46
Avengers: Age of Ultron (Marvel, 2015), 78

Bammer, Angelika: New Formations, 112
Barnes, Marian, 33, 45
Barthes, Roland, 15; *Mythologies*, 114, 160n31
BBC (British Broadcasting Corporation), 6, 28, 54, 59, 142, 145
Beauty and the Beast (Disney, 1991), 34, 40
Bedtime Hour (CBeebies), 26–27, 50, 52–53, 55, 57, 59–60, 69, 72
bedtimes, 14, 26–27, 43, 49–54, 59–61; and *In the Night Garden*, 61–62, *63*, *64*, *65*, 66–69, *70*, *71*, 73–74

Bedtime Story (CBeebies), 52
Benbow, Kay, 56
Berry, Mary, 158n78
Big Brother (Channel 4, 2000–2010; Channel 5, 2010–18), 88, 92
Bignell, Jonathan, 56
binge-watching, 84–86
Black Lives Matter, 144, 145
Blunt, Alison, 74
Bochner, Arthur, 24
border crossings, 16, 20
Bowlby, Rachel, 113
breastfeeding, 85
Briggs, Matt, 56
British New Wave, 122–23
Brown, Steven D., 34
Brunsdon, Charlotte, 23, 26, 84, 162n81
Buffy the Vampire Slayer (WB/UPN, 1997–2003), 146
Buonanno, Milly, 120

Camberwick Green (BBC, 1966), 155n61
Campbell, Sue, 132–33
cannibalism, 94–96
care, 22, 25–27, 33, 35, 37–38, 74, 86, 109, 135–38, 141–42 153n21; and children, 50–51, 53–57; and Disney, 42, 44–46. *See also* parents
Catastrophe (Channel 4, 2015–19), 28–29, 111, 128–29, *130–31*, 132–34, 138–39
Caughie, John, 4, 5, 38

CBeebies. *See* Bedtime Hour
Channel 4 News (Channel 4, 1982–), 139, 144
Cheers (NBC, 1982–93), 114, *115*
childlessness, 7
children, 5–6, 7, 54–57; and bedtimes, 13–14, 26–27, 49–54, 59–61; and disability, 25–26, 33–34, 35, 38–40; and Disney, 40–46, *47*, 48; and *In the Night Garden*, 61–62, 63, 64, *65*, 66–69, *70*, 71, 73–74
Children's Hour (BBC, 1922–64), 54, 59
chrononormativity, 7, 10, 128
cinema, 90, 116, 122–23
complex television, 12
contamination, 83–85, 88, 142
continuity, 14–16, 27, 29, 53, 67, 69, 71, 78, 87, 125, 134, 136, 142
Couser, C. Thomas: *Vulnerable Subjects*, 37
COVID-19 pandemic, 29, 139, 140–46
crip time, 11, 39–40, 148n35
Cucumber (Channel 4, 2015), 16–17, *18–19*, 20–22, 138
culture, 120
cyclical time, 8–10, 23

Davenport, Andrew, 61, 64, 66, 73–74
Davidson, Michael, 48
Davidson, Peter, 117, 122; *Distance and Memory*, 124–25
Davies, Russell T., 16, 149n56
daytime television, 23, 147n3
Delaney, Rob, 128
dementia, 123, 135–136
disability, 3, 7, 11, 37, 110, 128–29, 132; and children, 25–26, 33–35, 37–40; and COVID-19 pandemic, 143–44; and Disney, 40–46, 48; and infantilization, 151n34; and kinship, 133–34; and queer theory, 148n35
Disney Home Video, 6, 25–26, 33–35, 40–46, 48
DIY SOS: The Big Build (BBC, 1999–), 110
Doc McStuffins (Disney Jr., 2012–20), 73
Doctor Who (BBC, 1964–), 161n54
domestic space, 10, 12–15, 23, 50–52, 57, 90, 110. *See also* home
Douglas, Mary, 96, 101, 109, 125; *Purity and Danger*, 83
driving, 24, 114, 116, 118
duCille, Ann: *Technicolored*, 147n3
duration, 4, 5, 7, 22, 24, 60, 104, 134

Eakin, Paul John, 37
EastEnders (BBC, 1985–), 1, 3, 142
eating, 27–28, 80–85, 86–94, 105–6; and *Hannibal*, 94–97, *98–100*, 101, *103*, 104–5; and metaphors, 84–85; and performance, 101–2
elderly, the, 6, 7, 135, 136
Ellis, Carolyn, 24
Ellman, Maud, 105
episodic television, 12
escape, 122–23
Evans, Elizabeth, 80
everyday, the, 8, 9, 13, 13–16, 137; and *Cucumber*, 16–17, *18–19*, 20–22; and digital television, 78, 80; and family, 31; and fantasy, 26. *See also* bedtimes; eating

familiarity, 5, 14, 49, 104–5
family, 13–14, 25, 31, 32, 33. *See also* children; siblings
fantasy, 26–27
Fear Factor (NBC, 2001–6), 92
Felski, Rita: *Doing Time*, 8–9, 11, 14, 20, 137, 148n21
Feltz, Vanessa, 20–21, 149n55
feminism, 8, 9, 10, 37
food. *See* eating
Forgacs, David, 40
Freeman, Elizabeth, 7, 10
Friends (NBC, 1994–2004), 113–14, *115*, 136, 160n27–28
Frolova, Ksenia, 6

Galetti, Monica, 91
Galloping Gourmet, The (CJOH-DT, 1969–71), 104
gardens, 66, 68, 154n47
Garland-Thomson, Rosemarie, 129, 132
Gauntlett, David, 81
gender. *See* men; women
General Hospital (ABC, 1963–), 147n3
generational divides, 5, 27
George Clarke's Amazing Spaces (Channel 4, 2012–), 110
Geraghty, Christine, 24
GIFS, 104–5
Ginsberg, Faye, 46
GLOW (Netflix, 2017–), 89, 91
Goodley, Dan, 41

Good Place, The (NBC, 2016–20), 11
Graham Norton Show, The (BBC, 2007–), 143
Great British Menu (BBC, 2006–), 90
growing up, 5, 11, 25, 26, 34; and disability, 38, 39–40, 48; and Disney, 40–41

Hannibal (NBC, 2013–15), 25, 28, 82, 157–58n69–72; and eating, 94–97, 98–100, 101, 102, 103, 104–5
Happy Valley (BBC, 2014–), 122
Hartley, John, 83
Hastie, Amelie, 90
Have I Got News for You (BBC, 1990–), 143
Heidegger, Martin, 8; *Being and Time*, 153n21
Highmore, Ben, 21
Hill, Annette, 81
His Dark Materials (BBC, 2019–), 126
Hollows, Joanne, 90–91
home, 13–14, 15, 108–14, 116, 123–25
homesickness, 3, 16, 114, 115, 117, 120
home video. *See* Disney Home Video
Horgan, Sharon, 128
housewives, 9, 12, 23

identity, 7
illness, 7
industrialization, 10
In the Night Garden (CBeebies, 2007–9), 5, 26, 27, 50, 52, 55; and bedtimes, 61–62, 63, 64, 65, 66–69, 70, 71, 73–74
intimacy, 5
Isher, Wolfgang, 132
iteration, 4, 9, 11, 15–16

Jackass (MTV, 2000–2007), 92
Johnson, Catherine, 71
Jones, Owain, 67
Jones, William, 50, 53–54
Joyrich, Lynne, 10–11

Kafer, Alison, 48, 128–29
Kavka, Misha, 86, 91
Kerr, Graham, 104
Ketchum, Cheri, 90
Kilgour, Maggie, 81, 85, 94
Kittay, Eva Feder, 44; *Love's Labor*, 33, 34
Kramer, John, 35
Kuhn, Annette: *Family Secrets*, 31

Last Tango in Halifax (BBC, 2012–), 28, 111, 117–18, 119, 120, 121, 122–25, 137–38
Lavis, Anna, 90
Lawson, Nigella, 91
Lefebvre, Henri, 8
Levine, Elana, 147n3
Life Animated (Motto, 2016), 41–42
linear time, 8–9, 10–11
Line of Duty (BBC, 2012–), 146
Lion King, The (Disney, 1994), 33, 34, 46
Lipman, Caron, 112
literature, 4, 10; and bedtime stories, 50, 59, 60, 68, 69
Little Mermaid, The (Disney, 1989), 34, 40, 41, 42, 151n37
live broadcasting, 14, 15
Location, Location, Location (Channel 4, 2000–), 109
loops, 9, 11, 15, 40, 104–5; and *Cucumber*, 16–17, 18–19, 20
Loose Women (ITV, 1999–), 143
Lopate, Carol, 23, 137
Lost (ABC, 2004–10), 8
Lotz, Amanda, 12
Love Is Blind (Netflix, 2020–), 140
Love Island (ITV2, 2015–), 140
Luke, Tony, 93
Lury, Celia, 80
Lury, Karen, 15, 60, 61

McCarthy, Anna, 104–5
McCulloch, Derek, 54–55
Magic Roundabout, The (ORTF, 1963–73), 155n61
Man v. Food (Travel Channel, 2008–10), 28, 82, 91–94
Mary Poppins (Disney, 1964), 46
MasterChef: The Professionals (BBC, 1990–), 90, 91, 105
Mattingly, Cheryl, 42, 44
mealtimes. *See* eating
Meigs, Anna, 83
Mellencamp, Patricia, 25, 26, 135
Meltzer, Ariella, 35
memory, 31, 34, 87–88, 132–33
men, 122–23
metaphors, 83–86
Michalko, Rod, 34
Michelis, Angelica, 95

Mikkelsen, Mads, 102, *103*, 104
Mills, Brett, 12
Mitchell, Juliet, 38–39, 45
Mittell, Jason, 8, 12
Modleski, Tania, 9; *Loving with a Vengeance*, 23
Mol, Annemarie, 27, 55
Monty Python's The Meaning of Life (Universal, 1983), 88
Morley, David, 86
Morse, Margaret, 114
music, 43–44, 78; and bedtimes, 52–53, 62, 64, 66

Naficy, Hamid, 83
Nash, Catherine, 112
Natov, Roni, 66, 68
Needham, Gary, 10
Netflix, 84, 85–86, 88, 125, 141
Newman, Michael, 38
Nick Jr., 50, 53, 60, 71
Nikolajeva, Maria, 68
nonlinear television, 12

Oswell, David, 55

Pajanimals (Sprout, 2008–13), 50, 57, *58*, 67, 68–69
Pallant, Chris, 34
parents, 26–27, 50, 52, 59–60
Pearce, Lynne, 24, 89, 116, 133; *Devolved Identities*, 111, 112
performance, 101–2, 104, 105
Pertierra, Anna Cristina: *Locating Television*, 116
Pets Factor, The (CBBC, 2017–), 140
photography, 31, 32, 33, 35, *36*
Pocahontas (Disney, 1995), 45
Pointless (BBC, 2009–), 141
politics, 160n43
pollution, 83
Powell, Helen, 109
preschool television, 5, 25, 26–27, 59–60. *See also* Bedtime Hour; *In the Night Garden*
Probyn, Elspeth, 81
property programming, 109–10
punctum, 15

Queer as Folk (Channel 4, 2000–2005), 16
queer theory, 7, 10, 11, 38, 148n35

Radstone, Susannah, 116, 117
Rapp, Rayna, 46
reading, 4, 24
reality television, 83, 86, 92, 140
Reavey, Paula, 34
repetition, 4, 5, 8, 9–10, 11; and bedtimes, 53–54, 61–62, 64; and children, 27; and Disney, 40, 41, 42, 43–44; and home, 109–10; and soap operas, 23
retreat, 15–16
return, 15–16, 23, 27; and *Cucumber*, 16–17, *18–19*, 20–21
rhythms, 51–53, 56, 62, 64, 66, 73
Richard Osman's House of Games (BBC, 2017–), 141
Richman, Adam, 92–93
ritual, 88
Roth, Wolff-Michael, 4, 7
Rueschmann, Eva: *Sisters on Screen*, 38
Runswick-Cole, Katherine, 41, 46

Saturday Night and Sunday Morning (Reisz, 1960), 122–23
Scannell, Paddy, 53, 54
Schechner, Richard, 101, 108
Schormans, Ann Fudge, 37
Schwartz, Claire, 8, 112
Sconce, Jeffrey, 113
security, 3–4, 71. *See also* anxiety
Sendak, Maurice, 69
sex, 85–86
Sex and the City (HBO, 1998–2004), 82, 128
Shacklock, Zoë, 10, 120
siblings, 35, 38, 38–39, 45
Silverstone, Roger, 26, 51, 53, 74
"Sing-Along Songs" (Disney, 1986–2006), 43–44, 151n41
sitcoms, 11, 113–14. *See also Catastrophe*; *Friends*
Sky, 77–78, 79, 80, 82
soap operas, 4, 9, 23, 24, 132, 147n3. *See also EastEnders*
Spigel, Lynn, 31
Stacey, Jackie, 8; *Writing Otherwise*, 122
Stanley, Liz, 5, 37, 107, 137
stares, 129, 133
Steemers, Jeanette, 59
Stewart, Kathleen, 14, 15, 125
Stockton, Kathryn Bond, 38

studio audiences, 143
Suskind, Owen, 41–43, 44, 48

Tatar, Maria, 50, 62; *Enchanted Hunters*, 59, 60
Taylor, Diana, 101, 102, 104, 105
Taylor, Janelle, 136
Taylor, Liz, 68
technology, 4, 6, 13, 55–56, 77–78
Teletubbies (BBC, 1997–2001), 15, 56, 61
television, 13–16, 22–23, 134–37; and autobiography, 4–7; and bedtimes, 53–54; and binge-watching, 84–86; and care, 25–27, 37–38, 153n21; and children, 54–57; and companionship, 1, 2, 3–4; and COVID-19 pandemic, 141–46; and digital, 77–78, 79; and eating, 27–28, 80–84, 86–94; and home, 109–10, 113–14, 116; and rhythms, 51–52; and time, 7–13, 125, *126*, 127. *See also* advertising; Bedtime Hour; *Catastrophe*; Disney Home Video; *Last Tango in Halifax*
temporality. *See* time
30 Rock (NBC, 2006–13), 82, 91
Tiger King (Netflix, 2020), 141
time, 7–13, 125, *126*, 127, 148n21; and *Cucumber*, 16–17, *18–19*, 20–22; and disability, 39–40. *See also* bedtimes
Titchkosky, Tanya, 34
"Toddler's Truce," 59, 153n31
Tomkins, Silvan, 89
Toy Story (Disney, 1995), 42, 73
trauma, 21
Tronto, Joan, 55

Tryon, Chuck, 77, 84
Turner, Graeme, 78, 80; *Locating Television*, 116

Varley, Ann, 74
video art, 10
videocassette recorders (VCRs), 35, 43
Villarejo, Amy, 51; *Ethereal Queer*, 10, 147n3

Wainwright, Sally, 117, 122, 123, 124, 160n38
Wallace, Greg, 91
Waller, Alison, 4; *Rereading Childhood Books*, 87
Wareing, Marcus, 91
Watch with Mother (BBC, 1952–75), 59, 64
Webb, Alice, 59–60
West, Amy, 83, 86
White, Mimi, 28, 113
Williams, Raymond, 113
Williams, Rebecca, 104
Winn, Marie, 84
Wise, Sue, 137
Wogan (BBC, 1985–92), 54, 56, 152n13
Wolff, Janet, 8; *Writing Otherwise*, 122
women, 8, 9, 123, 161n68; and eating, 82; and pregnancy, 128–29, *130–31*, 132–34. *See also* feminism; housewives
Wood, Anne, 61–62
Wood, James, 111–12
Woods, Faye, 118, 123
Woolly and Tig (CBeebies, 2012–14), 73

Yorkshire. *See Last Tango in Halifax*